White Collar Politics

White Collar Politics

Martin Oppenheimer

Monthly Review Press
New York

Library of Congress Cataloging in Publication Data

Oppenheimer, Martin.
  White collar politics.

  Bibliography: p.
  Includes index.
    1. White collar workers—United States.   2. White
collar workers—United States—Political activity.
3. White collar workers—Europe.   4. White collar
workers—Europe—Political activity.   I. Title.
HD8039.M4U5695   1985   322′.2′0973   84-25570
ISBN 0-85345-659-3
ISBN 0-85345-660-7 (pbk.)

Monthly Review Press
155 West 23rd Street
New York, N.Y. 10011

Manufactured in the United States of America

10 9 8 7 6 5 4 3 2 1

How many illusions can be built on the simple fact that one holds a pen in clean hands and can initial forms, tons of forms! What a sorry affirmation of one's self! . . . how many white-collar workers still have the illusion that they belong to a "superior" world—because they scribble notes and sort papers instead of screwing bolts in a factory!

—Pierre Vallières,
White Niggers of America

Contents

Acknowledgments

This work is a synthesis that stands on a foundation built by many others. The ultimate architect is Karl Marx. The groundwork was prepared by a series of thinkers in dialogue with him, particularly Lewis Corey, C. Wright Mills, and Harry Braverman. The recent contributions of two writers, Erik Olin Wright and Richard F. Hamilton, proved critical in challenging my own thinking and in helping me to develop some of the theses around which this book is organized. The work of several of my students, notably Laurie Beth Dopkins, David D. Eisenhower, and Michael Yarrow, has sharpened my thinking along several theoretical dimensions, as has my ongoing debate with my colleague and friend Dale L. Johnson concerning the "class nature" of the middle strata.

I also want to express my thanks to several colleagues who read earlier drafts of this work, especially Val Burris, Dale Johnson, and Andrew Zimbalist. Sandra J. Coyner was of great help in providing information and clarifying my thinking on white collar theory. Chapters 2 and 3 are based in part on an earlier collaboration between us. These colleagues are not, of course, responsible for the shortcomings of the final product, or for the fact that I did not always take their advice.

Some parts of this book have appeared in earlier versions and various formats in the folllowing: *Social Policy*, July/August 1970 and January/February 1975; *Monographs of the Sociological Review* (Britain), December 1973; *Social Scientist* (India), November/December 1975; *Insurgent Sociologist*, Winter 1981; and in several places in *Class and Social Development*, edited by Dale L. Johnson (Beverly Hills, Calif.: Sage, 1982).

I am grateful to the Rutgers University Research Council for several small grants, and to the university for two faculty study leaves that enabled me to find the time for sustained work. Two lectureships, one at the John F. Kennedy-Institut of the Free University of (West) Berlin in 1976, and a Fulbright-Hayes appointment at the Westphalian-Wilhelms University of Muenster in 1982, helped me obtain access to German materials and also provided time and space away from the stresses of normal academic life, without which this work would not have been possible.

Editorial assistance, affectionate support, and an occasionally critical kick in the pants were provided by Hannah Fink; my editor at Monthly Review, Susan Lowes, provided invaluable support, assistance, and comradely criticism.

1
The White Collar Issue: Introductory Remarks

Introduction

This book attempts an assessment of the political role of the white collar strata, especially their potential contribution to the kind of social change associated with the socialist tradition.

The socialist assumption is twofold: First, there is a ruling class that dominates the mode of production and the political state; second, its existence implies its negation, a class or classes that, in concert, have as their objective mission the overturn of the ruling class and its state, and the substitution of a new form of class society and a new form of state responsive to it. In turn, that new form of class society, in the socialist premise, is one that will ultimately eliminate all forms of class oppression and exploitation and presage a democratic, humane, warless, and relatively prosperous world.

In the contemporary world there are two forms of class rule, two modes of production that coexist and interact, even as they contest with each other over as yet unaffiliated parts of the world: the capitalist mode of production, of which the United States, West Germany, and Japan are the leading models, and the bureaucratic collectivist, or state capitalist, mode, of which the Soviet Union is the leading model, and the People's Republic of China a variant, and which the capitalist mode often calls "communist." These two basic modes differ most fundamentally in that under capitalism the ruling class is one of private owners, with the state mediating among ruling-class fractions that may have somewhat varying immediate politics but are concerted in their overall long-term interest; under communism there are few private owners. The state owns—hence it is those who control the state, that is, the bureaucracy as a group (not as individuals), that constitutes the ruling class. What these two modes have in common is that both exist at the expense of, and in contradiction to, the working class of producers; and that both to survive must expand their boundaries at the expense of uncommitted sectors of the world, and/or at the expense of the other. Hence, both are in some way imperialist forms, existing not only by exploiting their own internal working classes and other class groupings, but also by exploiting the working and peasant classes of other societies. Capitalism does so 'rough the domination of the multinational firm, coupled with political alliances with repressive governments responsive to profiteering, governments that seek to maintain propertied classes in power in their own countries. Communism does so, usually, by aiding revolutionary forces that overturn governments responsive to capitalism. Those revolutionary forces then become targets for takeover by contesting state bureaucracies—local, Soviet-oriented, and Chinese-oriented. Rarely do such forces succeed in maintaining their national independence while at the same time successfully thwarting counterrevolutionary elements supported by the previous regime (often with the aid of the U.S. government).

The two major modes of production generate a series of fundamental contradictions: that between a nation's ruling classes and its working class (plus peasants or small-scale farmers); that between the major nations' ruling classes in concert and their working and peasant classes on a world scale; that among the major nations' ruling classes when they are in conflict over strategic areas, market and/or military; and, closely related, that between the exploiting nations and the dominated nations of the third world, whether they are colonies, neocolonies, or branch-plant economies.

It is the first of these contradictions that is my subject. I will focus on the United States, still the center of world capitalism, and will limit the discussion to the capitalist mode of production.

In the United States, and in the Western world more generally, then, if there is a ruling class, what is its negation in these closing decades of the twentieth century? Is it still the traditional blue collar proletariat? Or have blue collar workers been coopted, historically displaced in the dialectical process by the peoples of the third world or by their U.S. counterparts among the nonwhite poor? Or have shifts in technology created a new white collar working class as the leading potentially revolutionary force in Western society? Or must we look to some combination, some coalition of classes and fragments of classes?

These questions are based on the socialist assumption that fundamental, revolutionary change is the prerequisite for a world without oppression and exploitation, without warfare and misery. Outside the socialist framework other assumptions can be argued: either that there are no contradictions; that no fundamental change can or need be made; or that "sectoral" contradictions such as race or gender, rather than class, are the critical factors in social change. While these arguments will be touched on in the course of the book, my focus will remain on the issue of class because for socialists (particularly those informed by Marxian assumptions) class continues to be the critical variable in social change, and the most important tool of social analysis.

While the issue of which class or grouping is to be the chief agency for fundamental change is not a new one, it has become more urgent in recent years due to the failure of liberalism, on the one hand, and the virtual disappearance of many insurgent movements, on the other. Nor is this an academic issue, for linked to one or another prognosis is a strategy and a set of tactics for politics of action in the next few years. It is, for example, the answer to this question that divides Weatherpeople from revolutionary socialists from social democrats from Eurocommunists from "hard-line Communists," Communist Party members. In today's world the search for an agency of change has become *the* critical issue for the entire left, using the term "left" in its broadest sense. It has become so in part because of the failure of the Western working class to become a revolutionary force, a class in the subjective sense, "for itself." Implied, therefore, in any discussion of agency is an examination of this failure, and this is the topic of chapter 2.

The "debate" concerning the political role of the middle strata of society vis-à-vis the ruling class, on the one hand, and the traditional blue collar working class, on the other, appeared on the political stage in the late 1800s. At that time it became apparent to a number of social thinkers that a phenomenon treated only sparsely by Marx, Engels, and their generation was about to become a tremendous factor in societies of the Western capitalist sort.

From that time to this, the inescapable fact dominating all labor force statistics has been the numerical and proportional growth of the so-called white collar occupations relative to the growth of the blue collar occupations (and of course to farm owners, who are, as a group, decreasing both as a proportion of the labor force and in absolute numbers in virtually every Western country). This fact, one argument has it, is alone responsible for the failure of the Western working class to become a revolutionary force, for in this view white collar work is synonymous with the rise of a new form of middle class—and the "middle classicization" of society, the disappearance of the sharp schism between bourgeois and proletarian. Theories such as this will be examined in chapters 3 and 4. The overall trends, their subordinate components, and their causes, both macrolevel (the United States as the administrative center of world imperialism, for one) and microlevel (technological changes in the nature of office work, the "paperless" office, and the proletarianization of lower level white collar work, among other factors) will be discussed in chapter 5.

A fact thought startling a few years ago, but now acknowledged by all observers, must accompany any analysis of the development of the white collar strata: The numerical growth of these strata is closely associated with the increasing participation of women in the labor force. About half of all white collarites are women; over 60 percent of all women in the official labor force in the United States are in white collar occupations. This relationship between gender and job will be analyzed in detail in chapter 6.

A critical set of problems for any student of the class divisions of society has to do with definitions. First, what are the boundaries between classes—what marks one class off from another? Second, in what ways are classes split into segments or fractions? And third, are such segmentations sufficiently fundamental that we can identify two, or even more, real classes within a set of seemingly similar occupations? This problem is exacerbated when there are occupations that do not actually "produce," in the traditional sense, anything concrete. Many of the modern "professions" fall into this category. What professionals "do," how they contribute to the process of production, is not always clear. (My children can describe to their friends what I do; many of their friends, however, cannot do so for their parents.)

Moreover, styles of work among professionals often differ markedly from one another. Some are highly independent; others are subjected to the same laws of the marketplace as those that cover the most poorly paid laborer. What does it mean, then, to be a professional today, in class terms? What is likely to happen to the working conditions of that 15 percent of the U.S. labor force classified as professional—a percentage, incidentally, nearly the same as that for factory production workers? This issue will be addressed in chapter 7.

One of the indices of the political development of any occupational segment in Western society is the degree to which its members are trade unionists. The socialist assumption, again, is that unions constitute a potential lever for social change, no matter how minimal: Therefore no class analysis can be complete without an inquiry into the position of unions, as instruments of class interest, within the society. The general nature of unionism in the U.S. context is discussed in chapter 2; the specifics of white collar unions are detailed in chapter 8.

Politics of course transcends any one specific form of political behavior, such as trade unionism. Indeed, focusing on overt political behavior—such as membership in parties and unions, or strikes, or the response to attitude surveys, or electoral behavior—actually misses, even evades, a great deal of real politics that takes place not under the scrutiny of social scientists but at far less formal levels such as in workplace and in family relations. The "politics of everyday life," which has to do with power relationships between men and women, parents and children, workers and supervisors, is often the fabric that reveals real politics and gives clues to political potential. Politics frequently takes form in such phenomena as popular music, joking, or linguistic devices that protect the oppressed both from their oppressors and from social scientific snooping. Even the lack of overt political behavior is a form of politics, an abstention that is a political statement for those who are sensitive enough to take notice.

Data concerning political behavior are therefore limited. Nevertheless, they are indices to attitudes, and occasionally clues to potential behavior in other areas. Chapter 9 will summarize some of the more important findings concerning a number of political attitudes and behaviors, such as party voting preferences, with some attention given to cross-national data. Many of the theses advanced by the writers discussed in chapters 3 and 4 can be tested here: Are white collarites really conservative, liberal, radical? Which ones are which? and under what conditions?

The concluding chapter summarizes the book's main findings, and discusses their political implications.

The thesis of this book can be summarized briefly: People existing in contradictory class locations can be expected to develop contradictory consciousnesses. The different people and occupations that can be subsumed under the broad category white collar (*tertiaires* in France, *Angestellte* and *Beamte* in Germany) are not located in the same single class; clusters of them exist in different classes, some of which are in contradiction to one another, and many individuals straddle more than one class, at least in an objective sense. While classes in their aggregate constitute distinctive units, there are many individuals at the "outer edge" of every class who find themselves in extremely ambiguous positions. This is especially true for white collar people.

For those who wish to analyze the world from a Marxist class perspective, the very concept "white collar" is misleading, for it suppresses the idea of class and disguises class differences among white collarites. Since different white collar occupations have different class locations, or are sometimes located simultaneously in different classes, "consciousness" as revealed in political attitudes, voting behavior, cultural views, and even myths will vary from segment to segment within the white collar grouping, depending on location. A particular set of occupations (a segment or fraction) may confront contradictory problems at a given moment, or may be different from, or even in conflict with, other segments.

The extent to which this thesis differs from others will become apparent in the course of the discussion. It denies that the white collar occupations as a whole, or in their predominant configuration, are merely appendages of the bourgeoisie. It also denies that they constitute an independent "new" middle grouping, a "third way," apart from bourgeois and proletarian, for society. It denies that they are, in their entirety, a "new" working class, historically destined either to replace, or align with, the "old" working class as a revolutionary force. They are all of these and none of these, because the grouping consists of many different class fractions, some simultaneously. Hence to try to identify a single political mission for people located in contradictory class position is futile. What must be done is to try to identify the class positions and the class interests—objective as well as subjective (that is, as they are articulated today)—of the different fractions that make up the white collar occupations, and to develop tactics that will unify the more working class of these fractions with one another and with the still quite large blue collar working class for the purpose of creating a movement for fundamental social change. The purpose of this book is to contribute to this project.

On Definitions

Two key terms that necessarily recur in any discussion of the middle strata deserve some clarification before we proceed to the body of this work: "class" and "white collar." Almost as much confusion has been generated by these terms, and their misuse, as by the more structural problems of social trends and occupational changes. Indeed, terminology itself—the process of labeling—has become a "real" factor in what many radicals perceive as "false" political or social consciousness within the ranks of the white collar occupations.

To make the issue even more complex, not only is there a widespread misunderstanding both of the term "class" and of the idea of "white collar," but one class, the "middle," is often assumed to be synonymous with white collar. All of these issues must be carefully delineated. A class is not necessarily a clustering of occupations; nor is a clustering of white collar occupations a class, or even (unless by historical accident) part of a single class.

Mainstream sociology generally holds that middle *class* is equivalent to middle *stratum,* or layer, usually as measured by some set of objective or subjective indices such as income, education, prestige, occupation, or attitude, or some combination of these. These indices, while rooted often enough in class membership, are not in themselves indices of class, which is something quite different. Class is not a quantitative measurement along some mathematical continuum, but a qualitative measurement representing groupings that are distinct and separate from one another (despite what may be a closeness arithmetically) by the fact that their basic relationships to the mode of production are different from those of other classes and are objectively in *conflict* with those of at least some of those classes. A class may also be subjectively in conflict with other classes to the extent that it is organized politically (in a party, in unions, in employer groups, etc.) for the purpose of conducting a struggle in defense of its interests.

If we conceptualize this relationship diagrammatically, we see that the expressions "distinct and separate" and "broken off from one another" are true only in a figurative sense. Classes look like a "normal" or bell-shaped curve in the distribution of a set of objective indices that Marxists call "relationship to the means of production," the most important being occupation in the general sense of source of income (see Figure 1-1). The term "class consciousness" in turn assumes that class takes the form of a similar curve in the distribution of some set of relevant political attitudes and behaviors (some of which will be analyzed in chapter 9). These distributions, if our theory is right, should, at the center of the "bell," differ from those of other classes, even though they overlap at their outer edges. In that sense, classes are qualitatively distinct from one another, but the breaks are not clean. The existence of those outer edges indicates that there are many individuals within a class who find themselves in very unclear positions, in

Figure 1-1. *Illustration of how classes may differ in the distribution
of a set of indices, such as political attitudes*

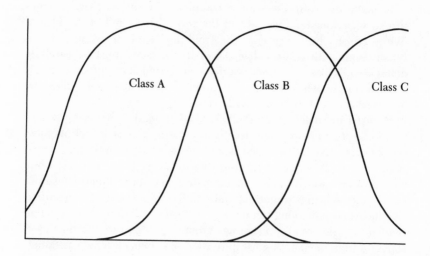

that they partake only partially of the objective (and therefore subjective) criteria of "their" class: They are in contradictory class locations,
in more than one class at a time. They are marginal members of their
class(es). This problem, as noted above, is particularly acute for those
with white collar occupations.

While it is true that many of those in white collar occupations land in
a statistical "middle" with respect to certain objective and subjective
indices, this is insufficient to make them a "middle class." Not all white
collar occupations are middle class; nor are all those who fall into the
middle ranges of some distribution of indices necessarily white collar.
In fact, I shall argue that white collarites, when examined as a whole,
do not follow the "normal curve" that would be required if they were to
be defined as members of a single middle (or any other) class. Some are
members of the upper or ruling class, others are middle class in the
historical sense of "petty bourgeois," others are working class, and, as I
have suggested, still others are of mixed-class membership. All of this
is obscured by government data lumping them together as white collar.
What, then, do I mean by "white collar" and "middle class"? By white
collar I mean those occupations characterized by *relatively* higher educational requirements (as imposed, often, by the society and not inher-

ently by the job), and by *relatively* clean, nonmanual work (though in fact most lower level white collar workers do manual work, such as typing). These occupations are *disproportionately* in administration, in the services sector (commerce, exchange, finance), and in government; those who work in them rarely *directly* produce commodities for the market. More often they produce (train) other workers, assist in getting commodities to the market, and control the flow of information concerning other workers; that is, they are neither *primary* (extractive, agricultural) workers, nor *secondary* (manufacturing) workers; they are *tertiary* (reproductive, planning, accounting, social control, welfare, administrative) workers.

Within this broad spectrum of occupations, some clearly differ from others along *class* lines. For my purposes, I shall define three classes as participating in the white collar occupations: (1) owners and upper management, i.e., the upper class or bourgeoisie, which derives its income from the capital that it controls and from the profit that that capital generates; (2) the old and new middle class or petty bourgeoisie, the former being the remnant of the old self-employed middle class and the latter being the supervisory and upper supervisory employees of modern business and government, embedded in capitalist social relationships in which their primary function is to sustain the profits of the firm and to exercise social control of, and over, the workforce; and (3) the new working class, which ranges in occupation and income from professionals (including many lower level supervisors), on one end, to clerical and sales workers, on the other. Most professionals, and everyone else in the new-working-class category—with the exception of some commission salespeople—derive their incomes from the sale of their labor power on the market for a wage, like other workers.

The new working class is a very substantial grouping among all white collarites. Eliminating those white collar strata that actually belong to another class or classes, we are still left with a rather large and amorphous grouping (perhaps 40 percent of the U.S. labor force—Oppenheimer 1979). However, this grouping is differentiated internally because some of its members have "contradictory locations" (Wright 1978), that is, they occupy positions straddling the working class and the new middle class because their jobs share some of the objective characteristics of different classes. It is further differentiated by economic *sector* (primary, secondary, tertiary), and between *private* and *public* sector. Even though most of the new working class work in the tertiary sector, this is divided between private and public, one based on profit making, the other on taxation, and this can lead to contradictory political attitudes and activities. In addition, the private sector is differentiated into what have come to be called "core" and "peripheral" economic areas: Dual labor market theory argues that in capitalist society significant differences exist between what are basically monopolistic (highly unionized, capital-intensive) industries and competitive (relatively smaller, nonunionized, labor-intensive) firms (O'Connor 1973).

The boundaries of the new working class, even without considering the fractions that exist in contradictory locations vis-à-vis other classes, are not easy to define. In the United States, most labor force data are figures collected and published by the government. This creates an immediate problem: Classifications exist without reference to (and possibly in an attempt to obscure) the question of significance, power, and control, that is, social class. The concept "ruling class" does not exist for the Bureau of Labor Statistics, so that the entire ruling class of the country is subsumed under the broad classification "white collar." The traditional capitalist class of large owners is buried within one category of white collar occupation, that of "managers and administrators," which also includes the neighborhood "Mom and Pop" grocery store. At the other extreme, that of the white collar mass, job classifications are sufficiently imprecise that tens of thousands of white collar workers are classified in "service occupations," and are not part of the white collar category at all. Police officers, for example, are "service workers," but police desk workers, who are more properly white collar workers in their day-to-day functions, are still policemen and are classified as service workers.

What this means is that our information on the number of white collar workers is imprecise at best. Using union figures to find out how many white collar workers are unionized is also misleading, since many white collar unions (such as the American Federation of State, County, and Municipal Employees—AFSCME) have both service and blue collar members (only about one-third of AFSCME is white collar), and numerous service and blue collar unions have white collar members, who are sometimes not counted in separate white collar units. The Teamsters, Steelworkers, Automobile Workers, Electrical Workers, Seafarers, Machinists, and many others organize white collar workers, while unions such as AFSCME and the National Union of Hospital and

Health Care Employees organize everybody from doctors to social workers to garbage collectors and janitors.

Another problem occurs when we try to pin down white collar occupations into the four general classes or strata used by the government: (1) managers, officials, and proprietors, now called managers and administrators in U.S. Census data; (2) professional and technical workers; (3) clerical workers; and (4) sales workers. First, a number of occupations in these categories are not white collar. Transportation baggagemen are considered part of the clerical category. Why are they not classified as service workers, gray collar? Second, many occupations that are indeed white collar should be classified differently by stratum. Airplane pilots and navigators are considered professional, but railroad conductors and ships' officers, pilots, pursers, and engineers are considered managers. Many sales workers, such as advertising people and real estate brokers, are far closer to being proprietors than they are to being five-and-ten-cent-store clerks. Third, specific occupations vary in their class content, but are nevertheless lumped together. College presidents, professors, and instructors are considered a single occupation. Presidents should certainly be called managers.

In short, the overall concept of white collar is fuzzy, and within that category it is harder still to identify in any strict sense who exactly is part of the new working class. Does this not argue for the elimination of white collar terminology, and its replacement with more functional labels that are linked more empirically to class positions? The logic of my analysis does indeed point in that direction. On the other hand, the term has become a social fact that in turn affects perceptions of class realities, false though some of those perceptions may be. It cannot simply be wished away; it must be dissected theoretically and empirically so that we can understand what elements of the white collar concept have political usefulness. While the concept is often misused to mystify class realities, it would be foolish to assume that there is no reality at all to the distinction between white collar, and other collar color, life and work.

Conventional social scientists, in making white collar synonymous with middle class, do so in order to argue that the United States is a middle class society, one in which fundamental social change is unwanted and unnecessary. Some Marxist theoreticians (e.g., Poulantzas 1975), though arguing for change, have also managed to define most white collar workers out of the working class. They have argued that the term working class involves more than just the sale of labor power for wages; that, in addition, a "worker" must be "productive," that is, must generate surplus value (rather than merely helping to realize it for capital, or performing other auxiliary functions). So Poulantzas concludes that "salarized nonproductive workers" are not workers but form a separate, new, petty-bourgeois class. While this argument may sound esoteric, it has political implications. If it is true that most white collar workers are not workers, then the working class as it is presently constituted, or likely to be constituted in the foreseeable future, cannot become the primary agent for fundamental social change. Other tactics, either more elitist or more coalitional, will have to be developed. (These approaches will be discussed in detail in chapters 3 and 4.) But if white collar workers are indeed workers, they can, together with the more traditional working class, form the mass base for revolutionary change. Obviously each of these theses implies a different set of political tactics in the here and now.

The latter view, contrasting with that of Poulantzas yet also based on Marxist assumptions, argues that large numbers of white collar workers are indeed members of a working *class* (as distinct from being simply an occupational stratum that can be distinguished from blue collar operatives, let us say, by the fact that for the most part they do "non-manual" labor). The assumption here is that while class may involve a stratum, or several strata, of occupation(s), something more is involved: a class is identifiable by (1) a common position relative to the means of production and distribution, that is, a common source of income based on the relationship between an individual and the economic mode of production; (2) an interest different from, and sometimes hostile to, that of at least one other class because of that different position relative to the economic system; (3) consequent separate life-styles; and (according to some theorists); (4) a consciousness of membership in that class and a political organization that expresses that consciousness (Anderson 1974: 50).

According to such a Marxian line of analysis, which involves both objective and subjective criteria, some white collarites constitute part of the working class because one dimension of their relationship to the economic system is that of selling their labor power in return for a wage (as contrasted, say, with those who own the means of production and derive their income from profits). But is that position an antagonistic one, in that white collar workers produce surplus value that is appropriated by another class, the bourgeoisie? Here it may be well to consult Marx, who says (in Volume 3, chap. 17, of *Capital*):

> The commercial laborer does not produce any surplus-value directly. . . . His wages are therefore not necessarily in proportion to the mass of profits, which he helps the capitalist to realize. . . . He adds to the income of the capitalist not by creating any direct surplus-value, but by helping him to reduce the costs of the realization of surplus-value. In so doing, he performs partly unpaid labor.

In short, Marx is saying that white collar employees, unlike blue collar industrial workers, do not produce a good that has a use value and an exchange value, and for the production of which they are paid only a portion of the exchange value—that portion on which they can, more or less, subsist and reproduce laborers for future generations. Rather, white collar workers help the capitalist to realize, or achieve, that portion which is *not* paid to the production worker (the surplus value), and a portion of which is then translated into profits. In so doing, they also contribute something (indirectly) to the process by which the surplus value is attained, and they too are paid only a portion of that which is contributed by them, hence they too are exploited. But at the same time, whatever it is that they are paid must come in the first place from the productivity of the producing workers, that is, from that portion which the productive worker does not receive: in short, from surplus value. Hence the white collar worker would seem to be living off the gravy produced by the blue collar worker—insufficient gravy, but gravy nevertheless.

A number of writers who follow in the footsteps of Marx have pointed out that the development of modern technology makes such a clearcut differentiation between production (the generation of surplus value) and other aspects of the process of translating production into surplus value, and profit, difficult indeed. In fact, if production is seen as a *process*, which no Marxist would deny, it is artificial to separate the primary (extractive), secondary (manufacturing), and tertiary (service) sectors in the contemporary integrated economic system. Production has become a societywide—indeed, a multinational—phenomenon, in which all wage earners who are socially necessary to the process (that is, who cannot be dispensed with under current conditions) and who are not paid the value of what they produce, (assuming that it can even be measured) directly or indirectly participate at some level in the creation/realization of surplus value. An automobile produced in a factory by an operative is absolutely useless in this society unless it can be transported and sold. Even though the teamster, the dispatcher, the billing clerk, and the salesperson add nothing concrete to the original product, they are, in the context of present society, indispensable to the process by which it is realized as a commodity. To some extent, the involvement of many kinds of workers in the process of production (including even marketing) is inherent in any economic system more complex than simple barter between an artisan and a customer. However, the division and specialization of labor has today reached a level not imagined by the thinkers of the nineteenth century: The increasing size of private firms as well as the state, in both numbers of employees and capital; the geographic expansion of markets from locality to nation to the world and the requirements of coordination, planning, and control (administration) have all contributed new layers of personnel. Moreover, technological developments (in part designed to assist in the administration of both people and other technologies) often require labor power in which the distinction between producer and realizer is not readily visible. Is it not artificial to say that the worker who inspects the product as it comes off the line, or even the worker who stitches the fabric on the seat, "produces," while the worker who drives the car onto the sales lot merely "realizes"? Each one, whether the collar be blue, gray, or white, is a necessary but not sufficient part of the overall process.

In addition, there are two processes that are indispensable to the overall process of production, even while they are removed from production in any direct sense: the reproduction of the productive forces of the society (new workers), and the reproduction of the social relations of production (the socialization process by which we become indoctrinated in the modes of behavior appropriate to our individual roles in the productive process). Without the reproduction and socialization of the labor force, there could be no process of production. Anyone connected to those processes is in some sense a worker, including housewives and, more to the point of this discussion, public sector workers, clerks, and teachers. None of these directly produce anything, but all are connected, in varying ways, with the process of production.

To argue that all these "indirect" producers live off the productivity of the original productive (i.e., blue collar) worker would, in today's economy, miss the point. As Harry Braverman put it in *Labor and Monopoly Capital:* "Although productive and unproductive labor are technically distinct . . . they form a continuous mass of employment which . . . has everything in common" (1974:423). If the relationship is one of *process*, then it is no longer fruitful to seek original causes.

But what of public sector workers, who live off the taxes paid by (all) workers? Indeed, this problem creates tensions, or secondary contradictions (hence tax revolts), but it does not negate the facts: (1) Most governmental functions are indirectly part of the process of production, the reproduction of the labor force, the reproduction of the relations of production, or the military protection of the present productive system; and (2) taxation is a way of socializing (that is, spreading among the population) certain costs of production that would be inefficient if left to individual firms. Rather than paying the worker less and having each firm run schools for the children of its workers, the worker is paid more and is taxed to have children schooled in a central place. The schooling is part of the productive (in this case, reproductive) process, and the schoolteacher as much a worker as the parent.

This brings us to the question of *subsistence*. It is sometimes said that white collar workers, particularly those at the upper levels, are paid more than the average worker and exploit to that degree. Yet with but few exceptions everyone in our society is paid a subsistence income. By subsistence is meant, very clearly, that which is required to live, to reproduce the labor force (at approximately one's own level), and, by implication, to reproduce the relations of production required at one's own level. If we are enabled, somehow, to acquire *more* than this form of subsistence, we reproduce labor at a higher level than our own. This is called upward mobility. Conversely, if we suffer bad fortune, we reproduce labor at a lower level—downward mobility. Naturally we seldom reproduce at precisely our own level, as individuals, but in the aggregate the labor force is reproduced more or less as is required by that generation of technology. One consequence of large-scale national planning is that this can be done more efficiently, that is, people can be socialized according to projections, rather than having the process left to individual whim. (For example, the state can control the output of institutions of higher education.)

While it is true, then, that virtually everyone contributes to the generation/realization of surplus value, directly or indirectly, it is not true that this makes everyone a worker, or that we therefore have a classless or single-class society. Who is not a worker? Those who live entirely or predominantly from profits (which are derived from surplus value)—landlords; coupon clippers; dividend collectors; persons whose income is based in part on stock options and other sources stemming from profits; those whose high incomes are unrelated in any meaningful way to subsistence, or to any reasonable calculus of production costs (the two are much the same)—for example, the twenty-five highest-paid "executives" in 1980, whose "earnings" ranged *upward* from $1.5 million per year each (*Business Week*, 11 May 1981). It is this section of the bourgeoisie whose incomes are not a necessary cost of production, but are instead based on the profitability of the firm (without which their incomes would collapse to a reasonable subsistence level, or the firm would declare bankruptcy).

Included among the categories of those who are not workers are those who are self-employed (the traditional petty bourgeoisie, or "old middle class"), whether they employ others or not. Some live off the labor of others plus their own labor; others live only from self-exploitation, which is in a sense contradictory, since only schizophrenics can be both workers and capitalists at the same time—but then political schizophrenia is in fact one of the recurring problems of the petty bourgeoisie.

What about high-level governmental administrators? Here the argument is a bit more complex. Indirectly, insofar as their incomes are significantly above subsistence even considering what is required to "reproduce" an administrator, this "super-income" is derived from taxes paid by workers and is based on a form of exploitation. But since the workers are paid wages sufficient to pay taxes (so as to socialize certain costs), top administrators are really being paid collectively, although indirectly, by the bourgeoisie. The difference between these high-level earners and ordinary civil servants, who have been characterized here as workers, is that the fundamental interest of the top administrators is to be responsive to the economic interests that dominate government, and that are responsible for their super-wages (through their manipulation and control of the political parties that control the legislatures that determine their pay).

Some supervisory work is essential to any process of production; such supervisors are also workers. Other supervisory work is unique to the extraction of surplus value, and still other "managerial" work is dedicated solely to controlling the labor force—an aspect of maximizing extraction (for example, "public relations," union-busting, redesigning the work process for the purpose of splitting workers apart ethnically, or for "de-skilling" them). As Richard Sobel has put it: "A distinction must be made between socially necessary . . . supervision and the managerial work involved in the extraction of surplus. While production need not be organized hierarchically, production of scale must be organized, and production with supervision is not inherently capitalist" (1982: 291). Ulf Kadritzke, who discusses this issue at some length, argues, "To the degree that capital constantly revolutionizes the technical and cooperative conditions of the work process in order to . . . increase the proportion of surplus value relative to necessary labor, the inner structure of the productive labor force changes. . . . With the increase of productivity and the associated integration of mental labor with the determinations of capital, the circle of productive workers widens" (1975: 86).

The argument, then, is that it is no longer feasible to divide the labor process for analytic purposes into those who "generate" versus those who "realize" surplus value, and to then argue that the latter grouping is in some sense "less working class" than the former. Today's integrated process of production, which includes the services sector and government, makes every wage earner a contributor, at some level, to the overall process (as are some nonwage earners, that is, housewives, who are not in the official labor force). The fundamental class distinction that must be made on the objective level is between all of those who are paid, directly or indirectly, at a contemporary cultural subsistence level to produce and reproduce, and those whose incomes are derived from profit. The latter include those private and public sector "managers" whose primary function is the long-term survival of the capitalist system—including the managers of our domestic and foreign military institutions.

These two classes, the workers and the bourgeoisie, continue to constitute the major classes that are in contradiction in our society. The Marxist assumption is that the social ills rooted in the exploitation of one class by another—war, poverty, racism, sexism—can be cured only by the elimination of that system of exploitation. The force to bring about such a revolutionary change is the class that is exploited—the working class, despite the complexity of its configuration. If there is to be fundamental change, it continues to be the working class—the producers (and reproducers), plus those whose contradictory or marginal class location makes their interests coincide to some degree with those of the working class—that must make it. The working class continues, albeit in a new form, to have the numbers, and to control the technological resources of day-to-day working life, to accomplish basic change.

Figure 1-2.
Class and fraction structure
in the United States

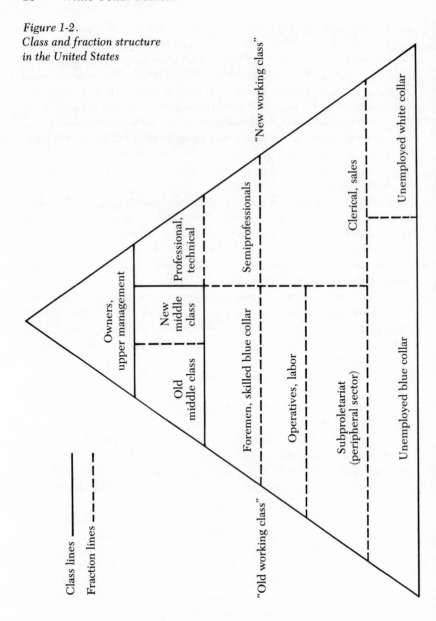

If we agree (a rather big "if," even within the left) that the working class, in its present complexity, continues to be the primary agent of fundamental change, several important issues remain to be resolved. Since the white collar occupations have become central to modern society, what segments of those occupations—and the people who hold them—constitute a part of the working class in terms of the criteria discussed above, and are therefore available for recuitment into movements for change? And what circumstances, including workplace conditions, the general economic picture, the political environment (including the degree of cohesiveness of both ruling and subordinate classes), make allegiance to the project of change more likely?

Certainly one part of any answer to these questions requires a look at a broader issue: Why has the working class in the United States not been recruited into a socialist project up to now, despite a tradition of militance and a series of historical conjunctions during which mass mobilization for fundamental change would have been expected? The lack of such a development, or even of significant progress toward independent working class politics, is surely one component of our present political environment. This past must be better understood if we are not to remain bystanders in the struggles to come. The next chapter deals with that issue.

2
The Problem
of U.S. Exceptionalism

Virtually all discussion of the politics of the white collar strata since the 1890s has been motivated by the "search for agency"—the question of which classes or strata (or other groupings based on ethnicity or gender) have the potential for becoming significant political actors, either alone or in combination. The fact is that the traditional (blue collar) working class has not become more class conscious, much less revolutionary, anywhere in the Western world. If anything, recent events suggest the opposite. Moreover, in proportion to other segments of the labor force, the working class is becoming smaller. What this means is that one of the main pillars of the Marxist theoretical structure (and therefore political strategy) is open to question.

In Western Europe and Canada, the working class had traditionally been present on the political stage in the form of at least one political party that is clearly based in it and that has at least a rhetorical commitment to some form of socialist transformation. Further, trade unions have played a significant role in support of such parties. To that extent, the traditional working class has been a class-conscious class. In the United States, however, the working class and labor movement have been absent from politics as an independent force since at least the early 1920s. This absence (as well as the decline of such forces in other Western countries) raises two questions: Why, in the United States, is there not even an independent working class party and labor movement? And what political role will the growing white collar sector of the labor force play?

The Crisis of the Labor Movement

Organized labor is in decline as a proportion of the labor force, as a significant political factor, and as a movement at the cutting edge of social progress, just at a time when the state of the U.S. economy is having a devastating effect on the labor movement and the working class as a whole—this time, unlike in the 1930s, with the state closely collaborating with capital to undermine the gains that labor has made over the past fifty years. As the *New York Times* pointed out in its Business Section (31 May 1981), noting the inability of labor to deal with the crisis of unemployment: "Organized labor—20 million strong, possessed of billions of dollars . . . has become an oddly quiescent giant . . . [it] neither understands workplace trends nor . . . is able to come up with imaginative strategies to counter them." Quoting Anthony Mazzocchi, one of the more imaginative and progressive labor leaders, the article goes on to indict the labor movement for having "no program, not doing any organizing, not having any vision."

At the most immediate level, organized labor, while continuing to grow very slowly in numbers, now represents a smaller proportion of the labor force than it did in 1940—between 20 and 25 percent, depending on the definition of "union." Some of its traditionally most militant unions (Automobile Workers, Electrical Workers, and Garment Workers, among others) are declining in absolute membership in the face of unemployment and "deindustrialization"—the flight of industrial capital from traditional manufacturing centers and an overall shift of the economy from manufacturing to the tertiary sector. The labor movement has been notably inept in dealing with "Reaganomics," even in its milder form under former President Carter. It has, for instance, done virtually nothing to cope with many factory closings, such as the one in Mahwah, New Jersey, where nearly four thousand auto workers were laid off in June 1980.

Moreover, despite a few spectacular wage gains and an overall rise in dollar income (such that 60 percent of all U.S. family units now earn between $20,000 and $50,000 annually), unions have not been able to improve the real after-tax income of the U.S. wage earners, which has remained unchanged since 1965. Further, lower-income families have not improved relative to other strata: Their real incomes too have remained unchanged over the last twenty years. Large numbers of occupational groups lose real income at a rate of 3 to 6 percent a year, including unionized workers and those in the state sector. As of mid-1984, the inflation rate had declined under Reagan. The unemployment rate had also declined, to about 7.4 percent. However, U.S. unemployment rate figures are notoriously unreliable and considerably underestimate actual unemployment. The overall rate gives no indication of far higher rates for specific groups and communities, such as black youth in urban areas, who suffer a rate of around 60 percent by most estimates, or places like Michigan, where the rate is probably close to 20 percent. Further, the average length of unemployment has continued to climb, to a post–World War II record of twenty-two weeks in June 1983. Nor does the overall rate count "discouraged workers," those who have given up looking for jobs.

How has organized labor responded to these deteriorating conditions? In the absence of a concerted approach, individual unions have been forced to make a broad variety of concessions, or "givebacks," ranging from wage cuts or freezes to the surrender of a variety of fringe benefits to increased workloads. Unions (or workers) have in a few cases purchased plants threatened with closing but the new management has often instituted the same wage freezes or cuts that the workers rejected under the previous owner.

From 1979 to 1984, employment in manufacturing, construction, and mining, three of the sectors of the economy where unions are strongest, declined by nearly 2.4 million. During the same period, jobs in wholesale and retail trade and in services more generally, sectors where the percentage of organized workers is far lower, increased by more than 4 million.

The labor movement has compensated for its rapid losses among blue collar workers by organizing in that sector of the labor force that is growing: the white collar sector—specifically, the services sector, including government employment, and (disproportionately distributed in white collar occupations) among women. But even here, organizing has been slow, and the number of new white collar members has not compensated for the loss of members in other sectors.

Those unions that exist in the white collar field are, moreover, weak when compared with unions in manufacturing. Public sector unions are often crippled by laws forbidding or inhibiting the right to strike, as well as the right to struggle for a closed or union shop. Many of the larger of these unions have come into existence "on the cheap," that is, by federal executive order, without the kind of struggle that makes for a militant membership. With a few exceptions, they have gained little for their members: White collar economic conditions, often determined by state and local political and tax-income considerations (the relative health of government budgets), do not appear to differ much between union and nonunion settings. Again with a few exceptions (in "protective" jobs such as police, fire, and garbage collection), white collar workers, especially in the public sector, have little clout even when they do strike: "Consumers" become hostile because of the withdrawal of such "necessary" services as publicly supported babysitting—the school system. This is particularly true when it comes to health-care workers, who are often chastised as virtual public enemies when they threaten strike action. The labor movement has been incapable of developing alternative "clout" tactics that would enable white collar workers to score real gains without dividing them from the taxpaying community, with one exception: Public sector unions are now increasingly taking the road of political lobbying (both in Washington and in the state capitals). While this strategy does not ally them with other taxpayers, it does generate results in the form of regular cost-of-living adjustments and such fringe benefits as health insurance. At the same time, however, the public's view of unions as "just another pressure group looking out after its own" is reinforced. Moreover, the lobbying approach rarely involves the rank-and-file; on the contrary, it creates a new layer of bureaucratic experts within the unions' leadership.

What has happened to a labor movement once considered one of the more radical in the world, with one of the most violent histories of any labor movement? Why does the United States have no radical labor movement, or even a mass social-democratic political formation that has the support, say, of half the traditional working class? Why is there no movement with the capacity to find a way out of the present economic stalemate?

U.S. Exceptionalism

All explanations of the present state of political development of the U.S. working class end at the same place: the "theory" of U.S. "exceptionalism." The meaning of the phrase "level of political development" is usually limited to several rather imprecise indices: some public opinion surveys, election results, union policies, and a set of miscellaneous behaviors such as strike data. Indeed, when pressed, observers are forced to concede that what they really mean by "political development" is the *absence* of behaviors normally considered part of political development in other countries: a *socialist* trade union movement, and an *independent labor party*. Alone in the Western parliamentary world, the U.S. labor movement is seen to lack both.

We assume that the U.S. labor movement is different because it lacks a socialist trade union movement and an independent (working class) labor party, that is, that in other Western countries there *are*, in fact, such formations. Is that really true today? Where in the Western world is there a trade union movement whose socialism goes beyond campaign rhetoric, and where is there a labor or social-democratic, or even mass-based communist party, that is based on the principle of working class power? We further assume, at least socialists do, that to have such a movement is the precondition for the development of a socialist society. Is that really true today? Can a socialist (social-democratic, labor party, electorally oriented, reformist, multiclass) movement in fact achieve socialism within the confines of late capitalism?

If it is true, first, that other Western countries lack a real socialist and independent working class movement, and second, that even where there is such a movement it is incapable of transforming society, then much of the exceptional nature of the United States is not so exceptional after all (cf. Przeworski 1980). But in fact, despite shortcomings, the political milieu in Western Europe and Canada permits a level of discourse about politics that is unimaginable in the United States at the present time. In other words, the potential for "real" socialism exists in countries where socialism is part of legitimate political discussion, as is not the case in the United States.

It is often argued that the reason for this lack of a socialist consciousness is that there is no radical culture, party, or labor movement; and, conversely, that the lack of such a culture, party, or movement stems from the workers' "embourgeoisified," or "false," consciousness. Unfortunately, this is an insoluble chicken-and-egg dilemma. A more dialectical and integrated explanation is needed. The theory broadly known as exceptionalism attempts to provide that.

There are generally two overlapping dimensions to the exceptionalism argument, the embourgeoisement thesis and the segmentation thesis. These in turn contain several sets of assumptions involving both structural and political or cultural features. Although in any overall analysis neither of these features exists in isolation—each affects and is affected by all the others—for practical purposes I shall temporarily describe each dimension of the theory separately.

The Embourgeoisement Thesis

One of the most common arguments for the lack of a radical labor movement in the United States is some variation of what Shalev and Korpi (1980) call "opportunity theory," an idea closely related to the concept of embourgeoisement. The historian Frederick Jackson Turner laid the foundation for this theory in an 1893 essay entitled "The Significance of the Frontier in American History." Turner argued that the frontier promoted a unique individualism by promising perpetual opportunity for those willing to take advantage of its conditions. "Since the days when the fleet of Columbus sailed into the waters of the New World, America has been another name for opportunity . . . a gate of escape from the bondage of the past" (Turner, in Ginger 1961: 118). The existence of free (or cheap) land acted as an "escape valve" for the discontented masses of the industrial northeast in the 1800s and early 1900s. The frontier philosophy persists even today, with many seeing the Sunbelt or Alaska, or outer space, as the "last frontier."

It is doubtful that many actually escaped, since most immigrants stayed where they happened to land rather than pressing onward. Moreover, it was pre–Civil War immigrants from northwestern Europe who could afford the transportation westward to find cheap land, while later immigrants—including those of peasant origin—were less fortunate (Rosenblum 1973: chap. 3). Nevertheless, the "Turner Thesis" was a powerful rationalization for individualism and opposition to collective action.

The Turner Thesis was soon elaborated on by a number of labor theorists in the early 1900s, particularly John R. Commons (beginning in 1905) and his many students, the best known of whom was probably Selig Perlman (1922, 1928, 1935). In brief, the new labor theorists argued that the absolute and relative (relative to Europe) affluence of the U.S. working class, including the unique opportunities for individual advancement within and between social classes, makes radical alternatives not only unnecessary but ideologically unfeasible.

The frontier thesis, as well as most conventional opportunity theories, thus focuses on domestic economic expansion and opportunity, as if these existed in a conflictless, benign laboratory that inevitably molds the social character of all U.S. workers in a middle-class ideological direction. It was, and still is, a singularly idealistic focus that misses the material underpinnings of whatever bourgeois consciousness does permeate the working class. Any real understanding of the relationship of consciousness to the "unique" nature of the U.S. economy and its alleged opportunities must transcend that limited approach and understand that the idea of economic expansion has to be linked to a theory of imperialism. This link is missing from the work of virtually all "labor theorists," who therefore remain standing on the first step of an analysis, valuable though that first step may be in overcoming naive notions of inevitable working class radicalism.

The rapid expansion of the United States westward, which involved acquiring land from other nations—sometimes peacefully but often militarily, was quickly followed by the defeat of the slave-holding South, and then, with the Spanish-American War of 1898, by expansion overseas. And so the external colonies of Puerto Rico and the Philippines were added to the continental conquest of Native Americans and Mexicans. By the mid-1920s, Hawaii, the Philippines, and Puerto Rico had become dependent on the metropolitan country—even for those foods they had once grown themselves. Immense profits from sugar, tobacco, and coffee poured into the continental United States, providing, as had happened in Europe two centuries before, a vast base for capital investment and industrial growth. This is not the place for a lengthy analysis of dependency theory; suffice it to say that British workers were not the only ones in the Western world to profit indirectly from the colonization and exploitation of "backward nations." Unlike European workers, however, the relative prosperity of workers in the United States rests on an empire that through economic penetration, with occasional military backup (direct or indirect), has continued to expand uninterruptedly since 1776.

Moreover, the resulting U.S. domination, firm from 1945 until about 1975, has benefited from the military defeat, or exhaustion, of several previously powerful empires—Spain, Germany, and Great Britain in particular—in each case without a single enemy bomb being dropped on the continental United States, and with comparatively lower casualties in military manpower. Expansion into Canada, where some 50 to 60 percent of the economy is in U.S. hands, has become a significant component of this development. It was not until the Indo-Chinese War in the 1970s that the United States suffered its first defeat abroad. It is clear that the prosperity of monopoly capital—particularly its multinational wing—has permitted it to surrender wage levels to unionized workers that would not have been possible under other circumstances. Further, economic expansion has created shortages of certain kinds of labor, whether of railroad workers, engineers, computer programmers, or secretaries, that enabled these workers to demand a high price for their labor. This was one of Commons's points in arguing that U.S. unions mainly focus on bread-and-butter issues, for what need is there for a more radical program as long as it is possible to obtain a high price for one's labor?

The political development of a class, the level of consciousness of its class interest, reflects not only short-run material realities but also the configuration of the class forces in which people find themselves. In the United States, one of the most important of these historical factors, noted by numerous observers, is the absence of precapitalist class structures and social institutions. This absence is crucial to an explanation of proletarian movements in the United States, which Mike Davis labels "depoliticized" (at least in contrast with European movements). In Europe the "working classes were forced to conduct protracted struggles for suffrage and civil liberties" (1980:9), while in the United States popular suffrage existed virtually without property qualifications from 1832 on (for white males). In Europe, the working classes, in the context of weak middle classes, played leading roles in the overthrow of aristocracies and the establishment of bourgeois class rule; in the United States, the bourgeoisie, with no powerful aristocracy to defeat, carried through its own revolution without requiring the help of "plebeian wings or 'surrogates' to defeat aristocratic reaction and demolish the structure of the ancient regime" (ibid.: 11).

The lack of a feudal tradition in the United States had two consequences. First, the newly formed working class did not constitute itself an autonomous political force as it had done in Europe. Second, the deeply ingrained sense of class (and class oppression) so prevalent in Europe as the result of feudalism's harsh practices was less developed in the United States (except in the plantation South under slavery). Yet the embourgeoisement thesis (including its component parts—the frontier, the relative affluence, and the absence-of-feudalism theses) fails to explain U.S. exceptionalism. There can be little doubt that petty-bourgeois aspirations and perceptions have been a constant in the history of the U.S. working class, and continue to be significant among large segments of that class today. This is true in part because a limited reality underlies those perceptions. But to overgeneralize from that limited reality, as labor theorists do, is a mistake, for each component of the overall thesis has been challenged on factual grounds.

The frontier thesis, to the degree that it is valid, works largely as a component of the growth and geographical expansion of industry, and not as Turner had surmised. All countries undergoing capitalist development, therefore, have such a "frontier"; the United States is exceptional only in that the industrial frontier is larger. As Mike Davis points out, it was not the farm frontier that was relevant but the industrial one: "It was this expanding urban-industrial frontier—rather than the Turnerian agrarian frontier—with its constantly replenished opportunities for small-scale entrepreneurial accumulation, that provided material sustenance for the petty-bourgeois ideologies of individual mobility that gripped the minds of so many American workers" (ibid.: 19). In short, "boom-town" expansion after 1850 constantly undermined the historic continuity of class relations in the traditional industrial centers. As for the relative affluence of the U.S. working class, Rosenblum (1973) has shown that U.S. workers actually improved their position less than did workers in four other Western countries between 1860 and 1893, and less than those in three other countries between 1860 and 1939 (workers in France, Sweden, and Great Britain all did better). Moreover, Norway also lacked a feudal tradition, yet had for a long time a markedly radical labor movement, while Denmark, with a strongly feudal tradition, has relatively moderate labor and social-democratic movements. Further, the franchise was obtained without serious struggle in Norway even before a real industrial labor force was formed. There was relatively little of the extreme repression of the labor movement characteristic, say, of Austria, yet the Norwegian labor movement was syndicalist (like the Industrial Workers of the World in the United States), and the Norwegian socialist party was the only one in the Western world in which the majority voted to join Lenin's Third International.

Embourgeoisement or opportunity theory also holds that mobility (blue collar parents have white collar children, or blue collar workers become white collar workers) indicates a move from proletarian to petty-bourgeois existence for so many people that to expect class consciousness in the traditional sense is foolish. While it is true that there have been changes in the nature of work, a series of counterforces undermine the effects of this sort of "opportunity." These will be described more extensively in chapters 5, 6, and 7, but briefly, technological improvements may produce greater alienation (not to mention unemployment) for many groups of workers and a deterioration of working conditions and incomes affects even professional workers. We must be careful not to generalize to the entire working class the advancements possible for limited fractions able to take advantage of new technologies, or able to protect themselves in guildlike unions or professional associations.

The Fragmentation Thesis

The second major thesis underpinning the theory of U.S. exceptionalism is that of the extreme segmentation or fragmentation of the working class in the United States. Although all working classes are segmented in some way—by skill level, gender, religion, language, race, and quasinational or ethnic differences, as well as by their different structural places in the economy (state versus private sector workers, to give a common example), no working class in the Western world suffers from all of these segmentations as deeply and as extensively as the U.S. working class.

The lines along which one segment of the U.S. working class is pitted against another are legion: white against black, native born against immigrant, Protestant against Catholic against Jew, skilled against unskilled, unionized against unorganized, employed against unemployed and welfare recipient, private sector against state sector, blue collar against white collar, urban against suburban, male against female, and those working in "protectionist" industries against "free traders." Many workers are in more than one segment and thus have overlapping hostilities. These differences have political consequences, some of which are played out in the major political parties or unions; many, however, are reflected only at the level of interpersonal behavior, voting, and so on.

The relationship among skill level, ethnicity, and unionization is a good illustration of the way such interactions work.

Jobs are not distributed randomly among races and ethnic groups, or between the sexes: All occupations have distinctive ethnic and gender distributions; all groups have distinctive occupational profiles, developed in response to particular conditions, such as industrial development, labor shortages or surpluses, the availability of immigrant or ex-slave workers, the need to contain wages in the interest of capital accumulation, and the availability of prejudice to rationalize discrimination based on some form of racial, ethnic, or religious labeling. In the steel industry, for instance, a virtually unbridgeable gulf separated English-speaking workers who controlled the skilled jobs from Eastern European immigrants, with consequences for consciousness: "Eager to dissociate himself from the Hunky (Hungarian), the skilled man identified with the middling group of small shopkeepers and artisans, and with them came to regard the merchants and managers as his model" (Brody 1960:121). The language problem was deliberately manipulated by employers to control the labor force, and the early American Federation of Labor (AFL) was hard put to overcome this obstacle, particularly since it officially advocated restrictions on immigration, and many of its affiliates barred blacks and Catholics! Nevertheless, during all of its organizing campaigns, the Steelworkers and its predecessor unions (of which twenty-four claimed some jurisdiction in the steel industry in 1918) studiously translated their leaflets into the dozens of languages represented in the steel mills, hired organizers who spoke them, and held rallies with speakers in the requisite languages. The great steel strike of that period foundered, however, on the rocks of immigrant divisions, when many of those still oriented to a return to Europe (next summer, next year, with their savings guaranteeing an upward mobility back home) continued to work (Rosenblum 1973: 160).

By the 1920s, craft labor had been displaced by an extensive division of labor (commonly associated with the term "Taylorism") in most major industries. The assembly line had been introduced in the automobile industry by Henry Ford in 1914. The identification of specific jobs with specific nationalities was common in the steel industry (Stone 1975). The subdivision of jobs coincided with the appearance of immigrant workers, so that each ethnic group came to be associated with a particular job, and each job with that ethnic group. Similarly, as new technologies created new kinds of jobs, the availability of a particular ethnic, gender, or racial group tended to lock that group into those jobs, and identify those jobs as "belonging" to that group (as in the case of women and typing). This fragmentation of work along ethnic and other sectoral lines had two consequences: It made union organizing more difficult, and it diverted "workers' consciousness from a class orientation and replace[d] it with an identification with one's stratum in society, producing status consciousness" (Wachtel 1975:107).

The most divisive line of segmentation in the U.S. working class has without a doubt been race, and racism has been *the* most persistent obstacle to working class unity. Racism is not merely a matter of miseducation leading to individual prejudice. That is of course true, but it does not explain the persistence of a racially skewed labor market, such that the black community as a whole suffers a rate of unemployment (during times of *prosperity*) roughly the same as that suffered by the *entire* population during the worst of the 1930s Depression. Nor does it explain how blacks with the same job titles as whites earn significantly less and how Spanish-speaking people suffer similarly.

The theory of a "dual labor market" provides a perspective on this development. It argues that the structural division of capitalist economies into "core" (oligopolistic, capital-intensive, relatively unionized) and "peripheral" (competitive, labor-intensive, relatively nonunionized) sectors coincides with race: Nonwhites are overrepresented in the peripheral sector, which is generally characterized by jobs requiring less skill and lower levels of formal education. Certain jobs and job levels are associated with certain groups (because those groups are available at the time those jobs appear), and these groups then become locked into these jobs because of discrimination—they are prevented from obtaining the skills needed for other jobs. In this way, blacks and Hispanics have become identified with low-paying jobs, unemployment, and welfare, creating further prejudice on the part of other workers who feel they are paying for the welfare. Several studies have demonstrated how discrimination against these minorities holds down overall wages (e.g., Willhelm 1980), yet racist practices and beliefs persist throughout the population, including in the labor movement.

Racism as a phenomenon that affects working class unity must therefore be seen as having two complementary aspects: the institutional racism that is rooted in the structure of the (dual) capitalist economy and the persistence of racist beliefs and practices within the working class and within the unions. Racism is not merely an invention of Wall Street to divide workers from each other, though it is often that. It is not merely an ideology historically absorbed by elements of organized labor to maintain a monopoly on certain "prestigious" jobs or to create such a monopoly where it did not exist before, though it has been that. It is not merely an aspect of distorted or displaced "nativism" through which a segment of the workforce seeks to obtain or maintain a "one-up" position in the prestige system, though it is that. Nor is it merely a result of a threat that jobholders feel from a reserve army of the unemployed in a time of a shrinking job market, though, cyclically, it has always played that role too (the number of lynchings is closely correlated with the price of cotton prior to World War II). The consequence is that blacks, who find themselves disproportionally in the peripheral sector, are in a permanent economic depression, making black labor qualitatively different from white labor inasmuch as many blacks are outside the class system altogether. It is this that pits the black unemployed against the white employed.

A second kind of fragmentation pits private sector workers—some 83 percent of the employed labor force—against the 17 percent that is employed in the public sector (plus all those receiving some form of assistance). The critical issue here is taxation, and the belief among many private sector workers that they are being forced to support wasteful governmental expenditures. Of course, many in that 83 percent also receive some form of subsidy, such as college scholarships, or work for corporations receiving government contracts, so that this resistance is not total. Indeed, although workers often claim to be opposed to the welfare "safety net," they support a wide range of specific assistance programs, perhaps because they or their relatives are beneficiaries. Nevertheless, the private-public division is a reality, and creates antagonisms within the working class. In a period when real income is at a standstill, taxes become a nasty question and politicians who talk of "budget cutting" are popular.

The third major segmentation within the U.S. working class is a geographical one. It takes several forms: between urban and suburban workers (this overlaps with racial segmentation), between workers in the industrial or "smokestack" states and those in the "sun belt," and between workers in the United States and those in third world countries that come within the orbit of multinational capital. The divisive issue of immigration policy is related to this third division, as is the argument between protectionists and free traders on the subject of tariff and other restrictions on foreign imports.

The common denominator among these geographical segmentations is the role of technological change and what has come to be called "deindustrialization." This is the outmigration of predominantly younger, better-educated whites from the central cities to the suburbs, the gradual depopulation of the Northeastern industrial corridor in response to the pull of jobs created by new technology in the South, Southwest, and West, and the unemployment of those remaining as factory work gradually moves out of the continental United States to areas of lower labor costs. Those workers who are left behind cannot be retained for new technologies because they lack the education (and training programs) or because they are too old. The industries that are left behind are labor-intensive and find themselves competing with cheap labor abroad. The Northeast becomes bimodal: white collar tertiary workers, who tend to live in the suburbs, and the unskilled, who live in the urban centers. The cities become poorer and poorer, their tax bases deteriorate, their services decay—leading to the further exodus of everyone who can afford to leave. Gradually, the cities become welfare enclaves, disproportionately nonwhite, centers of poverty and crime.

On a larger scale, manufacturing flees to areas of the world where labor is cheaper and more "stable," that is, less unionized, and where governments are more amenable to acting as social control agents.

First they go to the U.S. South, where "open shop" laws predominate, preventing unionization; then to Puerto Rico, Mexico, Jamaica, Taiwan, etc. U.S. firms continually export their labor costs, at the expense of U.S. jobs and of those firms that cannot compete with foreign labor. Thus U.S. investments in underdeveloped countries expanded from $5.75 billion in 1950 to $52.7 billion in 1980 (*Dollars and Sense*, December 1981). Although investment in Western Europe has, in recent years, been growing at a rate even faster than that in Latin America, profit rates continue to be highest in third world countries. Politically, as Vuskovic (1980) reminds us, the consequence of this policy of accumulation means that "we can expect an increase in authoritarianism, repression, and the separation of larger and larger sectors of the population from the political process" in these third world countries. The Reagan approach to "human rights" is an index to this development.

A further consequence of deindustrialization on working class solidarity and consciousness has been an end to the "urban village"—the traditional working class community that supported strikes and in which large numbers of people had similar jobs working at the same or similar firms. The suburbanization of the working class has meant that blue collar and white collar workers live together. It means long commutes and low-density housing, and less of the social interaction characteristic of urban neighborhoods (which were, in addition, ethnic enclaves). It also means more concentration on home ownership and greater dependence on the consumer "necessities" required to support suburban life—cars in particular. Whether the suburbs ever become new working class villages is not the question. Some have. The point is that the suburban life-style has added still one more obstacle to identifying as working class.

It might appear that the embourgeoisement thesis is contradicted by certain aspects of the fragmentation theory. Does imperialism's profit trickle down to "embourgeoisify" the working class, or does fragmentation function to impoverish it? Does the United States's vast industrial capacity enrich the working class, or are we at the edge of economic disaster? Yet to ask the question is to answer it: The working class is a contradictory, ambiguous phenomenon. It is fragmented so that some work for sectors of capital that make some fractions relatively better off, and others work for sectors whose dynamic makes these fractions worse off. Many workers rise, intra- and intergenerationally, to white collar and semiprofessional jobs; others fall, to disappear into the unemployed or lumpenproletariat. Some workers increase their skills and autonomy, while others become de-skilled, their jobs more and more subdivided and simplified, and their wages reduced. These two major structural features of the American working class—relative opportunity for many, plus fragmentation of the class as a whole (which reduces opportunity for many others)—combine to divide the working class, and constitute a monumental obstacle to the development of an independent working class politics.

Superstructural Institutions

The embourgeoisement and fragmentation theses involve elements of material culture Marxists term "substructural." They stem from basic economic institutions, including the level of technology and the way the economy is structured under capitalism. These productive forces, and the way they are organized, are assumed to be somewhat more independent and determining than other institutions, termed "superstructural." Among the superstructural factors that have been suggested as being significant in influencing the level of working class consciousness and organizational activity (including socialist activity) in the United States are: the particular political structure (the role of the state), the specific nature of trade unions, employer policy, the role of the cultural apparatuses (including academia and the media), and the role (and mistakes) of the left. While none of these is an isolated phenomenon, all reflect and affect the level of working class and socialist activity. In short, each of these superstructural elements contributes to U.S. exceptionalism.

EMPLOYERS AND THE STATE

From the beginning of the labor movement, employers developed strategies for containing it. First, they were able to take advantage of the decentralized structure of the state. In the United States, at least prior to the New Deal, political jurisdictions had "virtual autonomy in wielding police power, with the prime object of protecting life and property (rather than, as in Europe, preserving the state). These circumstances often rendered local police forces actually or effectively agents of employers" (Shalev and Korpi 1980: 47). Together with the frequent use of strikebreakers, vigilantes, and private guards, employers used government to repress labor. This strategy did not change significantly until well into the New Deal, when some fractions of capital began to see collective bargaining as a useful way to co-opt militancy and create a stable and reliable workforce.

Paralleling this strategy of resistance, employers rewarded conservative labor leaders and co-opted them politically (through the Democratic Party), while the state vigorously repressed radical elements within the labor movement. Nonradical labor leaders found it easy to participate in the Democratic Party and to become part of the "spoils system" of big city political machines. In addition, the two-party federal system embedded in the U.S. Constitution made it extremely difficult for third parties to become legitimate. Excluded from the ballot and from the legislature, minority parties remained largely impotent. The trade unions gained access to significant political influence only with the New Deal, which was partially dependent on their support. But this only confirmed and strengthened the alliance of union leaders (and the majority of their members) with the Democratic Party, making it even more difficult to develop independent political action.

THE UNIONS

Despite the Depression and the wave of union organizing that accompanied the New Deal, the militancy of the labor movement was quickly tamed and AFL-type bureaucrats restored to the powerful positions which they hold to this day. Mainstream union leaders came to see their role as that of bringing in immigrant workers without their radical traditions, while at the same time opposing further immigration; developing a partnership with the Democratic Party and the state in order to squeeze out concessions; advocating racial equality to protect members from strikebreaking, while condoning racial bars within the unions themselves; and supporting reform within the political structure while allowing portions of their own structure to become, and remain, corrupt and linked to organized crime.

Conservative, "economistic" unionism, more concerned with protecting the jobs of its members and officials than with organizing the working class, has led to criminal infiltration and to a marriage with U.S. foreign policy. As Herbert Hill has observed (*Nation*, 27 June 1981):

> Since the end of World War II, the U.S. government has assisted and protected union leadership groups that either aquiesced or engaged in corrupt activities, because of the services of such groups at home and abroad in the areas of foreign policy and national security. The govern-

ment repeatedly gave vital support to the union leaders who endorsed
and actively helped implement U.S. foreign policy. . . . within this context, the underworld was able to advance its own power and influence so
that the spread of labor corruption now extends to the highest levels of
the AFL-CIO, as well as to the independent unions like the Teamsters.

A part of the reason for the role of unions in foreign policy is structural: The unions that are most vocal in foreign policy are those with
the most immediate interest in it, particularly in military contracts.
But in the longer run, as Berger notes, "Labor leaders came to share
the ideals which largely dominated American foreign policy after 1897
and did so because of their acceptance of corporation capitalism and
their belief that the vital interests of the unions would be served in the
process" (1979:202). Soviet Communism was perceived as inimical to
the interests of American unions, and the ferocious anticommunism of
Jay Lovestone, Meany's foreign policy advisor, corresponded precisely
to the needs of American foreign policy in the days of the Cold War,
though this is not as much the case today in the era of East-West trade.

In this country, as in other countries, it is true that "if the trade
union remains an elementary organ of struggle, it has also evolved into
a force for integrating the workers into the corporate capitalist system,"
through the medium of collective bargaining (Aronowitz 1973: chap.
4). This contradictory role makes it impossible to ignore unions, and
equally impossible to accept them as is—even their most progressive
wings. Yet American unions' lack of imagination in the face of the
present economic crisis is unique among all union movements in the
world. If we place this situation in a historical context that includes the
many elements that make up American exceptionalism, we can see
both that this lack of imagination is the logical culmination of the
unique American development and that the structure, ideology, and
strategy of unions are a significant element, in turn, of that exceptionalism, affecting many of the other elements.

IDEOLOGY

This brings us to the role of ideology, so crucial in all discussions of
"embourgeoisement." Not only do major ideological apparatuses dis-
seminate an overarching mythology, but the left has also played a part
in obscuring or mystifying reality in order to rationalize particular
modes of action or inaction. Often, ironically, this stance has simply
been the mirror image of "hegemonic" ideology.

Academic social science has contributed more than a little to the mystification of labor's realities. As Laslett has pointed out, until World War II "most labor theorists looked at the working class from the point of view of the role played by unions viewed as institutional mechanisms" (1979:5), that is, labor theory was trade union leadership theory. Little work was done on rank-and-file workers, nonunion workers, workers' private lives, opinions, or culture. The existence of a working class culture was either denied or confused with the culture of poverty; immigrants, blacks, and the common class elements were lost. Perhaps this is not surprising given that labor scholars have traditionally been advocates of the assimilation of immigrant cultures—indeed favoring the homogenization of all cultures into a "middle class," "American" culture.

Labor scholarship has thus contributed to the idea of "classlessness" in the United States. By ignoring the study of working class culture and the radical tradition in immigrant culture, U.S. scholars helped to create the middle class myth, just as, by ignoring radicalism within the labor movement, they helped to create the myth that U.S. workers and their unions are merely and necessarily job conscious, and bread-and-butter oriented.

Social science has also contributed to the classless or middle class myth by denying the validity of the concept "class" altogether and by substituting for it—as do sociology texts to this day—the term "stratum." Stratification theory (which sometimes uses the term class, but in a way that denies any conflictual component) sees people as being quantitatively different from one another, rather than as clustered in classes that are qualitatively differentiated and in conflict. If there are no classes (as Marxists understand the term), there can be no conflict; if no conflict, then no classes.

The stratification concept results in, and from, a particular form of labeling, originated in part by the U.S. Bureau of the Census. Just as in Germany the notions of *Arbeiter, Angestellte,* and *Beamte* are historical artifacts, so in the United States the idea that white collar is differentiated from blue collar is a politically determined distinction, not one inherent in the jobs themselves. Moreover, the explosion in the number of job titles since the 1840s does not necessarily reflect an explosion in the number of different jobs. In fact, the reverse is sometimes the case, as when a job becomes fragmented in order to differentiate "women's work" and "children's work" from "men's work," even when the work itself is the same. A label is thus reified; artificial differentiations between jobs become accepted as real. Equally important, they have real consequences, so that after a while the label does indeed reflect a new reality.

The myth that the United States is a classless, or a middle class, society is reflected in the widespread perception that in this society everyone can be upwardly mobile if they work hard. The idea of individual upward mobility, sometimes called the Horatio Alger myth (after a fictional hero who went from rags to riches), places the responsibility for success, as well as failure, on the individual rather than on societywide factors, and is therefore logically counterposed to the idea that people can improve their lot through collective, or classwide, action. The idea of a classless society in which individuals can succeed through hard work dominates the popular media, appearing in television "soaps," pulp novels, and popular songs. It is underlined by the biased treatment given the history of trade unions, the growth of industry and monopolies, the role of the state, and even philanthropy in materials used to teach school children. Jena Anyon, who studied seventeen widely used secondary school history texts, noted that these

> textbooks not only express the dominant groups' ideologies, but also help to form attitudes in support of their social position. . . . poverty is a consequence of the failure of individuals, rather than of the failure of the society to distribute economic resources universally. This ideology encourages education and other actions that attempt to change the individual while leaving the unequal economic structures intact. Finally, textbooks promote the idea that there is no working class in the United States, and contribute to the myth that workers are middle class. (1979:382)

The widespread belief that the individual is alone responsible for the failure to achieve upward mobility, for remaining poor, for being unemployed, has dramatic consequences for mental health, as Richard Sennett and Jonathan Cobb (1972) have demonstrated. When people follow the rules, and still fail to succeed, they come to see themselves as inadequate, a perception that is constantly reinforced by the cultural apparatus.

The media may do their best to keep the myth current, but it would not be so widely accepted were there not some facts to support it. Virtually every working class child knows of at least one close relative who has been upwardly mobile (or at least horizontally mobile, from blue collar to white collar, which is often perceived as upwardly mobile). And indeed the United States has been the land of opportunity for enough people enough of the time—for whatever particular historical reasons—so these beliefs continue to accompany even the thinnest and most superficial objective opportunity.

Radical (including Marxist) theory in the United States has failed to understand the realities, no matter how limited, of embourgeoise-ment; has failed to comprehend the seriousness of working class frag-mentation (particularly the tenacity of ethnic loyalties, and the reality of the dual labor market); and has failed to incorporate the question of consciousness (subjective embourgeoisement) into theory. These fail-ures have persistently led to what Gabriel Kolko has called a "paralyz-ing and debilitating optimism" (in Laslett 1979). Lacking a theory to account for retreat and defeat, the organized left attributes the lack of revolutionary consciousness among U.S. workers either to sellouts by trade union leaders (the "labor lieutenants of the capitalist class" thesis), an "incorrect" party line (too opportunistic, too sectarian, too white and/or male chauvinistic—that is, bad propaganda), or, in the case of segments of the "new left," a Marcusian write-off of workers in the United States altogether as having become totally and hopelessly bourgeois.

How is it that the American left has been unable to explain the exceptionalist character of the U.S. industrial experience or provide a guide to social action? Is it, as Laslett suggests, partly because of an "American" aversion to theory? Or is it because the labor movement, for its own reasons, has made no demands on the left—after all, most of the left exists outside of it? Or is it because of an inability to understand the issues of race and nationality?

All of these are true, but all root the failure of theory in theory itself, rather than in material reality or history. But there are also historical-material underpinnings of the left's failures. It has confronted a series of conditions that, while not individually unfamiliar to other left move-ments, in concert have formed a unique configuration.

The formative period for the U.S. working class was one of large-scale immigration, including the immigration of many socialist and anarchist-thinkers. This led to a problem that Engels recognized early on: Socialist thought in the United States was rooted in European languages and terminologies. During the heyday of the U.S. Socialist Party, the influence of foreign-language elements continued to be dis-proportional and gave the party an "alien" hue that was manipulated by conservative elements. Later on, after the Russian Revolution, socialist and communist ideas revolved around European models of social change and socialist organization. Occasionally aware of the need to overcome the European stereotype in order to obtain the support of U.S.-born workers (who tended all too often to combine anti-Semitism, anti-foreignism, and hostility to the "corrupt" city), and to relate to the real problems of the United States in terms its workers could understand, the left grappled with the problem only at a superficial level— as, for example, in the 1930s, when the Communist Party chose Earl Browder of Kansas as its leader but the real leadership of the party remained in New York City. New York was, after all, the entry point, and often the resting place, for many immigrants, including radicals. This led to a "New York" bias by all left groups that persists today. Clustered in New York, the left devoted a large amount of its energy to infighting, seeming to believe that the United States as a whole could be understood through New York–tinted glasses—that what was happening in New York, with its high level of radical activity, was what was going on in the rest of the country. Part of the left's paralyzing optimism can be traced to this factor, since left culture is always stronger, providing a more positive image, in that city.

Perhaps the ingrown nature of the U.S. left would not have alienated it from the public to quite such a degree had the socialist movement been able to maintain a mass base after World War I. But the Socialist Party's industrial working class support was overwhelmingly foreign-born (the U.S.-born Protestant coal miners of Kanawha and Fayette counties, West Virginia, as well as some miners and railway workers in other parts of the country, were notable exceptions [Yarrow 1981]). The bulk of the party's nonimmigrant support was among small farmers in the Southwest, especially Oklahoma, and this eroded rapidly after World War I. Those industrial workers who at one point supported the Socialist Party went over to the New Deal, which seemed to many to incorporate reformist socialist ideals in a practical manner.

The resulting narrower composition of Socialist (and later Communist) Party membership made it hard for "real workers" to feel any sense of affinity with the culture of radicalism, rooted as it was in what seemed obscure, foreign-based languages and a petty-bourgeois, intellectual life-style. The estrangement of many radicals from real working class milieus contributed to their false optimism: Quite often the radicals were simply not in touch with the real attitudes of workers, including, among white male workers, the persistent undercurrent of racist and male chauvinist attitudes that would, in the 1970s, put at least some workers (although not a majority) in the camp of the superpatriotic, anti-feminist, antigay, antiwelfarist predecessors of the Moral Majority.

The Communist Party-USA has specifically been criticized on somewhat different grounds. Communist Party organizers in the industrial working class have been the most consistent, and are probably still numerically the largest group of left activists in the labor movement. They have often stood out in their bravery and dedication—even occasional martyrdom. On the other hand, the overall negative influence of the Communist Party on the left and on the development of socialist consciousness within the working class must not be underestimated. In the first place—and this is of greatest importance—the U.S. public identifies socialism with the Soviet model, an identification assiduously fostered by the Communist Party, and one that has been eagerly assented to not only by employers, but by both conservative and liberal trade union leaders. If "that" is socialism, the U.S. worker wants no part of it. Second, while individual Communist Party activists may adhere to the idea of workers' rights—at least in the United States—the party itself, through its various turns during the Stalin era, has on occasion managed to undermine as much as to promote unity. In one period advocating separate, Communist-controlled unions and attacking the reformist left of the American Federation of Labor (AFL) and the Congress of Industrial Organizations (CIO) for being merely social democrats, in the next period promoting a "popular front" approach so moderate as to make social democrats look like militant revolutionaries—even going so far as to support the no-strike pledge during World War II—Communist Party activists have survived in the trade union movement not because they have built a radical or socialist base, but because they are simply good trade unionists. That is, they have honestly fought for union demands and workers' rights. Their muted criticism of bureaucratism and corruption and their failure to build a base—which was related not only to their no-strike-pledge philosophy but to their defense of the Soviet Union—helped set the stage for their own expulsion from the unions during the McCarthy period. Today, the unions in which the Communist Party once had influence, even those from which they were not expelled, have virtually disappeared (in some cases because they are in areas of manufacturing that are decaying anyway).

Other radical groups that have tried to work in the trade union movement have fared even less well. The offshoots of the old Socialist Party have only a small influence within the leadership of a few unions, and less still among the members; other leftist groups work in the insurgent caucuses of a few unions—notably, despite intense repression and thuggery, in the Teamsters—but comparatively speaking the influence of U.S. radicalism within the trade union movement is probably at the lowest point since McCarthyism and the Korean War. The few black revolutionary movements inside the unions—like the League of Revolutionary Black Workers in Detroit—have foundered, mainly because they attempted to organize in opposition to union leaders seen by most members as relatively effective.

Unlike the situation in Europe, where nationwide federations of unions are aligned with particular political parties, all attempts in the United States to link unions with socialist politics or parties have been defeated. The explicitly socialist unions organized by Daniel DeLeons's Socialist Labor Party in the 1890s, the Industrial Workers of the World (IWW), the Communist Party's Trade Union Unity League in the 1920s, the black workers' groups, have disappeared, either because of state repression or because the mainstream unions were able to achieve some success. The CIO as a new union federation succeeded, only to merge with the AFL. Even the Communist-influenced Mine, Mill and Smelter Workers, descendant of the IWW-affiliated Western Federation of Miners, is now part of the quite conventional Steelworkers' Union. Dual or separate unionism, a logical response to the narrow business unionism of the AFL, has proven to be a dangerous diversion at best, another symptom of the paralyzing optimism that has repeatedly led the left to predict the imminent collapse of the system and the advent of revolution.

Exceptionalism and Consciousness

U.S. history seems to many Marxists and radicals to have dealt them a bad hand. The objective realities of relative prosperity and mobility for at least some workers combined with the fragmentation of the working class in a dozen different ways plus the acceptance by millions of workers of the "American dream" of a middle class life have together led to a political result that is a far cry from Marx's conception of a revolutionary proletariat at the heart of world capitalism. The Marxist assumption has always been that objective conditions affect consciousness, and that consciousness in turn affects reality, including political reality. If this is the case, then it might seem that nothing can be done; leftists are doomed by reality.

However, neither conditions nor consciousness are static. Both contain contradictory elements that, if understood, constitute the seed of opposition, and of the breakdown of what may appear to be the seamless fabric of capitalist power. In short, the apparent hegemony of bourgeois ideology, rooted in material conditions, can be challenged. Alongside each of the myths that so many accept exist potentially powerful counterideas that provide the ammunition for a rebellion of consciousness.

The fact that both reality and consciousness contain contradictory elements leads us to examine the theme of "dualities" in consciousness (Mann 1973). These exist at several levels. First, present-day beliefs and attitudes may come into confrontation with changing realities, making it difficult for people to make sure of the present and opening them up to new alternatives. Second, actual (aware) consciousness— ideas—may be opposed by latent nonconscious alternative sets of basic attitudes that are stored, dormant, in family, religious, or ethnic traditions. Third, actual consciousness itself has two sides, even within the same individual: one in which dominant ideology is accepted, and the other in which it is, in varying degrees, opposed. Such dualities of working class consciousness include the conception that we live in a classless, or overwhelmingly middle class, society, versus a persistent identification of people as workers (Legett 1968); a widespread skepticism concerning the value of collective action, versus an unequaled record of militant strikes (Brecher 1972; Lens 1973); a general opposition to "government handouts," versus support for most of the specific reforms associated with the New Deal, as well as for egalitarianism in general; a lack of profound dissatisfaction with work, versus widespread absenteeism, pilferage, sabotage, and malingering on the job; frequent (though not disproportional) support for right-wing populist candidates such as George Wallace, versus long-term voting for social reform parties (Carlson 1981); adherence to certain traditional values, such as family solidarity and the value of work, versus an orientation that favors leisure-time activities and retirement. The extent to which such sets of beliefs exist is a matter for investigation, but it is certainly not enough to say that since there is no radical mass party or labor movement, there is therefore no source of a coherent alternative interpretation of reality. Alternative schemes exist at many levels, political and prepolitical, religious and secular, incoherent and coherent. Indeed, the very confusion that workers feel may be one of the root causes of adherence to certain traditional values—not the least of which are patriotism and nativism (among white workers)—as refuges and rationalizations for the sacrifices made in a given lifetime (Sennett and Cobb 1972).

What this approach suggests is that the conservatism of many U.S. workers has been greatly overdrawn by political sociology, that within conservative appearances there may well exist radical inclinations. Indeed, as chapter 9 will demonstrate, even the superficial data at our command bear out the fact that embourgeoisement is far from uniform, overwhelming, and all-encompassing, even among those strata of the population long considered (according to the prevailing myths) politically hopeless—the so-called lower middle class or those in lower-level, white collar occupations.

This discussion of U.S. exceptionalism forms the context in which we can now examine the theories put forward about the white collar segment of the labor force in particular. The test of each of these theories must be its ability to explain the present political activities (or lack of activity) of the white collar part of the labor force, both within and without the labor movement. It must explain why some white collarites have become unionized, while others have not. It must explain why some vote for reform or even radical parties and others for conservative or even fascist parties, and under what circumstances. It must explain, in short, the contradictions and dualities of consciousness and behavior. The next two chapters will examine these theories as they have been spun out over the past century.

3
Theories of the Middle Strata: Elites, Vanguards, and the "New Class"

New class? New middle class? New working class? Professional-managerial class? Bureaucratic elite? Salariat? *Tertiaires?* Employees? Managerial revolutionaries? Intellectual prophets? No other occupational category has had so many contradictory labels and political missions assigned to it as has the white collar grouping. And no other continues to be so mystifying, so much the subject of controversy and debate.

Five basic views concerning the political mission of the new occupations that began to take shape in the late nineteenth century are in contention today: an *elite* view, which sees the top levels of these occupations as assuming now or later the leadership of society in an enlightened and efficient way, a view harking back to Plato's *Republic* and exemplified by B. F. Skinner's *Walden II* (1948); a *stabilizing* view, which assumes that most people in the labor force will achieve "middle class" life-styles based on white collar and other skilled jobs requiring advanced education so that they will be able to sustain a consensual middle-of-the-road democracy without significant alteration from the present; a *third-force* approach, which believes that this same group has an interest in reformist change, one that might conceivably end in a moderate form of democratic socialism; a *new-working-class* perspective, which proposes that many members of the white collar occupations will move leftward to join with, or displace, the blue collar proletariat as a major lever for revolutionary social change in an increasingly crisis-ridden capitalist society; and a *contradictory locations* approach, which argues that different fractions among the middle strata are located in different classes—some even in several classes at the same time—so that white collar workers as a whole constitute

45

neither a single class nor simply an appendage to another class, but rather a complex of shifting and conflicting segments (see, for instance, Sobel 1982: chap. 2; Wright 1978). The present chapter will deal with the first two of these schools of thought; the next chapter will deal with the last three, which are more change-oriented.

Elites and Vanguards

In a world in which social policy appears to many to be determined by men who are stupid, crooked, or at best inefficient, some intellectuals tend to see themselves as superior, enlightened beings who would certainly be able to do a better job. If present policymakers are unable to "deal with" chaos, with the utter corruption of cultural standards, then fascism provides an ideology to rationalize the intellectual's need for a quick and efficient solution. If fascism is too distasteful because of its racist and militaristic component, then vanguardist forms of communism are a substitute. If both fascism and communism invoke too great a fear of mass participation—hence of further disorder (and, possibly, of the abrogation of certain traditional intellectual rights, such as free speech)—a traditionalist conservatism, sometimes known as "eighteenth-century liberalism," can be invoked. Alternatively, fear of mass participation can also lead to an ideology that abjures ideology, a value system that preaches value neutrality, leading to technicism and even technocracy.

All elite theories advocate rule over society by experts who are educated and technically competent to rule, and who are selected by processes controlled by their own groupings. All, whether feudal-aristocratic or modern fascist, whether they stem from the impulses of European social democracy or the New Deal, from Stalin or Mao, share one important ingredient: a fundamental mistrust of genuine mass participation in important decision making, which they relate to the perception of an overriding need for efficiency.

Although all elitists share a commitment to elite rule in the interests of efficiency, two political issues divide them: First, what is the *purpose* of this efficiency, that is, what is the social goal of policymaking? This question divides, on the political-ideological level, liberals from rightists, and from some leftists. The issues are raised over such questions as: Shall the purpose be a more equalitarian society? Does this require the elimination of private enterprise? And/or shall the purpose be an orderly society? Does this require the elimination of civil liberties? Second, who shall be the *agents* of this efficiency, that is, who shall the experts be? Every dispute among those committed to rule by some upper stratum of the white collar grouping hinges on these two questions, even among those (on the left) whose rhetorical commitment is to mass participation: At the very moment that they advocate extension of democracy at home, they defend the rule of some group of party leaders/experts in some other nations.

With the exception of the "aristocratic critics" of mass society, most of the elite theorists discussed here are committed to a society that is to some degree more equalitarian, even at the expense of private property and the owning class. But even aristocratic theorists seek the good society, one in which war, violence, demagogy, and exploitation based on race, ethnicity, and gender will be moderated, if not eliminated. In that dream these elite theorists part company with fascism, which is based on an entirely different set of principles.

Elite theory goes back thousands of years but certainly among its more recent proponents, Comte and Saint-Simon are key. Both were forerunners of those who believe in the possibility of an "enlightened" technocracy on the one hand, and in the variety of centralized planning agencies associated with the social-democratic concept of "nationalization" on the other. Both saw the intellectual pioneers of modern ("positivist") thought, and the leaders of (classless) industry, as the carriers of culture and heads of society. There is a connection between this view and that of Edward Bellamy in the novel *Looking Backward,* an important socialist propaganda tract (1888); and between it and the views of U.S. sociologist Albion W. Small, particularly in his fictional *Between Eras: From Capitalism to Democracy* (1913), a book that Harry Elmer Barnes compared to Plato's *Republic;* and between it and B. F. Skinner's *Walden II.* They are all simple, relatively unsophisticated elitist views, whether of a more or less socialist bent. All were conceived in a tradition quite lacking in even a minimal rhetorical commitment to democratic participation by the masses in determining their own destiny.

This is not to say that alternative traditions were unavailable: The debate concerning "socialism from above" versus "socialism from below" had begun with virtually the opening gun of the French Revolution (see Wilson 1940). But the earliest proponents of elitist theory seemed scarcely aware of that alternative tradition, and did not bother to defend themselves against it. All shared the belief that philosophers, intellectuals, managers, and administrators could, by virtue of their wisdom (in some cases biologically acquired) and education, rule—and should do so.

The world after 1917 was a world in revolution, both from the left and the right. Many intellectuals identified readily with the leadership of the Third International or with the Third Reich. But others clung steadfastly to elitist theories and remained convinced that the masses were incapable of creating change—or at least positive change. This attitude was typical among those who have been called the "aristocratic critics of mass society," for example, Ortega y Gasset in *The Revolt of the Masses* (1932). What all of these thinkers had in common was the view that masses in motion are inherently destructive of rational, enlightened Western culture and its traditions; whether those masses are moving in a right or a left direction is irrelevant because they constitute, in terms of their content, a similar phenomenon that differs only on a formal level.

The aristocratic criticism has continued into the present (Hoffer 1951). Digby Baltzell (1964) takes it to another level. He argues that aristocracies must absorb or co-opt leading elements of the masses into elite structures if the cultural leadership of the historical aristocracy is to be maintained—as it must if the Western cultural tradition is to continue. Baltzell, like other aristocrats, accepts the fact that a power structure exists and takes that as a good thing. He wants to maintain that good by seeking to recruit the best, most talented elements of other strata to join the aristocracy, or, if not the aristocracy, the decision-making elite at least.

More committed to change, though still very concerned with the destructive potential of mass and class conflict, was Karl Mannheim (1936). For Mannheim, it was essential that intellectuals take a leading role in the reconstruction of society because they are relatively "socially unattached," or classless, and hence able to synthesize a progressive politics without dumping the "accumulated cultural acquisitions and social energies of the previous epoch" (1936:154), while at the same time defending themselves from the extreme attacks of both right and left. Classless, standing above the petty interests of classes and other interest groups, intellectuals represented universalistic progress. Their "common educational heritage" provides their independent, free-floating, and progressive consciousness. Mannheim warned intellectuals not to attach themselves to any of the real classes in society, for they would then lose their ability to determine the direction of society for themselves.

What is striking about Mannheim's analysis is that it comes in a work that made the term "sociology of knowledge" popular, yet his view of intellectuals is fundamentally in contradiction with the remainder of the book, which argues forcefully for examining the social roots of all ideas—an argument based on the work of Marx. Mannheim sneaks a benign, humane intellectual elitism on his readers before they are even aware that he is the ideological descendant not only of Marx, but of Plato and Comte.

Even more benign, at first blush, is the work of Thorstein Veblen. Best known, of course, for *The Theory of the Leisure Class* (1899), Veblen did not specifically nominate technicians as society's crucial change agents until 1921, when he wrote *The Engineers and the Price System*. Veblen's view was simple enough, and obviously affected by the Russian Revolution. He discussed the technical nature of modern industry.

> . . . those gifted, trained and experienced technicians who now are in possession of the requisite technological information and experience are the first and instantly indispensable factory in the everyday work of carrying on the country's productive industry. They now constitute the General Staff of the industrial system, in fact; whatever law and custom may formally say in protest. . . .
>
> Therefore any question of a revolutionary overturn in America or in any other of the advanced industrial countries, resolves itself in practical fact into a question of what the guild of technicians will do. In effect it is a question whether the discretion and responsibility in the management of the country's industry shall pass from the financiers . . . to the technicians. . . . There is no third party qualified to make a colourable bid. . . .
>
> The chances of anything like a Soviet in America, therefore, are the chances of a Soviet of technicians. (Lerner 1948:440–441)

A very remote chance, though Veblen, since such people are a "harmless and docile sort, well fed on the whole, and placidly content with the 'full dinner pail' which the lieutenants of the Vested Interests habitually allow them." Nevertheless, given "Harsh and protracted experience . . ." (ibid.:441).

It was an attractive view, particularly to engineers and technicians. In 1932, at a point when that harsh and protracted experience had already lasted three years, Howard Scott's movement, technocracy, exploded on the public scene (Elsner 1967). Scott, who used a lot of engineering and physics terminology, called for technologically trained people to form the nucleus of a new revolutionary movement. In 1919 or 1920 he was apparently in touch with the IWW, and supplied it with a report on the meat-packing industry, and possibly others—an interesting forerunner of early 1970s "people's research" groups. Two articles by Scott appeared in an IWW paper. Most members of Technocracy, Inc., were skilled workers or professionals, such as engineers. Scott had a "technet" of ham radio operators, a fleet of cars, and by 1938 was dressing organizers in neat gray uniform-suits. Technocracy, Inc., was antibusiness and somewhat populist, but it was not Marxist (at the same time, it did not spend much time attacking Marxism either). It was egalitarian in ideology, but attacked present-day democracy as inefficient, worthless, and corrupt. Its internal structure was highly authoritarian, and leadership was chosen from the top rather than elected. The organization stemming from Scott's Technical Alliance (later called Technocracy, Inc.) still exists but the New Deal ultimately drained the movement of any potential for mass support.

For Veblen and the technocrats, then, the elitist solution to society's main problem—the "Vested Interests" or capitalism—took the form of a "soviet" or council of technicians—an elite form of socialism, in the interest of the people.

The work of C. Wright Mills also fits into the elitist framework. While Mills is better known for his pioneering work *White Collar* (1951)—to which I shall return later—he had little faith that white collar workers *as a group* would foster change. In *The Causes of World War III* (1958) Mills isolates intellectuals and, in a manner highly reminiscent of Mannheim, lectures them on their social responsibilities. If only they were honest to the intellectual or cultural "calling," he says, they would reenter politics to "reveal the way in which personal troubles are connected with public issues" (153). They would become "consistently and altogether unconstructive" vis-à-vis the ongoing social order (157). In short, intellectuals would become a vanguard for change. Unlike the other thinkers surveyed here, Mills was not committed to elite *rule* of society, only to intellectuals' becoming the vanguard of a movement for change. He thus differed from both Veblen and Mannheim in that he was struggling to locate a mass base for change and subsequent rule.

Mills's view of intellectuals as a potential vanguard was based, as are a number of more recent elite theories, on the assumption that neither the blue collar nor the white collar working class could be mobilized as a force for change in the foreseeable future. Among writers associated with parts of the new left, it is university students or intellectuals who displace the proletariat as the primary vanguard element. It would seem almost inevitable that intellectuals—who for whatever reason see no hope for change as a result of mass action—must therefore pin their hopes on an intellectual and/or student elite.

Herbert Marcuse, the most prominent proponent of this view, pinned his hope for change on an alliance of alienated sectors of the population, particularly blacks and the lumpenproletariat (1964). As he stated in an interview during the Vietnam war,

> The opposition of American youth could have a political effect. This opposition is free from ideology . . . it is sexual, moral, intellectual, and political rebellion all in one. In this sense it is total, directed against the system as a whole. . . . Only in alliance with the forces who are resisting the system "from without" can such an opposition become a new avant-guarde." (1969: 372)

Marcuse was associated with the so-called Frankfurt School whose members are also referred to as "critical theorists." A more recent disciple of this school is Jurgen Habermas. Like Marcuse, Habermas holds that class struggle as it was once understood can no longer provide the chief dynamic for change in modern society. He believes, as do many liberal theorists, that "state-regulated capitalism, which emerged from a reaction against the dangers to the system produced by open class antagonism, suspends class conflict" (1971:107–108), so that we are more likely to see open conflict at the "periphery" of society, not among social classes but among the disenfranchised and superexploited both at home and abroad. These groups, he states (and here he is in contrast to Marcuse), cannot by themselves succeed in a revolutionary struggle but must form a coalition. At present, the only protest potential among nonperipheral groups is among students, especially those from privileged backgrounds, but since their protest is qualitatively oriented (rather than directed toward a larger share of the pie), it has the revolutionary implications needed to supply allies to the peripheral forces. Thus, while students (the professionals/technicians of the future) cannot by themselves constitute a revolutionary force, in alliance with marginal and third world elements they may succeed, despite the co-optative mechanisms of capitalist society.

Norman Birnbaum shares a similar view. He is blunt:

> As for the proletariat . . . it is neither in its culture nor its politics a harbinger of the future or a revolutionary force. Today's avant-garde in industrial societies will be found among the young, particularly students

(that is to say, those without immediate responsibilities or bondages to the existing order), and amongst intellectuals, those with a certain freedom from routine and a certain proclivity to employ their critical faculties. (1969:94)

There is a kinship between the views of Mills and Marcuse, Habermas, Birnbaum, and others of the critical-theory school, and those held by some members of the "end-of-ideology" school (e.g., Bell 1960). Although the former continue to believe that fundamental change is necessary (Mills leveling some of his most bitter attacks on Bell), and the latter hold that basic problems have largely been solved, they share the belief that the masses, particularly the industrial working class and white collar employees, have been sufficiently co-opted to eliminate them as a potentially radical force. This assumption has provided theoretical ammunition for a number of so-called third worldist writers, including Régis Debray, Eldridge Cleaver, and Huey P. Newton, who hold that the levers of change lie outside the metropoles, the centers of world capitalism, and are located instead in the third world, in the countryside, and/or among the subproletarians and lumpenproletarians on the periphery of economic activity in the technologically advanced countries. But the third worldists, unlike their critical-theory allies, do not look to intellectuals or students to be much more than incidental help—delegates, so to speak, of third world revolutionary forces.

Still another variant of the view that looks to certain upper white collar strata (particularly students) as a vanguard for change is that of the "counter-culturists." Slater (1970) and Roszak (1969, 1973) were leading celebrants of counter-cultural life-styles as portents of revolutionary change. But their approach lingers on in diluted form in many of the more recent discussions of the "Young Upwardly Mobile Professionals," the "New Man" (or Woman), and the "Baby Boomers" (*Business Week*, 2 July 1984), all of whom are alleged to have developed a new form of consciousness. Slater, who prefaced his chapters with verses from the Beatles, the Rolling Stones, and Bob Dylan, is well known for his work on advanced management theory, particularly around sensitivity training, and the development of new, more flexible structures for business organizations (sometimes termed "Theory Y"). It is not surprising, therefore, that he emphasizes modification of motivations, psychic change, and personal liberation. At the same time, he recognizes the need for institutional change. His indictment of our institutions, and of the mechanisms through which the Marcusian "one-dimensional man" is created, is a strong one, as is Roszak's or, for that matter, Charles Reich's in *The Greening of America* (1970), a work along similar, although rather more journalistic, lines. It is not until midway through the book that we begin to get an inkling of who is going to change all this: the alienated, psychic sufferers of the Dr. Spock generation, that is, the children of the educated middle class. This will be done through music, drugs, and new varieties of sexual expression, which constitute the "cultural revolution" and mount a fundamental, revolutionary challenge to rationalistic, technological, impersonal, alienated society. The hippie ethic is more radical, says Slater, than the political activist ethic, because the latter still partakes of the stern old code of postponement of gratification, task orientation, and rational thought. But the hippie is not realistic. The conflict between the two, both of which are wings of anti-establishment thought, is irreconcilable, and Slater refuses to choose—or, rather, he chooses both, while at the same time implying that in any case the change is coming about, willy-nilly, as the old culture is gradually permeated by the new. In the end, despite the poisonous viciousness of our present system, which is described in detail, Slater backs off from contemplating the kind of power that would be required to overcome it. We are left, one imagines, with playing rock music at management conferences. Fourteen years later Slater's hippies, now in middle-management ranks, were supporting Gary Hart, "greening" management by introducing participatory decision making, and, according to *Business Week*, developing a passion for "upscale products."

For Roszak it is also the young—"technocracy's children"—who are the hope of the future. In revolt against managerialistic, "think-tank" mentality, "technocratic America produces a potentially revolutionary element among its own youth." And the adult radical, confronted with a working class that is allegedly "the stoutest prop of the established order," must make a bid to become guru to alienated youth. As chief gurus, such figures as Norman O. Brown, Allen Ginsberg, Alan Watts, and Paul Goodman (but not Timothy Leary, whom Roszak early recognized as politically and personally erratic) were to become for the young what Marx, Engels, and Lenin were to an older generation of radicals. Even the religious "renewal" he began to see among young people in the early 1970s was a symptom of "incalculable value" (1973:xvii). The "visionary commonwealth" (by which Roszak appears to mean that we must leave the cities and organize ecologically sound anarchist communities—utopia) is opposed to all of the evils of contemporary society (ibid.:379ff.). The utopians, as always, produce accurate indictments and beautiful plans, but no inkling as to how to muster the forces, the power, to get from here to there.

The view that intellectuals and/or students are a vanguard (particularly for cultural—that is, noneconomic—reasons) and that their allies, if any, are to be found among other culturally alienated elements or groupings that are marginal to the economy must be carefully distinguished from the view that intellectuals, particularly students, constitute a vanguard force that actually foreshadows a much more profound social upheaval involving large segments of society, including the mass of professional and technical workers, other white collar workers, and the changing blue collar proletariat. This latter view more properly belongs in the section of the new working class in the following chapter.

The Stable Center?

In *White Collar* (1951), C. Wright Mills examined the basic political options open to the white collar strata, whom he called the "new middle class." One of these was that the new middle class would become a "major force for stability in the general balance of the different classes," and would therefore make for the "continuance of liberal capitalist society" (1951:290).

As with other theories about the white collar strata, this approach was foreshadowed in debates that raged in, around, and against German social democracy of the 1890s. Gustav Schmoller (1897), for instance, held that the growing proportion of the labor force that was educated and well paid would become propertied, and that this socially mobile group would come to constitute an expanding and contented middle class, a force for cultural and moral uplift.

Schmoller saw it as his political task to try to develop a rationale to combat the theories of class antagonism being advanced by writers such as Karl Kautsky and other Marxist advocates of class struggle. Schmoller and his "armchair" or "academic" *(Katheder)* "socialist" colleagues felt the need to develop a political theory that would propose social cooperation in the face of increasing class conflict at the turn of the century. In so doing, Schmoller made his mark as the theoretical founder of contemporary stratification (as opposed to class) theory (see Kadritzke 1975: chap. 1). Weber, Schumpeter, and many other German theorists followed in Schmoller's footsteps, at least where an analysis of social class was concerned. Weber (1919) thought that the *Angestellte*, the white collar employees, sought nothing more than to assimilate themselves to "society." Nothing, he thought, was farther from their ambition than solidarity with the proletariat. Similarly, Schumpeter (1929) saw no narrowing of the gap between employees and professionals (whom he saw as a "class in the becoming") and the working class. More recently, the work of Siegfried Braun (1964) echoes Schmoller, but with a more sophisticated wrinkle: The empirical fact that white collar workers exist in a state of internal conflict (between their status as wage earners and their status as administrative employees) results in contradictions of consciousness that neutralize them ideologically, so that they tend to identify with a political "golden mean" (cited in Kadritzke 1975:71). (We shall see, in chapter 9, to what degree this is true.)

One assumption underlying the stability approach is that of John Kenneth Galbraith's "theory of countervailing power" (in *American Capitalism* [1952]). "Private economic power," Galbraith wrote, "is held in check by the countervailing power of those who are subject to it" (1952:118). In a similar fashion, the political power of any interest group, stratum, or class is held in check by one or a combination of other strata, groups, and/or classes. Federal legislation protecting one group one day, and limiting another group the next, symbolizes the reality of countervailing power, leading to a balanced society. While white collar workers have not so far mobilized themselves to enter this contest, Galbraith predicts "that the next group to seek to assert its market power will be the genteel white-collar class" (Ibid.:154). Galbraith thus sees white collar employees as having a rather limited role: They are merely another group that, together with others, contributes to the balance of our society.

It is necessary to flesh this notion out somewhat if the white collar strata are to be understood as the *main* force for stability, that is, as the majority constituting the political ballast of the society. Several theorists go further than Galbraith. Daniel Bell, for instance, although he does not refer to white collar employees as such, clearly sees this grouping as part of that great U.S. middle class of educated joiners who have helped us arrive at a "political dead center" without this becoming a "dead norm" (1960:33). Bell's celebration (one cannot call it much less) of U.S. life and class structure is based on the belief, also shared by Galbraith (at that time), that more and more people are living better and sharing an educated culture. They do so, Bell argues, because inheritance no longer determines access to power, and because technical skill rather than property, and political position rather than wealth, "have become the basis on which power is wielded" (ibid.:42). Hence there is no longer a ruling class: It has split into an "upper class" and a "ruling group." The latter is a coalition in which elements of the middle class, particularly managers, play an important role. It is also a coalition that apparently reflects many individuals' working through organized collectivities—that is, interest groups—in order to affect politics. But, even more significantly, it is a coalition that makes decisions more on technical considerations than on substantively political or ideological bases.

The reality that Bell sees is a coalition of elite decision makers who reflect mass opinion in a general way and who make *specific* decisions based on technical rather than wider moral-political considerations. There is no ruling class. The only political question is which of our internal groups will bear the costs of any added burdens imposed (in the late 1950s) by the democratic method of countervalence.

As with Galbraith, the notion of a middle stratum or class as the main force for stability is present more implicitly than explicitly in Bell's work.

"Postindustrial" society implies a democratization of society as the vast middle class becomes educated; at the same time, it implies an "end of ideology" as social conflicts become resolved into technical questions to be solved by an elite that is a part of that new middle class.

Praderie (1968) made a similar argument. According to him, *tertiaires* are the employment wave of the future: By 1954, in France, extractive workers including farmers, the "primaries," constituted about 31 percent of the labor force, as compared with 34 percent for manufacturing workers, secondaries, and 35 percent for service sector workers, the *tertiaires*—with the latter on the increase. Praderie saw *tertiaires* as a new phenomenon, peculiar to postindustrial society, and not as part of the working class. On the other hand, *tertiaires* are not themselves an independent class: There are too many different strata among them in terms of work, income, and life-style. This nonclass grouping is inheriting a society that is rooted in a nonscarcity, noncrisis economy run basically by one stratum, the planners. While there are a few problems in the system, particularly a maldistribution of employment (so that there might be, for example, too many saleswomen and not enough secretaries), it is only necessary to iron out these kinks in order to have a basically stable, prosperous system in which the consumption-oriented *tertiaire* holds a plurality position in the balance of forces, as against the working class on the one hand and what is left of the owning class on the other.

A better-known version of this approach is that of Paul Halmos (1966, 1970). Halmos basically believes that a service or "counseling" approach is increasingly prevalent among all professionals, and that, since more and more occupations are becoming professionalized, this approach will lead to a more benign, cooperative society because the human service ethic pervades professional life. These professionals will "remain in the vanguard of moral change in society" (1970:197). Halmos declares himself, in distinction to his critics (especially radical sociologists, among whom he includes Mills, Marcuse, and Gouldner), an optimist: Humankind will survive, with the prerequisite for survival being gradual progress toward cooperation. Left critics of society contribute to the demise of humankind by the very style of their criticism: They negate and therefore contribute to hopelessness. In any event, the critics are wrong. If they would spend less time criticizing and moralizing, and more time engaging in the "personal service" (human services) professions they are constantly reviling, they would become more aware of the continuities and adaptations within society, trends that ensure progress and (hopefully) survival of the species. Conflict itself, it would seem, including class conflict, is more a metaphenomenon based on the ideological pessimism of radicals than a reality. While not the best of all possible worlds, it is not a bad world, and one that would be better still if radicals would stop interfering in their negative way.

Is There a New Middle Class?

Those who assume that the upper fractions of the white collar strata are an independent grouping crucial to the running of society can be subdivided into several political schools. Some see these strata as a vanguard for progressive change; some as a regressive force, an obstacle to change; and some (as we shall see) as a force for change in an evil direction. Still others see them as an element making for stability in the society. But whatever the approach, this group is distinguished both from the upper class and from the mass of society, and is seen to have interests distinct from both. The idea of an independent position has led to an attempt to conceptualize these middle or upper middle fractions as a "new" class formation.

Most of the theorists who use such terms as "new class," "new middle class," or "professional-managerial class" share, to some degree, the following assumptions:

1. The group under discussion is "middle" because it is neither capitalist nor traditional working class. That is, unlike all previous classes in history, it is defined by what it is *not*, rather than by what it is. The Ehrenreichs' use of the term "derivative class" is symptomatic (Ehrenreich and Ehrenreich 1979).

2. The new class creates its own independent ideology, that of meritocracy and professionalism. Gouldner, for example, argues that "unlike the old working class, [the new class] is basically committed to controlling the content of its work and its work environment, rather than surrendering these in favor of getting the best wage bargain it can negotiate" (ibid.:20). In somewhat contrasting terms, Bell (in Bruce-Briggs 1979) argues that members of this group are often opposed to merit systems and side with groups that are disadvantaged by culturally biased "merit" testing. Empirically, both variants are open to question: Many professionals are very much concerned with bread-and-butter job issues; many blue collar workers desire more control over the content of their work. Likewise, while some professionals side with their clients, others function more as social control agents (see Chapter 7).

3. Alongside such relatively benign ideas—merit, professionalism, self-actualization—various writers also hold the new class responsible for such disparate phenomena as the student movement, terrorism, regulatory agencies, and Naderism; the Cuban, Vietnamese, Chinese, and Cambodian revolutions; the concept of the vanguard party; Lenin and the Russian Revolution; and even Marxism itself. For theorists such as Gouldner or Irving Kristol and Norman Podhoretz, these phenomena are incomprehensible unless they can be understood as emanating from the new class (Bruce-Briggs 1979: chap. 1). The Ehrenreichs indict their professional-managerial class for being elitist, anti–working class, and responsible, owing to its "class outlook," for Leninism and the downfall of the Russian Revolution, as well as for every kind of bureaucratic action everywhere in the world. This is so despite evidence that revolutionaries of working class origin can be just as antidemocratic as those of middle class origin, and many profes-

sional-managerial (that is, middle class) people gave their lives for such democratic forms of socialism as workers' councils, council communism, anarcho-syndicalism, etc. In short, there is no "class correlation" with elitism, though it may indeed be true that many middle-class intellectuals are elitists.

For most new-class theorists, that group is believed to be in some sense anti-establishment and revolutionary, though not necessarily pro–working class. At the extreme, it is held responsible for both fascism and Stalinism—an assumption rooted in the aristocratic-elitist theories of Ortega y Gasset, Eric Hoffer, and others who decry all mass movements as being merely the manipulations by clever elites of the susceptible and ignorant masses. Most of those using labels such as "new class" do *not* see the upper segments of the middle strata as a force for progressive change; if they are a force for change at all, it is a bad one. This puts most such theorists in the camp of the aristocratic critics of mass society (for example, Ortega). A few, such as Ehrenreich and Ehrenreich, advocate anti-elitist, democratic forms of political struggle that will subvert the elitist proclivities of the professional-managerial group.

4. A further assumption underlying the argument of most new-class theorists is that this group, by virtue of its advanced education, is characterized by a separate educated culture—though there is no agreement on what this culture is. For Gouldner (1979) it is a "speech community" as well, with an "evolved set of rules, a grammar of discourse" called the culture of critical discourse (CCD for short). CCD provides the new class with a form of capital that gives it its unique class position in modern society. Since CCD is based on scientific rationality rather than on authority, it is in the interest of the new class to oppose censorship. Again, it is doubtful that any particular occupational group within the middle strata of society is disproportionally committed to rational rather than irrational discourse or is uniquely opposed to censorship.

5. In the Soviet orbit, according to Gouldner, the new class is the dissident group, the underground intelligentsia. Who, in this view, operates the Soviet state is not clear, since there is a very fuzzy line between the new class and those at the top. For Gouldner, the new class does *not* include management, the upper (politically appointed) state bureaucracy, or the guardians of the Soviet state—thus obscuring the issue of class in the Soviet Union as well as in the West. Writers such as Gouldner, as well as other recent contributors to new-class

theory, do not successfully differentiate between a "real" new-class situation in which the state controls the economy and a bureaucracy controls the state (in the absence of real institutions of community and worker self-management)—thus constituting the bureaucracy as a class (Djilas 1957), and the capitalist context in which the main dynamic continues to be private profit and capital accumulation for private ends. Only in one form of society does management constitute a new class: where it manages the state that commands the economy. Otherwise it is part of the capitalist class.

6. Who is included in the new class, then? What is the common core of this group, its common class characteristic apart from CCD and similar mystical notions about "culture as capital"? Depending on the source, it may include a large part of academia, all bureaucrats, employees of media, or "working intellectuals." Gouldner, in a table borrowed from the Ehrenreichs, lists managers, engineers, social and recreational workers, college faculty, accountants, auditors, government officials and administrators, editors, and reporters. An early contributor to the theory, Max Nomad, cites the following occupations for the Soviet Union, suggesting a confusion similar to Gouldner's: officeholders, technical managers and engineers, judges, savants, journalists, writers, professors, higher transport and postal employees, "Marx-theologians," army officers, actors, singers, scientific spies, bank accountants, and trade union and sports organizers (Bruce-Briggs, 1979:13).

For the Ehrenreichs, the professional-managerial class consists of "salaried mental workers who do not own the means of production and whose major function in the social division of labor may be described broadly as the reproduction of capitalist culture and capitalist class relations" (1979:12). This role may be explicit, as with teachers and social workers, or "hidden within the process of production," as with administrators, engineers, accountants, reporters, and such.

Numerous writers have pointed out that today production and reproduction are one thing, assigned to all workers. Engineers and reporters are only two examples of occupations that developed both in the process of de-skilling other workers and independently as part of changing technology (Noble 1977). These occupations, together with countless other professional-managerial class jobs, entail the generation of surplus value (directly and indirectly), its realization, *and* the reproduction of capitalist social relations, as do many working class occupations. In short, Braverman's (1974) (and Marx's) point that in today's world production is *social*, that even state workers participate in the accumulation of capital, and that the process of production is a single fabric in which functions cannot be isolated for most occupations and most workers contradicts the argument that some occupations can be identified as having a unique "reproduction" role.

Not only do occupations in the middle not constitute a class objectively, but these groups lack a common core culturally and their politics are often far from oriented toward change. Such groups are often even farther from being the anticapitalists the Ehrenreichs or Kristol see. While the record of the intellectual stratum, the group often identified as the heart of the new middles, varies from country to country and time to time, Bell argues that members of this group are generally regressive.

> In many countries intellectuals were a force for social stability, most notably in Victorian England. . . . Even the image of the Russian intelligentsia as either revolutionary, nihilistic, or dilletantish neglects the fact that other[s] . . . often vehemently opposed Westernization. . . . In the first four decades of the twentieth century, intellectual life in most European countries was usually dominated not by the Left, but by the Right. (In Bruce-Briggs 1979:172–73)

Bell's point is underscored when one looks at the dismal political record of German intellectuals, including the so-called value-neutral sociologists, the overwhelming majority of whom supported World War I in the most jingoistic fashion and (apart from those who fled) enlisted enthusiastically in Hitler's "New Order" as well (Papcke 1982).

Lipset's essay (in Bruce-Briggs 1979), devoted to celebrating the liberalism of U.S. academics, also concludes that "the more critical segment of the American intellectual community has not adopted a radical stance toward the legitimacy of American society and its basic institutions; a large majority endorsed the free-enterprise system in a 1977 faculty poll" (ibid.:85).

Moreover, if college education is supposedly an index to new-class membership and culture, what is one to do with the 17 percent of all manual workers who now have at least one year of college, and whose attitudes on all basic issues do not differ significantly from those of other workers? Gouldner includes college graduates who just happen to find themselves, given the state of the economy, in blue collar ranks within the new class. Are workers who have completed one year of college one-quarter new class? An Associate's degree one-half new class?

In short, there is very little evidence for a coherent leftist or other ideology among the new class. Gouldner is no more a spokesperson for the new class than is Kristol, Bell, or for that matter Mills, who antici- pated most of this discussion many years ago. Most students did not revolt in the glorious 1960s, most members of the new class did not march on Washington during the war in Vietnam, and most of the children of the rich do not become terrorists, fascists, or communists.

Ideologies derive, as Hacker says (in Bruce-Briggs 1979), from the way people engage in production (at various levels, it should be added). It is therefore not surprising that those who are engaged in producing symbols are exposed to an intellectual world not readily available to those in other lines of work. Indeed, as Schumpeter pointed out a long time ago, capitalism itself requires a critical frame of mind in order that invention, innovation, and growth can take place. And this critical frame of mind does not necessarily stop with the job at hand, once the dynamic is underway; it often goes on to criticize other things. None of this, however, requires the use of such terminology as "new class." It is all at least as old as the Protestant Ethic.

In this chapter, two positions have been reviewed: One argues that the upper strata of the white collar occupations constitute an elite, possibly a class that fosters change—whether for good or evil; the other argues that these strata are a force for stability, for the conservation of traditional social values. Aside from "Communist" societies—where it can be plausibly argued that a new class does exist, and constitutes a ruling and conservative force—the argument that these upper strata form a new class is in every aspect a weak one. Members of the upper strata—not to mention the entire white collar grouping—occupy dif- ferent class locations. Some are clearly part of the bourgeoisie, others are far closer to the working class (despite their relatively higher in- comes and greater control over their workplace), while still others are in several different, contradictory, positions at the same time. Conse- quently, no single political ideology can be said to characterize this elite group of Western society, and neither the change mission nor the stability mission are its exclusive outlook. Members of this elite have, in the past, been fascists, socialists, Communists, anarchists, and con- servatives—some within one individual's lifetime. But since the mate- rial interests and political persuasions of most "upper" members of society are on the conservative side (see chapter 9), we must look to a much wider population for a source of change. Let us thus proceed to examine theories that attempt to do just that: those that examine the wider population of white collar employees with respect to their mission for social change.

4
Theories of the Middle Strata: Radical and Revolutionary Masses and Classes

Introduction

Karl Marx did not devote much attention to the social role of "intermediate categories" such as clerks, functionaries, and the like, as Crozier (1971) and others have pointed out, although he did discuss these "commercial laborers" in terms of their relationship to the question of surplus value. The "white collar" question is therefore one of the very few in which debaters cannot rely on quotations from the source of Marxist thought. After about 1890, a debate commenced in European socialist circles involving two positions, that of Eduard Bernstein, who viewed the development of white collar workers as one of several class phenomena that contradicted, in his mind, Marxian assumptions concerning the polarization of classes; and that of Karl Kautsky, who held to the orthodox Marxian view that the laws of capitalism will drive the so-called petty bourgeoisie, including white collar workers, into the ranks of the proletariat. It is these two views, plus a variant on one of them, that will be discussed in this chapter.

The Bernsteinian tradition, which I term the "third-force" approach, shares with the stability view (discussed in the previous chapter) the assumption that in some way the white collar strata are a force in their own right, but differs from the stability view in that the group is seen as a potential force for (gradual) change. The more orthodox Marxian tradition, exemplified by Kautsky, and later in the United States by Lewis Corey (1935), assumes that these strata are part of the working class (or that significant portions of them are); or that they are "marginal," "in-between," "tail-enders," and *not* a force in their own right; that as a force for change they must align with other classes. Both the third-force and the stability assumptions imply that white collar workers are some form of "new class," or "new middle class," whether they use those terms or not, while those who argue some version of the more classical Marxian view see them as either merging with the traditional blue collar proletariat, as some form of "new" working class, or as a "mixed" set of groups, some being working class and others not.

Underlying both third-force and new-working-class views (and their variants) are certain interpretations of what the various writers see as empirical reality, both in the present and in anticipation. In turn, perceptions of reality are conditioned by the writer's own situation, including his or her immediate political interests—as will be demonstrated below. In short, ideas do not occur in a vacuum, as artifacts of pure thought. They are based on interpretations of reality that are in turn based on some "actual" reality.

Two themes recur in the context of this debate: the question of polarization and the related question of living conditions. Data indicating a lack of polarization, a maintenance or growth of middle groupings, are used by proponents of third-force (as well as stabilizing) views, while the same or other data, reinterpreted to show deepening schisms, are used by new-working-class theorists. Living conditions, measured by real income and mobility as well as on-the-job working conditions and other indices, also can serve to support different sides of the debate: Improving conditions, upward mobility, and a lack of development toward "proletarianization," including segmentation of jobs, theoretically correlate with a lack of polarization within the white collar strata and support a third-force view. Redefinitions of the concept "class" also undergird third-force theory.

A good example of this approach is that of Anthony Giddens (1973). His evaluation of the evidence leads him to conclude, first of all, that overall conditions for white collar workers continue to be significantly superior to those of the working class. Moreover, their work situations differ: "Even clerical workers participate in such a [command] hierarchy, and correspondingly . . . regard themselves as belonging to management" (1973:183). Computers, he argues, are leading to a general upgrading of skills for the middle class, which is therefore not splitting.

How does Giddens arrive at the label "middle class" in the first place? By deftly bourgeoisifying Marxist categories: A class becomes a "cluster of forms of structuration based upon commonly shared levels of market capacity," not a group of people sharing a common relationship to the mode of production, much less a relationship around the issue of exploitation. If classes are to be differentiated according to market capacity (what one offers for sale, and what one does, rather than the objective place in a class structure from which one's income is derived), then there are three classes: those who bring their ownership to the market, those who bring their knowledge, and those who bring their manual power—the second being the middle class. Although Giddens does not discuss the political consequences of his theory in any detail, it is easy to see how this can fit into the third-force or stability theories.

The Third-Force Theory

The fundamental assumption of reform socialism is, and has been since 1900, that schism or break between conflicting classes in capitalist society is neither likely nor inherent. This is because the polarization of society is contradicted by the persistence, indeed the growth, of intermediate social formations. In order for the socialist project to triumph, therefore, it must integrate these intermediate groupings. Bernstein's emphasis on legal, parliamentary action and his hatred for underground revolutionary tactis flows in part from this logic. There are other reasons for the strategy of social democracy as well, however: The relative prosperity of some portions of the Western European working classes, the institutionalization of trade unions and the legitimization of socialist parties, the success of the parliamentary strategy in gaining seats from 2 in 1871 to 110 in 1912 in Germany, all made it seem that reformist socialism worked (cf. Papcke 1979; Michels 1911). The reality, in the German case, was that the petty bourgeoisie, plus those working for wages in small businesses and for the state, continued to constitute a large and increasing proportion of the labor force (although it may have been shifting *internally*). In 1907, small producers and merchants, wage earners in small business, and state employees constituted 32.7 percent of the labor force, with another 10.7 percent being small-holding farmers; workers in large enterprises constituted 32.9 percent (Kadritzke 1975).

Bernstein, however, only foreshadowed third-force theory, even though it was consistently implied in the strategic approach of right-wing social democracy. Even in Germany, the prototypical social-democratic milieu, it was not until 1959, at the party's Bad Godesberg congress, that Bernstein's full program was effectively adopted with the dropping of the language of "class struggle." The U.S. milieu proved to be even more congenial to the development of this theory, in the guise of some of the labor theories mentioned briefly in chapter 2. Here, socialist theory and language was far less part of the culture, and a reformism without socialism more established as part of the political landscape.

The typical third-force view was posed by Selig Perlman:

> The middle classes, though greatly shaken economically, have stubbornly refused to accept the Marxian verdict that politically and socially they are doomed merely to choose between a capitalist or a proletarian hegemony. Instead, in some countries the middle classes have managed to find expression in an independent political power . . . which . . . may find expression either in Fascism or in a New Deal. (1935: 632)

In that same year (1935), Alfred M. Bingham, an activist in the Farmer-Labor movement of the U.S. Midwest, wrote a book (little remembered today) in which he laid out what amounted to an American Bersteinian view. The middle classes (note the use of the plural) of professionals, farmers, small businessmen, and the new middle class of salaried people working in finance, commerce, and for the government lack a working class consciousness. Rather, they have a different, independent psychology that gives them a stake in many aspects of the status quo. While they are ripe for fascism, they are equally ripe for a planned society that will fulfill their consumeristic dreams. Even though they cannot be approached through appeals to class, they can be recruited to an indigenous, U.S. brand of populist radicalism that emphasizes security, property rights, patriotism, and Puritanism as the context for a practical plan for social change. Bingham's main strategic point was that the middle classes and the working class must not be split by the class appeals of traditional socialists; rather, a united front between these classes is the only solution to capitalist crisis and the only alternative to fascism.

By 1935 the question of fascism (and its mass appeal) was very much on the agenda. No book on the subject of social class failed to address the issue of the Nazi victory and Hitler's mass support. Many writers asserted (and they continue to do so to this day—see chapter 9) that the middle strata provided fascist movements with their mass support, both in membership and in votes. This assumption was shared by Bingham, whose view was typical: "The impetus for fascism comes from disillusioned and desperate middle-class people . . . terrified at the thought of class war. . . . Fascism . . . is the last stand of the middle classes for capitalism" (1935: 105, 111).

Bingham was by no means alone in his view. Virtually every writer, from Communist to conservative, laid Hitler's victory at the door of the middle classes, or at least of the lower middle class. The Communists, of course, put the blame on the capitalist class, but argued that it was the lower middle class that allowed itself to be manipulated, while the working class remained relatively pure.

The assertion stems from the belief that the middle strata stand independent of both the working class and the bourgeoisie in part because of their unique mentality or "psychology." The middle strata have an anxiety concerning the actual or potential loss of status, a "status anxiety" or "panic" that makes them—or at least the lower part—susceptible to the demagogy of any authoritarian who promises to restore middle class prestige and its symbols.

There is little evidence of any fundamental difference in the political behavior of white and blue collar workers in the crisis of the 1930s. They differed in their degree of support for various political parties, but there are no data to support the argument that white collar workers acted as an independent political entity. They voted for various parties more or less in proportion to their numbers, tilting toward the moderate left in most cases (i.e., for the socialists in France, the New Deal in the United States—see chapter 9 for more details).

The political strategy that results from third-force theory, based as it partly is on alleged ideological differences between white and blue collar people, is an attempt to build a bridge toward the "panicked" white collarite in more or less the manner advocated by Bingham: toning down the socialist message in order not to frighten the new middle class away.

The war against Hitler brought relative prosperity to the blue and white collar workers of the unoccupied Allied nations. Contrary to many predictions, this prosperity extended into peacetime. Buttressed by the politics of anti-Communism, and by the extension of the U.S. economic empire, this prosperity reached back into Western Europe, particularly into the Federal Republic of Germany. An era began that many believed would finally lay to rest theories of class conflict and revolutionary change.

While many if not most new-class theorists belong, as I argued in the previous chapter, to the "stabilizing" view, seeing the new class as part of that great U.S. middle that is living better and sharing an educated culture—hence not particularly oriented to change—by the 1960s the question of social change and the issue of change agents once more appeared on the political agenda. It is here that third-force theory also once again emerged. David Bazelon makes the thesis explicit: "The decisive relation for the future," he posits, "will be that of the New Class and the Under Class" (1967: 20–21). By "new class" he meant all the propertyless and educated employees of oranizational life, the "working intellectuals" who gain "status and income through organizational position" (achieved by virtue of educational status). While it is not clear where this class begins and ends—Bazelon seems to exclude clerical and sales people at one extreme, and owners at the other—it does seem to include virtually the entire college-educated population that works for a salary. This is not just an elite—enlightened or evil; it is a large mass.

The mission of this large group, according to Bazelon, is to develop a coalition with enlightened businessmen, elements of the "underclass" (especially blacks in the civil rights movement), and New Dealers in politics to complete the New Deal. This is the first step in developing the new class's own ideology, which is more or less synonymous with left-liberalism.

This hypothesis is shared with only a slight difference of emphasis by European social democrats (and, in recent years, even by some Western European Communist parties): At some point in time this "completion of the New Deal" will become a qualitative change to a socialist society. The concept "moving equilibrium" may help us understand this approach. Liberals such as Bazelon, and social democrats such as Michael Harrington (1972), obviously do not hold that present-day society is functioning well, and that the new middle class wants to preserve it that way. Rather, the balance of society must be gradually shifted to the left, to progress, in an evolutionary mode. The idea that this can be done peacefully and piecemeal—the hallmark of social democracy—assumes that the capitalist system is fundamentally capable of dealing with its internal crises without either collapse or a turn to fascism: Socialism will be achieved qualitatively at some future date, as the sum total of a series of relatively small-scale reforms.

For this reason Harrington, although a socialist, must also be placed among the theorists who believe in a moderate solution requiring support from the middle strata of our society. His working coalition is not much different from that of Bazelon, though his final goal sounds more radical. The social-reform programs of Debs and Norman Thomas, he argues, have been absorbed with at least some success into the mainstream of U.S. culture and politics, even while their socialist advocates have fallen by the wayside. The mode of this absorption, and the strategy for its advance, is the alliance of the official trade union movement with the Democratic Party, which is, for Harrington, the rough U.S. analogue to the European social-democratic and labor parties.

But while this is a *mass* movement (according to Harrington), based in part in the blue collar working class (given the trade union focus), where do the white collar strata come in? Harrington argues that while the blue collar working class continues to be central to social change (precisely because it is not nearly so affluent as Galbraith and Bell want us to believe), this is only one element in the "democratization of power" that is required for progress. A second element is the new working class, which Harrington limits to the professional and technical stratum, and whose members are "middle class in . . . education and income, but often subjected to a production discipline like that of the workers" (1972: 442). The third element is college-educated people who are not technicians. These three groupings form the mass constituency for social-democratic politics, and for a socialist movement in the future.

Virtually every social-democratic program today is oriented toward that class-differentiated mass, on the assumption that appeals to the self-interest of the middle strata, based on concrete reforms, will attract them to a moderate socialist program, or at least prevent them from straying to the right. The types of welfare reforms (most of which are not structural, that is, not necessarily linked to a drive to raise more fundamental, radical issues) and the organizational contexts in which to fight for those reforms (the official trade union leaderships and, in the United States, the liberal wing of the Democratic Party) link Harrington's approach far more closely, operationally, to liberal theoreticians such as Galbraith than to revolutionary exponents of new-working-class theory such as Mandel (see below).

European social democracy, as Parkin rightly points out (1971), seeks to change the reward structure of society through "meritocratic" means: its goal is fairness in the competition for position in society, in order to "put the race for privileges on a more equitable footing." Egalitarian socialism, on the other hand, "is concerned with eradicating privileges, not with changing the principles by which they are allocated" (1971: 123). "Under meritocratic socialism," Parkin states, "classlessness would be produced by continuous, large-scale social exchange of personnel from one generation to the next. Under egalitarian socialism, classlessness would be produced by the distribution of reward on the basis of need and by the substitution of 'industrial democracy' for traditional authority structures" (ibid.). It is clear that meritocratic socialism is basically congruent with liberal reformism, while egalitarian (traditional, Marxist) socialism is fundamentally counterposed to it. Harrington's dilemma is this: Ultimately, like all social democrats, he is committed to the goal of egalitarianism. But practically, today, like all social democrats, he works for meritocratic change. This emphasis on reforms intended to develop "large-scale social exchange of personnel" over a generational period necessarily leads social democrats to advocate small-scale measures, rather than qualitatively radical, structural changes. Minute reforms of this kind often serve to stabilize the system overall, while changing small portions of it—in effect undermining qualitative change, at least in the short run. Politically, the tactic is to develop majorities that will force such changes to come about, a tactic that indeed prevents the development and espousal of more drastic change because the need to create majorities appears to require emphasis on minimalist programs.

The role of social-democratic theory, therefore, is to provide a leftist, radical rhetoric for the development of majority coalitions (including both blue and white collar workers) that will seek out a series of small-scale reforms leaving the general class configuration undisturbed. As Mills said of the U.S. party system, "The more variegated the public to which the patronage party must appeal for support, the more empty of decisive, antagonistic contents its programs will be" (1951:345). Much the same can be said today of the Western European social-democratic and labor parties. The egalitarian issue, which at this point in Western history cannot yet be a majoritarian issue, remains on the back burner.

Moreover, the dilution of socialist appeals in the attempt to attract an allegedly moderate new middle class leads to a critical weakness when it comes to the kind of crisis in which fascism flourishes, for it is precisely then that minimalist reforms, including the economic planning for which social democrats are famous, do not work. (Not that they seem to work well even under less drastic circumstances, as at present!) The point is made dramatically by Willy Brandt in his autobiography (1982), where he recalls how tens of thousands of workers were prepared to resist Hitler in the early months of 1933. In his hometown of Luebeck, spontaneous strikes broke out, culminating in an (illegal) general strike on February 3. The social-democratic leaderships (of party and union) rejected every appeal to take militant action for fear of losing middle class support. Indeed, on March 30 the party executive

announced its withdrawal from the Socialist International in order not
to be embarrassed by the Inernational's anti-Nazi pronouncements.

Revolutionary socialist or Marxist assumptions are different. Marxists are not opposed to majority coalitions or majority rule. Theoretically, however, Marxist parties are prepared to postpone sharing power
and fronting for a decaying liberal capitalism in order to develop majorities for a more fundamental form of change. This change, it is
assumed, can come about and be supported by majorities because of
the inherent long-run incapacity of even liberal capitalism to function.
To paraphrase Marx, a revolutionary party is doomed if it comes to
power when the class that it presumes to represent is not yet ripe for
power—it is doomed to represent those classes that are (still) ripe—
hence its function must inevitably be to suppress revolution at home
(even though sometimes supporting it abroad as Western European
social democrats support Nicaragua today).

Let us now turn to an examination of the body of theory that sees the
white collar mass as having the potential of becoming a revolutionary
class force, or at least joining with others in movements for revolutionary change.

New-Working-Class Theories

New-working-class theories, differences aside, share the assumption
that a mass of occupations at the botom of the "stratification" system
constitutes a social class that is in conflict with a minority at the top;
and that objectively, if not subjectively, struggles against that minority
for social dominance. The term "new" may refer to the newer "white
collar" occupations, or to the fact that all workers now find themselves
in a new technological era; the nature of the conflict may be predominantly cultural, or it may be economic; the leading elements of the new
working class may be white collar, or blue collar, skilled workers of
either collar, or the more proletarianized.

The pioneer in developing both new-working-class and contradictory locations approaches (see the following section) was the German
sociologist and socialist Emil Lederer (1912). In his most important
work, Lederer used the word "inbetweenness" (*Zwischenstellung*) to
explain the apparently contradictory position of white collarites who
were objectively workers yet subjectively hostile to the working class.
He saw their heterogeneity, their internal segmentation, and their
marginal position in the class structure as often leading to a false mid-

dle class consciousness that constituted an obstacle to socialist de-velopment. At the same time, he argued, there were two levels within the overall grouping: the upper stratum that was pro-bourgeois, and the lower stratum—"proletarians in false colors"—that had the poten-tial for aligning with the blue collar workers because of a growing similarity in their working conditions.

From 1918 to the mid-1920s, considerable radical organizing among the white collar occupations took place in Germany, and Lederer coined the term "proletaroid" to indicate the development of a prole-tarian consciousness among the lower strata. In 1928, at a general congress of German trade unions, Lederer predicted the decreasing importance of blue collar workers, due to their decreasing proportion in the labor force, and pleaded that more attention be given to organiz-ing the German *Angestellte* (roughly synonymous with white collar workers) in the face of the rise of Hitlerism.

Erich Engelhard (1939), another social scientist affiliated with the German Social Democratic Party, identified the ambivalence of the white collar employee as a major problem. These people held to mid-dle-class attitudes and sought (and to a degree attained) a middle class life-style, including the enjoyment of a "social esteem" to which blue collar workers only aspired, but at the same time suffered from the income limitations of all workers in the inflation-ridden Germany of the 1920s and in the depression of the early 1930s.

Fritz Croner, another social-democratic researcher, went into more detail as to why and how the white collar employee would develop proletarian consciousness. He argued, first, that the increasing concen-tration of industry would result in industry-wide collective bargaining, leading to an enlarged group consciousness among workers. Second, the rationalization of work would limit the individual's control over the workplace and narrow the scope of the job. Third, the white collar worker was already suffering unemployment of "hitherto unknown pro-portions." All of these factors would lead to increased union activity. Croner hypothesized that the white collar employee would move in consciousness from (1) a person who assists an employer (ideologically a "not-yet employer") to (2) new middle class (not a laborer, but a new class "between" the classes) to (3) a salaried employee (not a laborer, but part of the proletariat) (Croner 1928:5).

In outlining the history of white collar union activity, Croner pointed to the immense increase (98.2 percent) in salaried and civil service employment in the years 1907–1925; the figure for blue collar workers was 22.3 percent. White collar unions had formed their own federation, the socialist-oriented Arbeitsgemeinschaft freier Angestellten-Verbaende (A.f.A.), in 1917. It had participated in the 1923 general strike that had frustrated Hitler's attempted coup d'état and in such local actions as the 1926 strike of Berlin medical and sanitation workers. By 1927 the A.f.A. had 400,000 members (out of 1.16 million unionized white collar workers and out of a total of about 5.27 million white collar workers). Such data further undermine the "white collarites as mass base for fascism" thesis.

It was German social scientists, mainly of a left-wing persuasion (and generally employed outside the universities), who pioneered in analyzing the white collar strata; no doubt this reflected their very immediate concern with the political potential of this rapidly growing sector of the labor force in the context of a series of national crises spanning the interwar period. But while these analysts saw white collar employees as potentially proletarian (hence, potentially socialist), they also saw clearly the contradictions and conflicts, the "ambiguities" of white collar life.

In England, the view was less positive than in Germany. "The contemptuous term 'white-collar proletariat,' was coined specifically in the inter-war years to emphasize the pathetic self-deception of the black-coated worker who was seen as indulging in middle-class pretensions on a working-class level of living," observes Lockwood (1958:14). This attitude correlates with unionization figures in England; as late as 1951 only 25 percent of "blackcoated workers" had been unionized (ibid.:141).

The Depression did little to support either stability or third-force approaches, even though the political behavior of the mass of white collar workers was not spectacularly radical either. In 1934, Hans Speier, in exile in the United States but focusing on German materials, concluded that "the social level of the salaried employee sinks with the increasing extent of the group," thereby pointing to its increasing proletarianization. Yet the salaried employee attempts various rationalizations in order to maintain a social distance from the traditional proletariat, one of which is national chauvinism. The "social character" of white collar employees, Speier suggested, must be analyzed just as thoroughly as their purely economic, objective circumstances (Speier 1934).

In 1935 Lewis Corey, well-known figure of the U.S. left and at the time still an avowed Marxist, produced *The Crisis of the Middle Class.*

It was one of the first two books written in the United States on the white collar phenomenon (Bingham's being the other) and constituted the first systematic attempt to update Marxist theory in the light of shifts in the U.S. labor force. It remains a classical Marxist statement on the new working class. Corey wrote from the depths of the Depression, with fascism a rapidly rising force in both Europe and, to all appearances, the United States. Citing the dismal statistics regarding white collar workers, who had a 35 percent unemployment rate, made up one out of every five charity patients in New York hospitals, and made up 40 percent of those seeking relief jobs, Corey concluded that the middle class had become largely propertyless and that their fight had to become the same fight as that of all wage workers (1935: 15). Yet he also argued that the middle class was still, within itself, in ideological crisis. It was an intermediary class split into antagonistic upper and lower layers. The upper layer, or "old middle class," included "independent enterprisers" and self-employed professionals. But the new middle class was also divided, between an upper layer of "managerial, supervisory and technical employees in corporate industry [who] are wholly identified with monopoly capitalism and its reactionary aims," and "the masses of lower salaried employees . . . [who] waver between democracy and reaction" (ibid.: 148). Ideologically bourgeois, the middle class provides support for reactionary social goals in exchange for promises by the big bourgeoisie to provide economic security.

The disunity of the middle class, fostered by its heterogeneity, creates "wholly a split personality, tormented by the clash of discordant interests" (ibid.: 151). But since the present crisis is "permanent," "if and when their economic interests drive the masses of lower salaried employees (and professionals) to struggle for a new social order, they must necessarily unite with the larger class of the proletariat" (ibid.: 168). There can be no unity of action with the upper administrative layers, which "perform the function of exploiting the lower." Strictly speaking, then, the middle class is not a class at all: "It has no identity of *class* economic interests in terms of a definite mode of production, or economic order" (ibid.).

What needs to happen is that "the lower salaried employees (including the professionals) must split off consciously from the middle class, as they are already split off economically" (ibid.: 170). This process will be hastened by their proletarianization; "a typical large office is now nothing but a white collar factory . . . [also] the proletarianization of technicians is marked and inescapable" (ibid.: 250–51). Indeed, the masses of lower salaried employees (including salaried professionals) are *not* members of the middle class. . . , [or even of] the "new" middle class . . . [the latter] can include only the higher salaried employees, the managerial and supervisory, who perform the capitalist functions of exploiting the workers . . . they are capitalists in the institutional sense and their relation to production is clearly bourgeois. It is otherwise with the masses of lower salaried employees . . . . : they are economically and functionally a part of the working class: a *"new" proletariat.* (Ibid.: 259; emphasis added)

Here, in perhaps its most explicit terms up to that time, Corey posits new-working-class theory: The lower white collar strata constitute a new proletariat, hopefully destined to join the old (although as a dependent factor) in the struggle for socialism. Indeed, this is the perspective finally arrived at, years later, by Mills, though the latter was not so sanguine about the white collar proletariat's radical potential.

In passing, Corey explicitly denies the old Bersteinian view that the development of a new middle class proves Marx wrong about polarization and that the middle class is becoming a majority. The old middle class is shrinking; the new middle class is qualitatively different; and the lower salaried employees are neither new nor old middle class.

C. Wright Mills (1951) shared a number of Corey's assumptions. Though radical, his framework was not Marxist. However, Mills thought that the white collar strata had, ultimately, to align themselves with one or another of the major social classes or directions—capitalist or industrial proletariat, right or left.

It is Mills who laid the groundwork for most of the present discussions of white collar dynamics, and who first popularized the new-working-class view in the United States. Although he insisted on calling these strata the "new middle class," he summarized, in *White Collar* (chap. 13), all the alternatives that have been discussed: (1) The new middle class will develop into an independent political class, displacing other classes "in performance of the pivotal functions required to run modern society," hence becoming the next ruling class (in one respect or another the view of Veblen, Mannheim, Weber, Burnham, and partially Djilas) (1951: 290). (2) The new middle class will become a "major force for stability in the general balance of the different classes," hence "will make for the continuance of liberal capitalist society" (the dominant liberal view) (ibid.: 290). (3) The new middle class, due to its political outlook and life-style, is really bourgeois, and will remain a status rather than a class group: "They will form, as in Nazi Germany, prime human materials for conservative, for reactionary, and even for fascist, movements. They are natural allies and shock troops of the larger capitalist drive" (ibid.: 291) (largely the traditional Marxist view, including Eric Fromm and Wilhelm Reich). (4) The new middle class "will become homogeneous in all important respects with the proletariat and will come over to their socialist policy . . . a peculiar sort of new proletariat. . . . With the intensification of the class struggle between the real classes of capitalist society, it will be swept into the proletarian ranks. A thin, upper layer may go over to the bourgeoisie, but it will not count in numbers or power" (ibid.).

Mills gave careful attention to several other theoretical possibilities, but finally concluded, in a chapter significantly entitled "The Politics of the Rearguard":

> Nothing in their direct occupational experiences propels the white-collar people toward autonomous political organizations. The social springs for such movements, should they occur, will not occur among these strata . . . the white collar workers can only derive their strength from "business" or from "labor." Within the whole structure of power they are dependent variables. (Ibid.: 352)

Which one will it be? "Of what bloc or movement will they be most likely to stay at the tail? And the answer is," said Mills, "the bloc or movement that most obviously seems to be winning" (ibid.: 353).

Virtually all of the writers who contributed to the early development of new-working-class theory shared an approach to white collar workers that, while emphasizing the ambiguity of their situation, assumed that in one way or another this ambiguity would be resolved: either by the lower white collar strata finally joining the proletariat, or by their becoming part of a middle class majority, or by their supporting the upper layers of the middle class in an independent bid for power. Yet time has not served any of these theories well, and there is no reason to believe that renewed predictions along similar lines will fare any better. To this predicament Crozier asks "whether, after all, this ambiguity . . . is not on the contrary destined to subsist" (1971: 33). That is, if white collar employees' ambivalent behavior is so long-term, may it not be inherent in a social situation that is destined to continue? While white collar workers share many characteristics with blue collar workers, "it is at the same time a situation which facilitates identification with the world of the ruling classes" (ibid.). This persistent ambiguity is reflected in the ambiguity of the empirical data available to us even today—to anticipate an issue that will be explored in more detail later.

In Western Europe, in the 1960s, partly as an outgrowth of the student movement but also in response to the collapse of European social-democratic and labor parties as the champions of any significant, far-reaching social change (indeed, as these parties functioned to integrate the working class movements more and more closely with capitalism), a new wave of new-working-class theories developed, particularly in France.

What is significant about these, as contrasted with the work of Corey or Mills, is that here the new working class is no longer a minority or dependent partner of the traditional working class but has become a co-equal, or even the main, force for change.

Serge Mallet was one of the first to spell this out. The term "new working class"

> is given to those who work in automated industry . . . these are of two types: the new factory utilizes two kinds of workers—(a) those who are . . . the human correctors of the machine's failings; . . . (b) the office technicians, who are separated from production itself. . . . The enormous development of offices has created a veritable intellectual unity of production, in which the conditions of work resemble, more and more, a modern shop in which physical fatigue has disappeared. (1963: 58–59)

Mallet is saying that the new working class—or, better, the new form of the working class—is closely associated with automation, that modern technology creates a new kind of working class (incorporating all highly skilled workers, regardless of collar color), and that it is precisely their *easy* conditions of work (rather than their hardships, their alienation) that enables them to ask deeper questions about the structure of capitalism. Thus

> we see a growing consciousness which . . . brings the totality of the economic system into question and leads union organizations to go beyond the level of struggles for particular categories of workers and to move toward the demand for workers control over production, on the level of the company as on that of the entire society (1975: 46).

For Pierre Belleville (1963), too, the concept "new working class" means not so much that white collar workers constitute a new phenomenon, or even that all *tertiaires* or all personnel in automated industries are a new class, but that the form and nature of the *entire* working class has qualitatively changed. "New working class," for

Belleville, is thus a historical concept to differentiate it—all of it—from an earlier epoch. This new working class consists of

> all the salaried who, by their intervention of whatever nature, participate in industrial production. But the notion of industrial production must be taken in its largest sense. It is necessary to include, for example, . . . indispensable through auxiliary sectors. Maintenance workers in certain automated factories; . . . transport workers . . . workers and technicians in telecommunications . . . repair-service workers. . . . Distribution [today] is a simple prolongation of production into its last state. (1963:15)

In a more general way, "this extension of the notion of industrial production . . . is opposed to a rigid division between production and services, between secondary and tertiary activities" (1963:17).

Opposed to the new working class are their antagonists, the "collaborators": those who participate in authority, those who are responsible for decisions, even though salaried. What we have then is a new, integrated working class, quite different from the older, narrower, Marxian view that limits the concept "proletarian" to those who *directly* create surplus value, the industrial production workers.

Ernest Mandel, a Belgian Trotskyist, puts this type of analysis into a more formal Marxian context. His analysis begins with the students, whom he considers a new kind of social grouping. Mandel considers that "the student revolt represents on a much broader social and historic scale . . . [a] colossal transformation of the productive forces" (1969:49). But students are not an independent grouping: They will become "white-collar employees of the state or industry, and thus part of the great mass of salaried workers." While students are better able to free themselves from bourgeois social conditioning than are some other groups, ultimately they must integrate themselves into a genuine workers' movement (that is, apart from "the ossified and bureaucratized structures of the traditional workers' organizations") (ibid.: 51).

In a 1968 talk, Mandel had developed the idea of the new working class in particular in connection with the "growing crisis of the international money system" and the growing proletarianization of the white collar strata in response to that crisis. This would produce, he proposed, "reduced wage differentials . . . increased unionization and union militancy . . . rising similarity of monotonous, mechanized, uncreative, nervewracking, stultifying work in factory, bank, public administration, department stores, and airplanes . . . ," as well as equalization of the "conditions of reproduction of labor power," in the form of mass education extending to the college level (1968: 8).

Mandel therefore disagrees with Mallet in one important respect: the potential politicization of the new working class will come about in the traditional way, as the result of "proletarianizing" tendencies in the structure of the economy and society, and not because these new prole-tarians have been able to *transcend* their immediate conditions, or because those conditions have become so much improved that they are able, like Mannheim's intellectuals, to "rise above" that struggle in order to have a more global vision.

This disagreement, it might be pointed out, is not a new one, nor can it easily be resolved. It is part of a much older debate concerning consciousness and change: Do people create and join movements for change as their conditions become worse or as they become better? Worse or better relative to what? In the present context, is it not probable that some segments of the new working class are indeed improving their condition, while others are suffering deterioration?

The developments in new-working-class theory just outlined coin-cided with a new outpouring of research, much of which was in Ger-man, the mother tongue of both theory and empirical work on the new occupations. Jaeggi and Wiedemann (1966), for instance, clearly ap-proached new-working-class theory when they proposed that salaried employees constitute a single grouping with a common, perceived set of interests. Neuloh (1966) was even more concerned with the effects of automation than were previous writers and hypothesized not only that the boundary between office and factory work is quickly disappearing, but that technological unemployment among white collar workers is likely to reach catastrophic proportions. Other German writers have continued the exploration of the political implications of these new strata begun so long ago by Schmoller, Kautsky, and many others, both empirically (e.g., Lange 1972) and historically (e.g., Kadritzke 1975, and Kocka 1980). Lange (1972) and Witt (1975) both focus on the development of the upper layers of white collar life, including political and trade union developments among them.

In the United States, a structural context similar to that in Europe (involving the rapid growth of the student population, especially in the universities) and an immediate political need combined to draw atten-tion to the theory of the new working class. The political need came when the "old guard" of the Students for a Democratic Society (SDS), the authors of its 1962 Port Huron Statement and their followers, graduated from college, made their way into the labor force, and confronted the need to develop a rationale that would tie political action to their new locations. By about 1965 or 1966, the Radical Education Project had been created at the University of Michigan by older SDS members, and a series of conferences on radicals in the professions had been organized. As the authors of a key document, "With a Little Help from Our Friends," put it:

> Once we recognize the unviability of an orthodox career line, . . . there are three action alternatives open: we can take establishment jobs and seek other outlets for our human and political needs; we can "drop out" and work for the movement; or we can try to transform our professional roles from ones supportive of the status quo to ones that use their location to undermine it. (Haber and Haber 1969: 291)

But if the third alternative was to be viable, a political strategy or ideology was needed: The European new-working-class theorists filled that void, even though few of them were read in depth (especially in their original languages). U.S. theorists contributed relatively little of theoretical significance to the debate, with the exception of James Becker (1973). He argued that the same thing was happening in the white collar strata as was happening in the production sector: The proportion of capital to labor was increasing, creating the precondition for more intensive exploitation of what labor remains:

> The investment mechanism has promoted an enlarged and unproductive circulatory apparatus which is the main abode of the so-called middle class. This "class," however, falls into two distinct segments, each of which is in economic opposition to the other. . . . It is in actuality not a social class per se. It is but a divided fragment of the totality of social labor . . . its reality is a cleavage between administrative labor and the managers. . . . The contrast is between, on the one hand, the technicians and professionals . . . and at the other pole, the unproductive labor of the managers and the ruling class as a whole. . . . Administrative labor is not a part of managerial labor with which it is so often confused. . . . It is part of the working class, emerging as a definitive portion of that class within the managerial phase of development. (1973: 275–76)

The theory of the new working class, while hardly free from ambiguity or controversy, is based on the logic that white collar workers (who work predominantly in the services sector and in government) are an integral part of the productive processes. Although their consciousness of themselves as workers may "lag" behind that of their blue collar colleagues, it is assumed that they will "catch up," either because the nature of their work will become increasingly professional and subject to confrontation with the kinds of "meta-needs" posited by Mallet and others, or because the nature of their work, and life-styles, will become increasingly proletarianized, as hypothesized by Corey and others. Indeed, both tendencies may take place, and the white collar labor force be split into upper and lower levels.

Contradictory Locations

Lederer, Corey, and Mills all made the point that politically, as well as structurally, there are profound divisions within that "group" of occupations labeled "white collar" in the United States and *Angestellte* in Germany. Each of these writers described some form of split between the upper layers, which are closer to management and to the bourgeoisie, and the lower layers, which are closer, in both condition and consciousness, to the blue collar working class. Becker, quoted above, develops this thesis further, and Erik Olin Wright (1978) spells it out in the most sophisticated form to date.

Wright's analysis takes the form, in large part, of a rebuttal of the approach of the French Marxist Nicos Poulantzas (1975), whose argument was that only a minority of workers at the very bottom of the new occupations perform "productive labor," produce surplus value, and can be considered truly a part of the working class. The new white collar workers by and large, therefore, are antagonistic to the working class in that the former's source of income is at the expense of the latter, of the surplus value that they generate. (See chapter 1 for a more detailed discussion of this issue.) Poulantzas poses an important question: If the working class consists of all wage earners, blue and white collar alike, why has unity of that class been so elusive? His answer, however, that only a minority of wage earners are "real" workers raises an even more difficult issue: How can a minority working class create fundamental change?

Wright sets himself the task of examining the real differences not only within the working class but among those occupational layers just "above" it, in order to find out what impedes unity, and, on the other hand, what common interest can be discovered. First he attacks the assumption that surplus value is generated only in the production of physical commodities, an issue that was discussed in chapter 1. He argues that many positions in the labor force "contain a mix of productive and unproductive activities," so that many others besides blue collar workers in production have unpaid labor "extracted" by their employers (1978: 46–47). There are thus three main classes—the bourgeoisie, the proletariat, and a much smaller traditional petty bourgeoisie, but between them there are

> three clusters of positions [that] can be characterized as occupying contradictory locations within class relations: 1. *managers and supervisors* occupy a contradictory location between the bourgeoisie and the proletariat; 2. certain categories of *semi-autonomous employees* who retain relatively high levels of control over their immediate labour process occupy a contradictory location between the working class and the petty bourgeoisie; 3. *small employers* occupy a contradictory location between the bourgeoisie and the petty bourgeoisie. (Ibid: 63)

The conceptual handle on these contradictory loations is the degree of control each person has over *what* is produced, *how* things are produced, and the *legal* possession of the means of production. Those within the social division of labor who have at least some control over some of these relations find themselves in contradictory locations, and Wright estimates that this includes at least 40 percent of the labor force. This is probably an exaggeration, however, because Wright includes jobs "involving the execution of state policies and the dissemination of ideology," that is, much of the state sector.

In sum, according to Wright, once those at the "bottom" and those at the "top" of the labor force are stripped away, a residue of contradictory, ambiguous, constantly shifting strata and occupations remains. This residue, if we may call it that, is segmented in significant ways materially, forming obstacles to its ideological and political unity with other classes *or* within itself as a third force.

Building on Wright's analysis, it can be argued that both the public and private sectors are segmented into at least three strata of significance: direct policymakers (management); indirect (second echelon) policymakers (administrators, foremen); and policy executors (technicians, semiprofessionals). The first two fit into the contradictory position between the bourgeoisie and the proletariat; and the last is the group Wright calls semiautonomous employees and fits between the old petty bourgeoisie and the proletariat. It includes vast numbers of service professionals and semiprofessionals who participate at least partially in actual production (directly or indirectly) and who often have blue collar working class backgrounds.

I conclude from Wright's argument that the failure of the middle strata either to develop an independent politics or to align clearly with the bourgeoisie or the proletariat (in those countries where party identifications make this possible, such as England or France where there are clearly defined labor and/or socialist parties) can be accounted for by their contradictory status. Contradictory objective locations imply contradictory subjective politics. The task of a socialist movement is to develop strategies that will overcome the divisions within the working class and between it and its closest "contradictory" allies—who are, according to Wright's analysis (with which I agree), partially workers anyhow. The increasing rationalization of work, the fiscal crisis, the intensification of exploitation, all serve to sharpen the contradictory position of many people in the middle occupational layers and to place social change on their agendas.

This analysis implies an approach to the tactics of social change that is based on democratic assumptions. Elite theories ultimately fail because the elites of the new occupations—managers, administrators of the state sector, upper-level professionals—are not an independent grouping, but are, rather, part of the bourgeoisie, or, to the degree that they find themselves in a contradictory situation, ultimately too close to the bourgeoisie to break with it. Stabilizing theories fail because there is no homogeneous middle that can be identified as a separate class. Similarly, new-working-class theory is undermined by the fact that there are real differences between many of the "middle" occupations and the traditional working class, and also because there are too many fragments within the white collar occupations to allow them a class unity—middle or working. The contradictory-locations approach is, at this point in the historical debate concerning the political mission of the new occupations, the one that is most persuasive for two related reasons: The data do not support the other theories, yet they do provide strong ammunition for this approach. The realities of the lack of a homogeneous white collar "class" and the fragmentation of white collarites so that different segments belong to different classes, and some segments to more than one class at the same time, will be elaborated upon in the chapters that follow.

5
Trends: People, Paychecks, and the Paperless Office

Introduction

"The office today," stated a 1973 U.S. government report, "where work is segmented and authoritarian, is often a factory. For a growing number of jobs, there is little to distinguish them but the color of the worker's collar" (U.S. H.E.W. 1973:38). Twenty years earlier, Mills had written: "The new office is rationalized: machines are used, employees become machine attendants, the work, as in the factory, is collective, not individualized" (1951:209). The news is official: From every nation, including many so-called less-developed countries, the trend is the same—more and more workers in absolute numbers, and increasing proportions of the labor force in percentages, are engaged in office work, white collar work, the services sector, the state sector. And everywhere the talk is of the rationalization and segmentation of work, and the possible de-skilling of the white collar labor force. This is true not only at the lower level of office employment, but at the upper levels as well, where, according to Sobel (1982), professionals and even managers find themselves increasingly treated as employees, sharing much of the lot of other white collar workers.

This chapter and the next will be concerned with the "lower levels" of office life, while chapter 7 will focus on "professionals." This approach is based on the assumption that the upper and lower strata within the so-called middle occupational groupings deserve to be analyzed as separate components of the class process, quite apart from the internal divisions within each.

Two kinds of questions set the parameters of the discussion: First, what are the roots of the development of the myriad of new jobs called "white collar," "services sector," "public sector," or "tertiary"? Are these developments, as many writers believe, simply the outgrowth of inevitable technological change and progress? Or are they based on the historically specific location of the United States and some other Western countries as administrative centers of world capital, representing, on an international scale, a form of the division of labor? Or do they reflect the shifting social and political positions of preexisting classes, so that the emergence of the white collar sector is the outcome of a hidden form of class struggle (as argued for instance by Burris 1980a, 1980b)?

The second set of questions, which overlaps with the first, has to do with the specific form of labor associated with the modern office. Again, the question of technological change arises: Does the modern office represent progress, and is it therefore simply the most appropriate and efficient way to organize work? Or is it—also?—independently?—a form of labor organization responsive to the imperatives of capital? To put the issue more broadly: Is the segmentation of work, in both shop and office, the most efficient way to organize production, or are social relations and technology in the workplace organized the way they are in order to "de-skill" labor and keep the labor force divided (Braverman 1974)?

But putting the issue this way begs the question of who defines "efficiency." Efficient to what end, for whose purposes? If efficient means "cost-effective," then it is synonymous with an extensive division of labor because labor segmentation tends to drive down unit labor costs, hence maintains or increases profits—an important issue even in the public sector in a time of shrinking revenues. Moreover, under many circumstances, labor costs and profits are more important than quantity or quality of output. If, on the other hand, efficiency is seen in a broader way, in terms of social good, then it becomes synonymous with "effectiveness," the delivery of quality goods and services to people needing them. In that case, the segmentation of work associated, at the extreme, with the factory assembly line or with the word-processing "pool" may not be efficient at all.

If this second set of issues is to be dealt with, certain empirical questions must be answered. To what degree is work, at the lower levels of white collar life, being downgraded? Is at least some of it being upgraded? Are working and living conditions splitting the lower strata of the white collar occupations in the same way that professional life is being segmented (as I shall propose in chapter 7)? Or is it more valid to argue the "middle-classization" thesis—that these lower strata belong to a single new grouping (or even class) between the traditional working class and the upper class? In short, what does the "inside" of white collar life in the modern office actually look like?

Trends—People

Total white collar employment in the United States increased from 43.4 percent of the labor force in 1960 (28.3 million people) to 53.8 percent of the labor force in 1982 (53.6 million people); within that broad category, clerical workers increased from 14.8 percent (9.6 million) to 18.5 percent (18.4 million) while the number of blue collar factory workers has increased at a far slower rate—"operatives," the government category most closely associated with ordinary factory workers, constituted 18.1 percent of the labor force (just under 12 million workers) in 1960 but in 1982 amounted to only 12.7 percent (12.8 million workers) (see Table 5-1). Looking at this issue by economic sector, government (including local and state) employment increased 93 percent from 1960 to 1980; finance, insurance, and real estate by 100 percent. The trajectories of the core white collar and blue

Table 5-1. Overall Trends in the Employed U.S. Labor Force

	1965		1982	
	No. (in millions)	%	No. (in millions)	%
White collar	31.8	44.7	53.9	54.0
Mgrs. & Admin. +	7.3	10.3	11.8	11.9
Prof. & Tech. +	8.9	12.5	17.2	17.2
Clerical +	11.1	15.6	18.8	18.9
Sales	4.5	6.3	6.6	6.6
Blue collar	26.2	36.8	28.7	28.9
Crafts, etc.	9.2	12.9	11.9	12.
Operatives −	13.3	18.7	12.1	12.2
Nonfarm labor	3.6	5.0	4.5	4.4
Service +	8.9	12.5	13.7	13.8
Farm laborers −	4.0	5.6	2.8	2.8
Totals	71.1		99.1	

SOURCE: *Monthly Labor Review,* various issues.
+ Indicates steady increase in percentage.
− Indicates decrease.

Table 5-2. Trajectories of Operatives and Clerical Workers, 1960–1981

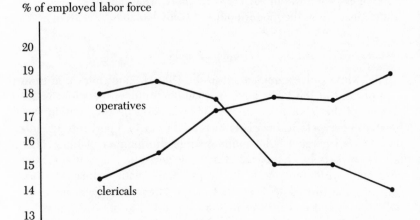

% of employed labor force

collar worker groups crossed around 1970 and, at least proportionally, were moving in opposite directions (see Table 5-2).

In a broad way, these trends have been under way since the 1870s and 1880s, both in the United States and in all Western countries (and since the 1940s, in such developing areas as Puerto Rico, Chile, and others). The general picture was described by Mills:

> In the early nineteenth century . . . probably four-fifths of the occupied population were self-employed enterprisers [including farmers]; by 1870 only about one-third, and in 1940, only about one-fifth. . . . Many of the remaining four-fifths of the people who now earn a living do so by working for the 2 or 3 percent of the population who now own 40 or 50 percent of the private property in the United States. (1952: 63)

In overall terms this configuration holds true for most Western countries. To cite but a handful of examples: In Great Britain in 1910 there were just over 3.3 million white collar workers; by 1971 there were over 10 million, during which time the total labor force expanded by less than 40 percent (Jenkins and Sherman 1979:18). In Germany, the proportion of *Angestellte* (encompassing most white collar employees, both private and public) increased from 3 percent in 1882 to 44 percent (Federal Republic only) in 1976 (Littek 1982:285–86). From 1950 to

1976 the number of white collar workers grew from 3.5 milion to 9.1 million; in that same period the civil service more than doubled. In Japan, white collar workers made up 11 percent of the nonagricultural labor force in 1920; by 1959 they constituted 26 percent—over 7 million out of nearly 28 million workers (Vogel 1963:6). Even in Italy, where the services sector has been slow to develop, the number of office workers increased from 480,000 in 1901 to 3.3 million in 1971—a sevenfold increase—while the number of factory workers only doubled in that time, from about 2.4 to 4.8 million (Invernizzi 1982:4).

In the United States, the proportion of white collar people who work for wages has increased steadily from 79.2 percent in 1940 to 90 percent in 1975 (Sobel 1982:205). But large numbers of people in some of the better-paid professional occupations remain self-employed—in 1970, 61.4 percent of doctors and 55.7 percent of lawyers. Overall, the proportion of professionals who are wage earners has increased from 81.6 percent in 1940 to 92.2 percent in 1975. At the lower levels of white collar life (clerical and salespeople), the proportion who are self-employed has always been very small—1.6 percent in 1940 for clericals, and 10.9 percent for salespeople. These percentages have increased only slightly in the thirty-five year period under examination.

Correspondingly, as Mills indicated, the proportion (if not necessarily the number) of self-employed—the "old middle class"—has fallen drastically. Burris (1982a) states that the drop-off in the United States was from 33.7 percent in 1900 to 8.4 percent in 1978 (for the nonagricultural sector only, it fell from 12.7 percent in 1900 to 6.7 percent in 1978). In Germany, the proportion in the agricultural sector fell dramatically from 49.1 percent in 1878 to 6.4 percent in 1978 (Littek 1982:304) although the proportion of small producers, tradesmen, and other small proprietors did not fall as dramatically (Kadritzke 1975:166).

Despite the general decline of the *proportion* of workers in old middle class occupations, Marx's prediction that the petty bourgeoisie would inevitably be crushed between labor and capital is true only if considerably qualified. In the United States, as well as in most other "advanced" capitalist societies, the actual *number* of self-employed, outside of agriculture, has remained stable, and in some cases has even risen. In countries such as France, Italy, and Japan, the self-employed account for between 10 and 16 percent of the labor force, and even in the United States, where the nonagricultural petty bourgeoisie is one of the smallest, proportionally, in the world, we are still talking about 6 or 7 million people (a slight decline since 1970, when there still were about 8.9 million sole proprietorships with reported business receipts of less than $100,000 per year) (Gioglio 1975).

Further, the much-touted "decline" of the old middle class varies widely from country to country. A very large proportion of it is the result of the modernization of agriculture—the penetration of the modern capitalist enterprise into the countryside and the destruction of the small-holding farmer population. Where this has not, for various reasons, taken place (e.g., Japan or Italy), the overall proportion of the old middle class continues to be high—as much as a quarter of the employed population.

The gradual increase in the proportion of people working in the white collar area is, therefore, accompanied by a number of internal developments. A proportional decline in self-employed middle class people is only one of these developments, even as the continued presence of large numbers of petty-bourgeois white collar people helps to segment the white collar mass between those who sell their labor power for wages and those who do not—and from those who do some of both.

A second major internal differentiation is between those white collar employees who work in the private sector and those who work for the state. The former are directly or indirectly involved in the process of production, in the realization of surplus value through the medium of commerce, or in related fields such as marketing. The latter are involved more in the reproduction of the labor force, and/or in the reproduction of social relations, and include teachers, social workers, police officers, technicians, secretaries, etc. The immediate source of income differs for each group: The former derive their income as part of the expense of producing a commodity; the latter derive their income from taxes, that is, from the income of other workers. The resentment that this generates against state sector workers was alluded to in chapter 1; what is important to note here is that the state sector has been steadily increasing as a source of employment throughout the capitalist Western world (quite apart from the state's monopolization of all employment in other parts of the world). This increase in state employment is closely related to the increase in all white collar services sector employment, and helps to account, numerically, for the increase of all white collar employment.

Generally speaking, the state sector is subsumed under the broader concept of services sector. Varying somewhat from country to country, this includes transport, trade, banks, and insurance. Once again, however, a problem of definition arises: It is impossible to separate goods production from services, since each has components of the other. Most authorities define a "service economy" as one in which "more than half its work force is employed in producing intangibles" (Shelp 1981: 13). The United States is often considered the first service economy, because it crossed that employment threshold in 1940. Western European nations leading in the proportion of civilian employment in commerce and services include, in descending order, Sweden, West Germany, France, Denmark, Norway, Ireland, Netherlands, Italy, Switzerland, and Spain.

In the United States the growth of the public sector and that of the services sector are closely related. From 1960 to 1975, one out of every three new jobs was in the public sector. State and local government employment increased from 6.1 million in 1960 to 11.6 million in 1975 to 13.5 million in 1980. There was a slight decrease in 1981 as the fiscal crunch began to hit local budgets. Federal employment grew to 1.9 million additional workers in 1950, 2.3 million in 1960, 2.7 million in 1970, and 2.8 million in 1980. The federal figure (which excludes the uniformed armed services) was 2.7 million in October 1981 (*Business Week*, 21 July 1975; *New York Times*, 27 December 1981).

Technology and Domination

The reasons for the growth of the state sector are complex, but a detailed analysis is not necessary in order to understand the basic trend. Most radical observers agree on three contributing factors, at least in the United States: (1) the gradual socialization of certain costs of production (that is, their spread among the general population through governmental intervention supported by taxes) in the era of monopoly capital, particularly in transportation, banking, research, the education of the labor force, and the regulation of commerce (including regulatory agencies); (2) domestic social control, that is, police and social welfare functions that are aimed at controlling criminality and unrest; and (3) the changing U.S. role in the world division of labor, particularly its role as military bastion against revolution and competing imperial systems.

Although the growth of the public sector (the state) and the growth of the services sector (especially transport and commerce) are related, they are not synonymous. The growth of the state is related to its function as mediator among the various fractions of capital and as guarantor of the overall profitability and survival of capitalism as a system (Oppenheimer and Canning 1979; Poulantzas 1978). The reasons for the growth of the services sector—the location of most white collar occupations—is more complex and has not been as thoroughly analyzed. As Burris points out (1982a), the most common explanation (by conventional social scientists, by radicals such as Mills, and even by technological-determinist "Marxists") is that industrialization's technological innovations willy-nilly lead to an explosion in demand for the kinds of workers needed to handle this machinery and the business and governmental relations required to operate, at an administrative level, such a complex structure. The modern firm involves a multiplicity of internal administrative relationships, must relate to other complex organizations, and must interact with the state. Technology is created to help do this and this in turn generates a demand for workers. At the same time, the proliferation of knowledge makes it impossible for single individuals to master any process in its entirety. Consequently, the work must be subdivided, and supervised and managed by yet another skilled group, administrators. The argument is thus that efficiency requires the subdivision of labor (specialization, whether in the factory, office, or for that matter in the professions) and its coordination by management.

This approach has recently come under fire. Burris, for one, and Clawson (1980) remind us that a number of historians have shown that much of the division of labor associated with modern industry came about not in order to improve quality and quantity, but as the result of management's attempts to undermine the bargaining position of labor and to assume greater control over the labor process. Similar data are available for white collar and professional employees (Kraft 1977).

At the same time, the argument (by Braverman 1974, and those following in his tradition, including Burris) that virtually all of the changes in class structure (the development of white collar occupations) and working conditions (specialization, the segmentation of work, the de-skilling of labor) are attributable to "the competitive struggle among capitalists, and between capitalists and workers, over the appropriation of surplus value" (Burris 1980a:24) appears to oversimplify this process and make it the simple result of managerial conspiracies, even though that implication is not intended. Blatant inefficiencies and costs, even in the capitalists' own terms of profit maximization, suggest that this approach is as overly deterministic as the earlier technogenic explanation. It is true that the extensive introduction of machinery and bureaucratic hierarchies that lead to an increasing division of labor is not inherently necessary. But it is also true that under certain circumstances technology has a life of its own and exerts a dynamic outside the control of any given firm or manager, even under monopoly conditions.

Clawson (1980) suggests a more productive, and dialectical, approach: "It is not capitalists who force bureaucracy on us," he argues, "it is the class struggle." That is, "if workers did not resist, if they were truly and fully socialized to be happy and obedient, capitalists would not need the enormous and complex apparatus that is bureaucracy" (1980:24). In short, technology and the way it is structured (bureaucracy) should not be approached as if they were either purely technical advances or solely attempts to control the labor process, but rather an integrated whole: Modern technology and its bureaucratic organization increase efficiency (by lowering production costs) both by introducing new devices and by controlling workers more effectively—indeed, technological advances segment work and control workers, but conversely the control of workers creates imperatives for the development of new technology that will aid in such control (Clawson 1980: 192–93).

An examination of some technological developments in the modern office will shed light on this issue and help us further to develop an explanation that combines the technological and class-struggle theories.

The Paperless Office?

The medium determines the message: If there is machinery available, a way will be found to make use of it. But this is true only under certain circumstances, and begs the question of what kind of machinery is invented and made available, for more than an abstract "necessity" leads to inventions. Rather, technological innovation appears and is made available only in response to the necessities generated by the demands of capital, at least nowadays. Noble rightly asks (in connection with "automated" machine tools),

> Is it just a coincidence that the technology tends to strengthen the market position of these firms and enhance managerial authority in the shop? Why did this new technology take the form that it did, a form which

seems to have made it accessible only to some firms? . . . Is there any other way to automate machine tools . . . which would lend itself less to managerial control? (Noble 1979: 20).

Is it merely a historical coincidence, to quote Glenn and Feldberg, that office automation is built on "programs which automatically make decisions and initiate sequences of actions, functions which were formerly reserved for human judgment"? (1979: 46).

No, these are not just coincidences and no manager would claim that they are. It is perfectly justifiable, indeed imperative, to control labor costs and to take decisions out of the idiosyncratic hands of individuals and put them on a totally rational basis, something that can best be done by a machine. Indeed, Max Weber would have applauded this shift as a step in the direction of legal-rational authority and away from personalistic authority (Weber 1946: 196). Moreover, the sheer size of many firms, an artifact of the tendency of capital to concentrate in fewer and larger units, tends to impose uniform measures of productivity and accountability, which in turn are better served by machines. Uniform systems of data collection tend to generate processes within the organization that have uniform data collection as their aim: Data that are amenable to machine utilization replace all other forms of data; productivity that can be measured in uniform ways replaces other forms of productivity, that is, productivity tends to be measured in standardizable units. Numbers replace all other forms of measurement, so that, for example, productivity in the social services is measured by number of cases closed (rather than quality of service), education by student bodies in a classroom (rather than by measuring "learning"), and telephone service by uniform units of operator responses per time span (rather than customer satisfaction or some other measure).

The growth of the office (both in terms of number of offices and persons per office) is therefore the result both of the overall growth of the services sector—in turn related to the rapid expansion of industry in the context of monopoly capital and the imperative of this particular historical form to generate coordinative and administrative functions, and of the availability of technologies that "fit" these administrative needs. These technologies (ranging from the first typewriter to the latest word-processor-computer system) affect the form of output of the services sector, which must be measurable, leading to "standardization." Finally, this process helps to shape working conditions. Technol-

ogy therefore responds to the need to administer labor, helps to determine the form and content of labor, and at the same time helps to
determine the nature of the product (numbers).

The old office, as Mills argued thirty years ago, is on its way out, and
the era of the new (automated) office has scarcely begun. "The next
step is clear," Mills incorrectly predicted. "A moving 'belt' replaces
desks" (1951: 197). Such an antiquated form of mechanization is no
longer required. The computer terminal has virtually replaced the
desk, pieces of paper are no longer passed around or filed, and the
paperless office is nearly here in many larger firms.

Yet before we herald the new era too quickly and chuck our manual
typewriters into the nearest ashcan, we should consider several caveats
to these predictions, made by management people and radicals alike.
First, the sheer expense of the new technology (including the costs of
transition time), even for very large organizations, has inhibited the
office "revolution." Second, many individual managers, not to mention
clerical workers, prefer traditional methods (partly because they involve traditional managerial authority structures and prerogatives,
such as the "private secretary"). Third, the equipment tends not to
work as well as advertised, and when it is "down" the entire organization stands still—there are no backup manual systems. As *Business
Week* (24 November 1980) pointed out:

> Manufacturers [of word-processing equipment] are finding it more
> difficult to maintain existing levels of support and service because they
> are facing an ever tightening squeeze on profit margins . . . just as big a
> hurdle . . . is the training of their customers' office workers to operate the
> machines.

In short, the machines cannot just be plugged in and the operation
continues. A lot of money (and time) must still be spent to get the
system going. "It costs an average of $60,000 to hire, move, and train a
typical computer programmer," *Business Week* reported in April 1981,
and while few businesses using computers actually need their own
programmers, they must still buy the service from someone. Although
the costs of data and word processing are steadily declining, at least
according to the manufacturers, and clerical costs are steadily increasing (an argument for the introduction of labor-saving office machinery),
there are still millions of businesses (at the smaller end of the small
business world) for which the cost of even a microcomputer is prohibi-
tive. Nor is the present state of the economy helping matters. Al-

though the data-processing field has been one of the last to be hit by
layoffs, even it has been forced to "retrench" (*Business Week*, 25 October 1982: 30, 86). Layoffs, furloughs, bankruptcies, and corporate
takeovers involving large-scale job "retrenchment" at all levels, from
top management to assemblers of computer components, have become
almost as common in some parts of the computer field as in the more
traditional manufacturing indu tries.

Finally, there is evidence of considerable job dissatisfaction among
the clerical work force using the new technologies. With improved
technical methods of monitoring clerical output, alienation has increased (Glenn and Feldberg 1979; *Dollars and Sense*, September
1981; *Business Week*, 24 November 1980). Moreover, there exists what
might be called "anticipatory alienation": the fear of the new technology, especially the fear of unemployment, has a negative impact in
anticipation of, and during the phasing-in of, automated machinery.

In the past few years, women's groups have drawn attention to the
health problems created by the computerized office, as well as those
that have long existed in all offices but have been ignored. Among the
longer-standing complaints are fatigue stemming from back strain
(from poorly designed chairs and other equipment), eye strain and
headaches (from poor lighting and fluorescent lamps), hearing problems (from the constant noise of office machinery), and ailments involving nerve irritation that results in weakness, numbness, and pain in the
hand (commonly called carpal tunnel syndrome). More recently,
chemicals in typewriter cleaners, stencil fluids, copying machine liq-
uids, and correction fluids have been related to eye and skin problems.
The introduction of video display terminals (VDTs), a component of
word-processing and other forms of clerical, design, and laboratory
work, has led to complaints of eyestrain, nausea, cataracts, stress, and
problem pregnancies. Preliminary indications from Swedish and
Norwegian union studies, plus at least one study conducted by the
National Institute of Occupational Safety and Health (NIOSH), all
point to a possible correlation between the amount of time spent at the
VDT and stress, eyestrain, and eye damage (Sorensen & Swan 1981).
But the evidence concerning cataracts is unclear: Real proof of damage
has been denied (*New York Times*, 12 July 1983). However, the NIOSH
study (of three West Coast newspaper offices) led to the conclusion that
eye damage could not be disproven either. In 1977 the New York
Newspaper Guild charged that terminals posed a threat to health and

Table 5-3. Estimated Percentages of Annual Expenditures on Computers and Peripherals by Sector for Three West European Countries, 1985

	W. Germany	Netherlands	Switzerland*
Manufacture	45	27	29
Banking	8.6	15	14
Sales	11	8.7	20
Govt.	8.5	9.6	8.5
Transport	NA •	9.3	NA
Total services	28.1	42.6	42.5

SOURCE: U.S. Department of Commerce, International Trade Administration, *Country Market Survey*, January 1982.
*Data for Switzerland are from 1983.

safety and took the matter to arbitration. The union lost, but the arbitrator's finding left the issue unresolved: The etiology of cataracts remains "undetermined," particularly since not enough time has passed to evaluate long-term exposure to microwave radiation.

Nevertheless, a new era is here, even though it is not as fully developed as either overly optimistic computer manufacturers or worried labor organizers think. In 1981 alone, U.S. manufacturers shipped about $10.4 billion worth of computers—just over 1 million units—a 29 percent increase over 1980. (Compare this with a mere $1.84 billion in 1972 [U.S. Department of Commerce 1982a]). Peripheral equipment sales were valued at over $8 billion, up 14 percent from the year before. Figures for other Western countries are comparable (see Table 5-3); a 22 percent annual growth in purchases of computers and peripherals is likely for West Germany from 1980 to 1985; in the Netherlands, the annual expansion rate has been about 25 percent, resulting in $1.5 billion in purchases in 1983. In Switzerland, 1985 purchases are projected to be $1.112 billion. Most important, computerized facilities are growing fastest in the services sector, where most clerical workers are employed.

The computer has enabled employers to set up entire integrated office systems. Today, about one out of five office workers (including executives) uses electronic typewriters, word processors, and printers; about 10 percent have computer terminals and computer-based telephone communications systems. The larger the firm, the more likely it is that clerical workers will have microcomputers and other computer-based devices (*Forbes,* 14 March 1983). A $10 billion market for office systems was predicted in 1979 (Wharton and Burris, 1983).

The primary reason for the introduction of this new technology is savings in labor costs. A second is improved managerial control and centralized decision making. The result is twofold: the de-skilling of lower-level clerical labor and the transformation of the traditional patriarchal office to one that is highly "rationalized"—with increased alienation as a result: "Work throughout the organization is structured by the requirements of the computer. Although the clerks may be less directly supervised, they do not gain autonomy. . . . They have little discretion to do the work as they see fit and they are under pressure to work quickly" (Glenn and Feldberg 1979: 57–58).

The extreme example of this process is the word-processing center, where women work (often on night shifts) without ever having contact with the "initiator" of the communication, and not only is the work boring and repetitive, but the pace is monitored by other machines, and by management, at a discrete distance (deKadt 1979).

The drive to maximize profitability by keeping labor costs down leads not only to the displacement of workers by machines and the fragmentation of work, but to an international division of labor. Clerical labor is cheaper in the less-developed nations, and the new technologies enable firms to export much of their menial work. For some years, key-punch operations (for example, to update large mailing lists or to transcribe simple questionnaires onto punched cards) have been carried out in Hong Kong, Taiwan, and the Philippines. It is cheaper to fly the raw data (on paper) abroad, have it key-punched by local labor, and fly it back to the United States for computer entry than to have the material punched domestically. Today firms can transmit information by satellite, have it typed into a word processor abroad, and then retransmitted to the United States. Manuscript pages can be sent using facsimile machines, typed, and readied for printing—all without the use of airplanes. For such labor, Barbadians, for example, are paid $1.50 an hour versus between $4 and $12 an hour on the "mainland."

A further aspect of the "electronic sweatshop" is the replication of the old putting-out system but using modern computer terminals: Housewives type letters and manuscripts, as well as other forms of data, on terminals at home, and are paid considerably less than full-time clerical workers. Such isolated workers are virtually unorganizable, and receive no fringe benefits, vacation time, insurance, etc. (*New York Times,* 3 October 1982).

Worse Off or Better Off?

Under these rapidly changing conditions, are the lower layers of the white collar occupations worse off or better off? It is important to keep in mind what we mean by "lower layers": those occupations that the government classifies as "clerical" and "sales" on the assumption that they require somewhat less formal education, pay somewhat less, and are somewhat less autonomous. By definition, therefore, we are looking at workers who are not as well off as the upper white collarites, including the so-called professionals (see chapter 7). We are also looking at occupations that are disproportionally female (see chapter 6).

It is also important to remember that worse off and better off are relative terms. The "whom" used as a comparison may be: upper white collar workers, blue collar workers, or "lower" white collar workers at an earlier time.

There are a number of indices that are used to measure these gaps: mobility (whether rates of moving up through the stratification system are improving), standard of living (measured in real income on the culturally determined assumption that the higher the standard of living, the better off people are), rate of unemployment, the nature of the job itself (the degree to which jobs are being subdivided or segmented), the degree to which jobs are more or less autonomous, and work satisfaction (examined through questionnaires). Most of these measures (with the possible exception of real income and unemployment rates) yield contradictory results, because the situation can vary widely from one white collar position to another, even within a fairly circumscribed group such as secretaries, stenographers, or telephone operators.

Overall, however, two shifts are clear: In general, the standard of living of the Western working classes has improved significantly since World War II; there has been a great deal of intergenerational mobility from blue to white collar. About 37 percent of sons of working class parents go into white collar occupations (Miller and Form 1980: 225); about 10 percent achieve "elite" status. At the same time, many manual workers spend part of their occupational careers in nonmanual jobs, and vice versa. In an earlier study, Lipset and Bendix (1959) reminded us that overall in Western countries there is about as much downward as upward intergenerational mobility, including lower white collar fathers with blue collar sons.

The implication in many of these studies is that white collar work, regardless of other conditions, is by definition "above" blue collar work, and that blue collar work is "below" white collar work. What we are dealing with, however, is horizontal rather than vertical mobility, for although white collar work may be cleaner (and sometimes more prestigious), this does not necessarily mean that it pays more or involves greater autonomy. If we hypothesize that people are better off as white collar workers than as blue collar workers, then we must look at such indices as income to see whether this is true.

Average annual salary increases for clerical workers have been below annual inflation rates for some time. During the March 1979–March 1980 year, when increases for clerical occupations went up at an almost unprecedented rate of 8.8 percent, the consumer price index went up 14.7 percent (B.L.S. *News*, 1 July 1980). In that same year average salaries ranged from $7,884 for the lowest-level file clerks to almost $20,000 for top-level personnel clerks. Bottom-level secretaries were earning just over $11,000 annually, an increase of about $2,500 in four years—but a decrease in actual purchasing power. Average gross weekly earnings (in 1977 dollars) are shown in Table 5-4.

Such wages (even before taxes) put significant proportions of employed people into the official "poverty" category. Some are rescued because they belong to family units whose total income puts it above the poverty line. On the other hand, female workers who are the sole support of their families are far more likely to find themselves truly poor: They are more likely to be part-timers, and even when full-time earn only about 60 percent as much as men at the same occupational level (Wharton and Burris 1983: 15).

The average annual rate of wage improvement for clericals has, in almost every year since 1961, been lower than that for professionals and administrative employees. In the public sector, this means that while all civil servants subsidize the state because their income in-

Table 5-4.   *Earnings, 1970–1980: Selected Sectors*

	1970	1980	% change
Manufacturing (blue collar)	$208.00	$212.06	+ 2
Wholesale, retail trade	149.80	129.65	− 15
Services	150.80	140.12	− 7
Finance, insurance, real estate	175.77	153.74	− 13

SOURCE: *Dollars & Sense*, July/August 1982.
NOTE: The averages include an unspecified number of part-timers; excluding them would raise average incomes.

creases lag behind the rate of inflation (even if they match or exceed this rate in any one particular year), lower-level and lower-paid workers subsidize the state more: the lower the base pay, the less the annual net increase. This prompts the state to restructure jobs so that lower-level and lower-paid workers are a higher proportion of newly hired workers (e.g., paraprofessionals displace professionals, community college degree holders displace B.A. and M.A. degree holders, etc.). Moreoover, the lower the base income, the more serious it is for the individual when income lags behind the cost of living: An administrator earning $50,000 can survive on a mere 3 percent annual increase when the rate of inflation is 5 or 6 percent; a clerical worker with a salary of $15,000 cannot afford such a lag. And women "contribute" more of this extra "tax": Among twenty-one white collar occupations surveyed by the Bureau of Labor Statistics in 1980, salary levels for women exceeded those for men in only nine occupations, while they were below those of men (by up to 10 percent) in all the rest (U.S. Dept. of Labor, Bureau of Labor Statistics 1980).

The incomes of most U.S. workers have not kept up with inflation and unionized state workers have done less well than organized blue collar workers in the private sector. However, this disadvantage is partly offset by the higher unemployment rate among blue collar workers, which over the years has been over twice that of white collar workers (see Table 5-5).

For specific white collar occupations—lawyer, librarian, clergy, chemist, aerospace engineer, teacher, university professor—there have been dramatic increases in the unemployment rate, in some cases as early as 1970. For others—public health specialists, some engineers, paralegal aides, for example—there has been a great increase in de-

Table 5-5.   *Unemployment Rates Among Blue Collar, White Collar and Professional Workers, 1959–1982 (in percent)*

	Blue collar	White collar	Professional
1959	7.6	2.6	1.7
1965	5.3	2.3	1.5
1970	6.2	2.8	2.0
1975	11.7	4.7	3.5
1978	6.8	3.5	2.6
1982	14.4	4.0	3.3

SOURCE: Paula G. Leventman, *Professionals out of Work* (New York: Free Press, 1981), p. 36; *Monthly Labor Review*, September 1982.

mand. Overall, the rate of unemployment among white collar workers rises and falls with the rate for the economy as a whole, though at a lower level. While there has long been speculation that white collar unemployment rates will eventually begin to approximate blue collar rates, this has not happened yet.

It is important to consider some of the reasons for the ups and down of white collar unemployment. "Human capital" theorists attribute unemployment to inadequate methods of anticipating demand and educating workers for jobs that will be available in the future. Either jobs are available for which there are no workers, or people are trained in overly large numbers for the available job market. In a relatively unplanned economy such as that of the United States, there is normally some lag between the development of a job and the availability of people trained to fill it. Moreover, as the word spreads that a particular need exists, more people are recruited than are required. By the time they have finished training and appear on the job market there is a glut, and the word spreads that this is no longer a desirable occupation; "manpower" shortages then develop, and the recruitment-training-oversupply cycle begins again. The engineering field has suffered this boom-and-bust cycle repeatedly in the past two decades, in part because of its dependence on military spending.

A second reason given for white collar unemployment is similar to one cited for all unemployment: technological displacement. It is asserted that the introduction of labor-saving machinery, particularly in an age of rapidly expanding computer use, displaces large numbers of workers who, for various reasons (age, residential immobility, lack of literacy, laziness), cannot be retrained and placed in the new technologies.

A third reason, which is closely related, lays the blame on the structure of the economy. White collar unemployment is said to have the same cause as blue collar: the gradual decay (deindustrialization combined with state fiscal shortages) of the entire economic system. (The role of the multinationals and the flight of capital from the Northeast to the Sunbelt and abroad was discussed in chapter 2.) The trade-off between inflation and unemployment tends over the long run to result, after each bout of the disease, in higher "normal" unemployment rates—a gradual upward movement of the so-called Phillips curve.

What is the impact of the new office technologies on employment, and on the job itself? Is there technology displacement or does the new technology create jobs? The short answer is that nobody seems to know. A more complex answer is that jobs are destroyed and other jobs are created at the same time. As far as the nature of the work itself is concerned, again the answer is complex: Things are coming up neither all roses or all thorns. For some at the lower end of the white collar occupations, working conditions are clearly worse, more alienating, more monotonous, while for others the job is becoming more interesting, involving, and challenging.

The impact of automation on employment is often disguised, as Seligman (1966) points out, by ordinary business expansion, which in times of prosperity absorbs many of the workers who might otherwise find themselves on the street. Moreover, there is often an increase in the need for service and maintenance during the first years of installation of new machinery. However, "once the system jells and is operating at full strength, growth in the work force is halted and may even decrease . . . jobs are simply not filled when girls [sic] transfer or quit" (Seligman 1970: 270). As in other sectors of industry, management sometimes deals with the problem of staff reduction by hiring women during the changeover period on the assumption that the problem will solve itself because younger women are assumed to quit at a higher rate.

A Fund for the Republic report in 1962 accurately pinpointed another problem: Even though the services sector will grow,

> service activities will also tend to displace workers by becoming self-service, by becoming cybernated and by being eliminated . . . the U.S. Census Bureau was able to use fifty statisticians in 1960 to do tabulations that required 4,100 in 1950 . . . service industries can now carry on a vastly greater amount of business without hiring additional personnel; for example, a 50 percent increase in the Bell System's volume of calls in the last ten years with only a 10 percent increase in personnel. (Michael 1962: 90)

As long as the economy is expanding, the effects of technological change on employment are disguised, "old" workers are absorbed into "new" occupations (at least at the lower levels), and expansion appears to create shortages of certain personnel. As the trained labor pool expands to meet these shortages, an oversupply tends to develop (as in engineering); the usual cycle of oversupply to undersupply and back (related to the expansion and contraction of related educational facilities) is underway. Then, as the economy stagnates, two tendencies develop side by side; cutbacks in capital investment (in office hardware) result in an oversupply of specialists, yet some firms introduce more machinery, including computers, in order to lower labor costs. Finally, these two tendencies are underlined by a flight of capital: Investment leaves the area and moves into areas of lower office labor costs (implying a utilization of simpler machine systems requiring less educated labor), just as investment in general moves to areas of lower labor costs in general—that is, to the third world.

The drive toward profitability in the private sector and the need to save money in the public sector operate constantly; in a period of stagnation and fiscal crisis, this drive becomes frantic, and results in "trimming the fat" from employment rolls (but not the salaries of top management). But for those who remain employed or succeed in becoming employed, the nature of the work becomes a critical issue, since this same drive results in an increased division of labor, segmentation of work, and de-skilling of some workers. In computer-related technologies, employees suffer increasing specialization and simplification of tasks, so that at the lower levels they approximate clerical labor (Kraft 1977); at the same time, the technology must be made accessible to less-trained workers, and must be made easier to use. The impact on professionals is clear: The automation of medical diagnosis, the introduction of "jurimetrics" to draft legal documents, the computerization of the administrative and counseling tasks of clergy and social workers, the substitution of computers for engineers in designing, all tend, in the long run, to make for fewer and cheaper workers whose work is less autonomous.

At the lower levels of clerical work, which are overwhelmingly female, the trend toward the elimination of routine jobs has been clear for some time. As a Women's Bureau study put it,

> Entry jobs, which are typically low skilled and routine, have been a prime target for elimination by automation in some fields. . . . In such industries as insurance and banking, the relative loss of low-skilled jobs has been especially hard on young women . . . and may have some influence on the persistently high unemployment rate of teenagers. (U.S. Dept. of Labor, Women's Bureau, 1970:5)

Nevertheless, as many routine jobs are eliminated, new—but also routine—jobs are created to meet the needs of the new technology. The proportion of low-level clerical jobs may not change much (Glenn and Feldberg 1979: 58), but that is small consolation to the individual who suddenly finds herself without one. It is at these lower levels that the effects of unemployment, well reported in research literature, are felt most: higher rates of suicide, homicide, stress-related disorders such as alcoholism, and admissions to mental hospitals (*New York Times*, 3 November 1982, summarizes five such studies; other studies, including those on professional unemployment and its effects, are discussed in Leventmen 1981).

The trend is not limited to the United States. As Littek et al. discovered in West Germany,

the application of electronic data processing, and a strong thrust for office rationalization as a result of the economic crisis, have increased the rate of technological and organizational change in office work . . . a threat to job-security of white collar employees so far unknown in post-war Germany [has] been the outcome.

They cite accounting as one example:

The unified function of a bookkeeper was parcelled out into detail-functions serving the centralized EDP [electronic data processing] department, so that traditional bookkeeping knowledge and talents were to a certain degree no longer required. A division of labor was made between bookkeeping department and central-EDP unit. (1981: 138–39)

Does this mean that the deprofessionalization or proletarianization of work is *the* trend? Or is it more accurate to speak of *polarization*, so that there is de-skilling for a large proportion of the white collar labor force (or, more precisely, the maintenance of a low level of skill) and the upgrading of a smaller portion at the top? Or are both of these expressions too extreme? Has there instead developed a *continuum* of working conditions between totally unskilled, routinized, alienating work at the one extreme, and relatively professional, skilled, autonomous work at the other, within occupations termed "clerical"and "sales"? Many "professionals" are finding their working conditions (quite apart from their standards of living) deteriorating so that, in these terms, they are more like clerks than not. Meanwhile, some clerks are becoming more professional, increasingly differentiated from those below them, even while they continue to be "workers." The study by Littek et al. emphasizes this point. The bookkeeping division of labor did not work out, and bookkeepers were supplied with video terminals. The result was a reintegration of the work process:

The consequences [of rationalization] are different depending on the type of white collar worker concerned: some of them are the "winners" . . .

with respect to their better work and employment conditions, others are put into a meaner competitive position [and] some . . . are completely thrown out of the labor market. (Ibid.: 148)

The artificial "line" between clerical and sales workers, and professional and technical workers, is becoming fuzzier even as people at the very bottom of the clerical field, and at the very top of the professional field, are moving farther and farther apart. Hence it is not surprising that "studies of office automation have produced varying and sometimes contradictory findings regarding its effect upon division of labor" (Faunce 1970: 93). Among lower-level clerical workers in electronic data processing work, specialization is contributing to more alienation; but at higher organizational levels there is more centralized decision making and decreasing specialization. Thus, "the accessibility of larger amounts of more accurate information makes it possible to manage organizations of increasing size without increasing the differentiation of organizational structure" (ibid.: 94).

If we turn to the working conditions among the lower white collar occupations, we can first look at the degree of autonomy and decision-making power on the job. Sobel (1982) finds that some 34 percent of clericals, and 12.7 percent of salespeople, supervise someone else, while 62.8 percent of clericals and 70.9 percent of salespeople have no supervisory functions. (The remainder are self-employed.) Sobel distinguished three strata among nonsupervisory "workers": "authorized employees," who report considerable authority and decision making in their jobs; "workers," who are closely supervised, lack decision-making powers, and have repetitive jobs; and "normal employees," a residual category between these two. Workers in all of these categories are members of a "central working class." Then there are the supervisors, who may be working class in some respects but find themselves in contradictory class locations. Among supervisors in the clerical category, about 31 percent are managerial, that is, they supervise three or more employees and have a say in promotion and salary matters. The rest are termed "nominal supervisors." Among salespeople, about half have managerial functions.

While only 9.5 percent of all white collar employees are "workers" (that is, work under conditions analogous to blue collar workers on assembly lines), this amounts to 23 percent of all nonsupervisory white collar employees (Sobel 1982: 173–74). Even among the managerial fraction, few in fact supervise more than a handful of other people.

Table 5-6. *Percentages in Various Occupational Categories:*
Total Percentages for Each Category and Proportions within
Nonsupervisory Employees (in parentheses)

Occupational levels	Total nonsupervisory	Authorized employees	Normal employees	Workers
Total (for entire labor force)	52.3	16.6 (31.7)	21.1 (40.3)	14.6 (27.3)
White Collar	41.3	13.6 (32.9)	18.2 (44.1)	9.5 (23.0)
Upper white collar	15.9	8.1 (41.5)	8.2 (42.1)	3.2 (16.4)
Professional	30.3	11.6 (38.3)	13.8 (35.9)	4.9 (16.2)
Managerial	5.4	3.5 (64.8)	0.9 (16.7)	1.0 (18.5)
Lower white collar	65.0	19.6 (30.2)	29.0 (44.6)	16.4 (25.2)
Clerical	65.8	16.3 (24.8)	31.1 (47.3)	18.4 (28.)
Sales	62.5	28.5 (45.6)	23.2 (37.1)	10.8 (17.3)

SOURCE: Richard Sobel, "White Collar Structure and Class," Ed.D. diss., University of Massachusetts, 1982, p. 173.

Table 5-6 summarizes, for all white collar occupational levels, the percentage of nonsupervisory employees, and presents figures for each of the three subcategories of "workers." The numbers in parentheses represent the percentages of nonsupervisory employees within each of the three "worker" subcategories.

It is often assumed that the growth of supervisory employment as a proportion of all employment indicates an upgrading of labor and a decrease in the more segmented kind of labor at the "bottom." Sobel examined the trend since 1945 and found a very clear increase in the proportion of supervisory compared with nonsupervisory employment in all white collar levels, although for clericals the trend shifted around 1970, when a slow decline in supervisory labor began (Sobel 1982:214, 215, 221). If, however, we bring the category "authorized employees" into the analysis, a somewhat different picture emerges. While the categories of "supervisory," "normal," and "worker" *all* increase over time, the "authorized" category decreases, though not in every sector of the economy. It may therefore be more accurate to say that the proportion of white collar workers at both ends is increasing, while that in the middle—autonomous workers—is decreasing.

Let us make a final attempt to look at working conditions in terms of job satisfaction. Between 1967 and 1972 alone some 556 surveys on this subject were published. The general conclusion was that there was no conclusive evidence of a decline in job satisfaction in the 1962–1972 decade, and that between 51 and 67 percent of clerical workers were either very satisfied or satisfied with their jobs, as measured by a wide-ranging set of criteria (U.S. Dept. of Labor, Manpower Administration 1974). White collar workers did not vary much from blue collar workers in terms of which aspect of the job was "very important" to them, both rating intrinsic factors such as "work is interesting" more highly than most extrinsic factors (with the exception of pay, which blue collar workers rated above all other factors).

Between 1969 and 1972 Gallup polls reported a drop in job satisfaction, as did many authors. Andrisani (1977), using longitudinal surveys from 1966 to 1976, also found a decline, but mainly from the category of "highly satisfied" to "somewhat satisfied" (1977: 92). This downward trend was more marked among white collar workers (as well as craftsmen, service workers, and farmers) than among factory workers. Among white male clericals those saying they were "highly satisfied" declined from 58.2 percent in 1966 to 45.9 percent in 1971; among white females it declined from 70.7 percent in 1967 to 68.7 percent in 1971. Among black females, however, it improved from 58.5 percent in 1967 to 65.6 percent in 1971 (ibid.: 70–71). There was a rate decline even among professionals, who consistently have the highest rate of job satisfaction. Within this stratum, the "highly satisfied" declined, among white males, from 71.3 percent in 1966 to 66.6 percent in 1971. There were no improvements in any category.

Despite an outpouring of pessimistic statements concerning the "increasing alienation" of American workers, including white collarites, surveys continue to indicate that most workers are *relatively* satisfied with their working conditions, despite these declines.

These overall responses disguise a good deal. Most important, the questionnaires are closed-ended and post no alternatives. The respondent is asked about satisfaction, but relative to what? Given no alternative, it can be surmised that the respondent gives answers framed in terms of his or her own experiences and/or expectations: The respondent is satisfied, compared with other jobs held, or compared with what is likely to become available, or given the wages, even though other aspects of the job may be terrible. No questionnaire possesses the issue in terms of: "If you had the chance to work under the following conditions . . . would you prefer that to the present situation?"

In addition, these survey results do not separate the responses of workers in different kinds of job situations or organizational structures. Crozier, in a study of six French insurance companies, found an interesting relationship between rank, work involvement, and dissatisfaction: "The more one rises in the professional hierarchy, the greater the tendency to be interested in one's work and to complain about one's position" (1971: 97). High rank and lots of involvement, yet many complaints? This finding, which is difficult to put into an overall satisfaction rating, makes more sense after analyzing a study that specifically focuses on organizational structure.

John Low-Beer found that over half of those handling paperwork in a "traditional, non-participatory . . . vertical" electronics firm said they would choose the same job again (Low-Beer 1978:76). How can this be? Low-Beer raises a critical issue, ignored by most surveys: benign structures (according to his research) do not necessarily make for happiness, or authoritarian ones for poor morale. There are, he argues, *two* job dimensions that must be considered as crucial determinants: the degree of involvement (i.e., decision making required) and the participatory or nonparticipatory nature of the organization, that is, its control level. If the job is involving but the organization is rigid, so that it prevents the worker from doing what he or she perceives to be a good job, discontent will result, as in Crozier's study. Conversely, if the job is monotonous, and the organization is supportive and participatory, the worker will seek to express discontent actively and will tend to become militant.

The corollary is evident: Exciting jobs in participatory organizations lead to relatively high morale. But the reverse does not follow, for involving jobs in rigid organizations do not lead to happiness but to an alienation that takes the form of withdrawal and resignation, rather than militant protest.

Clerical workers are the least satisfied, overall, of all white collar categories, and their satisfaction rates are declining. If it is true, as the literature informs us, that dissatisfaction is mainly based on the *absence* of certain extrinsic rewards such as adequate salary, security on the job, decent hours, and healthy environmental conditions, then the deterioration of clerical real incomes, the threat of unemployment, and increasing occupational health problems may be a partial explanation. On the other hand, since overall satisfaction rates disguise differences in the structure of the organization (whether private firm or state bureaucracy), it may be that many white collar workers who find themselves in semiprofessional jobs with relatively higher levels of authorization become more dissatisfied as the organizations rigidify, with extrinsic problems a secondary matter.

The increasing levels of control, which appear to coincide with (1) size, (2) the introduction of computerized control mechanisms, particularly in the areas of accountability and productivity measurement, and (3) the rationalization (making uniform) of the product, whether commodity or service, would, following Low-Beer, lead to conflict when jobs are involving but controls are rigid—hence to lower rates of job satisfaction.

To the degree that the number of employees in the state and services sectors continues to grow, to the degree that economic crisis "requires" job segmentation and limits salaries, and to the degree that the combination of computerization-centralization-rationalization affects these employees, increasing dissatisfaction would seem inevitable. The "bottom line" is that relatively educated workers at the lower levels of white collar life confront working conditions that are becoming more and more onerous. The coincidence of this proletarianization with the disproportional representation of women in this lower stratum creates a sex-linked class fraction that will be the focus of the next chapter.

6
The Hidden Proletariat: Women Office Workers

The theoretical issue concerning the class nature of white collar employees, says Braverman, has been "unambiguously clarified by the polarization of office employment and the growth at one pole of an immense mass of *wage-workers* . . . a large proletariat in a new form," which is overwhelmingly female in composition (1974: 106–07).

Are women office workers "working class" or "middle class"? What is the significance of women office workers as a social, economic, and political phenomenon? Five areas will be examined as we explore these questions. (1) How can we define women office workers, in the context of social class theory? (2) How has this group arrived at its present historical position? (3) What is its size and position relative to the rest of the workforce? (4) What are the present conditions of women office workers insofar as this has not been discussed in chapter 5? (5) What are some of the social and political implications of these conditions, particularly with reference to the women's movement and trade unionism?

What Is an Office Worker?

For the purposes of this discussion, an office worker will be defined as any person listed under the "clerical" category by the Bureau of the Census. This includes such occupations as library assistants, physicians' office attendants, bank tellers, bookkeepers, cashiers, bill collectors, vehicle dispatchers, railway mail clerks, file clerks, insurance adjusters, messengers and office boys [sic], office machine operators, payroll clerks, postal clerks, receptionists, secretaries, shipping clerks, stenographers, storekeepers, telegraph operators, telephone operators, ticket agents, and typists, as well as those sales workers who work in an office-like context (especially retail sales clerks who work primarily around office machinery). (Although retail clerks are often thought of as white collar, the work of grocery clerks, the largest single category of retail clerks, is in fact more like manual work. Department store employees correspond more closely to the definition of office worker, but they are a much smaller proportion of all retail clerks [Estey 1971: 57–58]).

In 1981, 34.7 percent of all employed women were in the clerical category; if sales (which is admittedly a vaguer category) is included, 41.5 percent of all employed women do some form of office work (U.S. Department of Labor, Bureau of Labor Statistics 1982: Table 648).

In what ways are office employees "workers"? That is, in what ways are they members of a working *class* (as distinct from being simply an occupational stratum that can be distinguished from "blue collar operatives," let us say, by the fact that they do mostly "nonmanual" labor)?

If we use Marxian lines of definition, which involve both objective and subjective criteria, women office workers constitute part of the working class because one dimension of their relationship to the economic system is that of selling their labor power in return for a wage— as contrasted with those who own the means of production and derive their income from profits. Second, office workers indirectly help capitalist enterprise to function, to generate surplus value, and to make a profit. They no more receive the full fruits of their contribution than do factory workers and are also exploited, as was pointed out in chapter 1. The conflictual nature of their relationship to this exploitative workplace is reflected at several different levels: in the nature of office social relations, in the organization of office workers into unions, and in such overt and specifically "political" forms as party membership and voting.

Many, though not all, women office workers are proletarian in a further way: Large proportions of lower-strata white collar women are married to blue collar men. Although the man's class does not determine the woman's class, the man's is a component of the social milieu in which the woman lives (and, vice versa, the blue collar man's life may be less traditionally working class when his wife is white collar). We have little data on how this relationship works. We do know that in 1960, 24 percent of wives of factory workers were clericals and that by 1975 this had increased to 32 percent, underlining the close links between the clerical labor force and the traditional working class (Hayghe 1976: 16).

Also, many white collar husbands, particularly those in the clerical stratum, have recent, if not current, blue collar family connections.

The Feminine Dimension

The woman office worker must be analyzed not only from the point of view of her membership in the working class, but also as a woman. The debate as to the "nature" of women as a social category is broad and far reaching (see, for example, Firestone 1970 vs. Mitchell 1971). While the debate is by no means settled, several points seem clear. Women are distributed throughout the labor force quite differently from the distribution of men. A "caste-like" occupational structure has developed over time: Each occupation, and every social class, has a different component or mixture of women, blacks, Jews, and so on, and every ethnic, racial, and gender group has an occupational "profile" different from every other one. Such distributions change, but slowly, leading Acker to observe that women "can be viewed as constituting caste-like groupings within social classes" (1973: 941). The term "caste" is not meant in a literal sense, but points to the relative lack of mobility of such groups, which are "stuck" in certain job categories.

The point that large proportions of women do office work has already been made; correspondingly, office and much other white collar work (especially at the lower levels of the authority structure) is disproportionally female. While women constituted 42.8 percent of employed persons in 1981, they were 65.9 percent of all white collar workers and 80.5 percent of all clericals (see Table 6-1); women constitute 90 percent or more of certain occupations. These proportions have changed little over the past decade (see Table 6-2).

In addition, we must take into account the issue of housework. Virtually all working women who are wives and/or mothers are also housewives, as are virtually all women not in the official labor force. The question of what class a housewife who is also in the labor force belongs to is as problematic as the question of what—if any—class she is in if she is not. It has generally been assumed that the full-time housewife is either in no class (since she does not sell her labor power for wages, and does not, at least to all appearances, produce or realize surplus value), or that she is in the class of the man to whom she is attached (by virtue of life-style). This proposition is supported in part by the arguments about the importance of the woman office worker's husband's job as an index to her membership in the working class.

Table 6-1.   Percentages of Major Occupational Groupings That Are Female, 1972 and 1981

	1972	1981
Managers, admin.*	17.6	27.5
Professionals	39.3	44.6
Sales	41.6	45.4
Clerical	75.6	80.5

*Change probably attributable to a very rapid increase in women bank and office managers.

More recently, however, it has been argued that housewives do, in fact, indirectly participate in the creation and realization of surplus value in that they are essential to the reproduction of the productive forces of the society (new workers), and to the reproduction of the relations of production (by means of the socialization process) (see, among others, Althusser 1971: 127ff.). For this, the housewife is paid (indirectly, through her husband, or directly, e.g., welfare) less than the value of what she is producing (which is a very long-term value). From this it would follow that most housewives are exploited in a technical sense. But housewife or not, the woman office worker is part

Table 6-2.   Percentages of Specific Occupations That Are Predominantly Female, 1972 and 1981

	1972	1981
Professionals		
Librarians	81.6	82.8
RNs & related	92.6	92.6
Teachers, excl. univ.	70.0	70.6
Teachers, pre-K & K	96.8	98.4
Clerical		
Bank tellers	87.5	93.5
Bookkeepers	87.9	91.9
File clerks	84.9	83.8
Secretaries	99.1	99.1
Stenographers	90.4	85.1
Telephone operators	96.7	92.9
Typists	96.1	96.3
Office machine operators	71.4	73.6

SOURCE: U.S. Department of Commerce, Bureau of the Census. *Statistical Abstract of the United States, 1982–83:* Tables 648, 651.

of a sex-linked stratum or quasi-caste, locked into certain job categories within the working class.

Women and Offices: Historical Development

From 1930 to 1942, under the auspices of the U.S. Women's Bureau, a number of studies of women office workers were produced and published (Byrne 1932; Byrne 1935; Erikson 1934; Maher 1932; Pidgeon 1930; Sullivan 1936; U.S. Dept. of Labor, Women's Bureau 1942). These studies, containing a wealth of information, covered the office, 5-and-10 cent store, and department store employment of women bookkeepers, stenographers, typists, clerks, salespeople, and the like, both at the macro and on the regional and city level, in selected places. Then, in 1953, Nancy Morse published the results of a survey of 742 employees in one white collar organization, 84 percent of whom were women. Aside from this, there was little *systematic* work on women in the clerical and sales strata until recently. Almost all of the other literature consisted of autobiographical accounts, exposés of specific job settings, short essays in the feminist literature, or fiction. The methodology followed by Mills in *White Collar* (1951) was standard: He based his work on his own personal observations and those of such novelists as Sinclair Lewis, John Dos Passos, Booth Tarkington, and Christopher Morley, using them to reconstruct an ideal-typical "folklore" of the "white collar girl": Born of small-town, lower middle class parents, she takes a business curriculum in high school and moves to the big city to seek her fortune and love. Failing at both, she settles into semi-adjustment in an office halfway between the midget office of the old-style firm and the superrationalized office of the modern conglomerate. Often substituting this kind of "career" for marriage, she becomes the corporate equivalent of a nun, serving her boss tirelessly until retirement. The degree to which this "typical" picture was true is virtually unresearched.

Only recently has an attempt to develop a social-historical analysis of the office, and its labor force, begun. Benét (1972), Davies (1974), Braverman (1974), and Glenn and Feldberg (1977, 1979) have analyzed the technological shifts that created the system of production, as Braverman puts it, that we today know as the modern office, with its (predominantly female) labor force. Benson (1983) has made a similar analysis for the department store clerical and sales labor force. The results of this research are summarized here.

Table 6-3.   Growth of the Clerical Force, 1870–1977 (in thousands)

	1870	1880	1890	1900	1910	1920	1930	1940	1950	1960	1970	1977
Total for clerical workers	91	186	492	770	1,885	3,311	4,274	4,847	7,632	9,783	13,714	16,106
As % of employed persons	.7	1.1	2.1	2.6	5.1	8.0	9.0	9.1	12.8	14.7	17.4	17.8
Female clerical workers	2	8	83	204	677	1,601	2,223	2,549	4,597	6,629	10,233	12,715
As % of all clerical workers	2.4	4.3	16.9	26.5	35.9	48.4	52.0	52.6	60.2	67.8	74.6	78.9

SOURCE: Evelyn Glenn and Roslyn Feldberg, "Proletarianizing Clerical Work," in Andrew Zimbalist, ed., *Case Studies on the Labor Process* (New York: Monthly Review Press, 1979), p. 55.

Table 6-4.   Stenographers and Typists in the United States

	Total	Percent female
1870	154	4.5
1890	33,400	63.8
1910	326,700	80.6
1930	811,200	95.6

SOURCE: Based on Margery Davies, "Women's Place Is at the Typewriter," *Radical America* 8, no. 4 (July–August 1974): 10; and Alba M. Edwards, *Comparative Occupational Statistics for the U.S., 1870–1940* (U.S. Bureau of the Census, 1943).

In 1870 there were but 91,000 (1 percent of the labor force) clericals, most of them males; by 1880 there were 186,000 and by 1890 there were almost a half-million. In July 1982 there were 18.4 million—18.5 percent of the employed labor force, four out of five of them women.

By the last decades of the 1800s, as business operations became more complex, the demand for office workers began to outstrip the supply. Was this complexity merely the result of the increased size of organizations, or did the nature of the labor process itself dictate a division of labor that introduced such large numbers of women at its lower levels? Braverman argues forcefully that management gradually began to substitute "the impersonal discipline of a so-called modern organization" for the intimate relations of the small office, and that office managership soon developed "as a special branch of management, with its own schools, professional associations, textbooks and manuals" (1974: 305). It was thus not merely size or complexity, but the imperatives of a profit-seeking management that led to increasing division of labor and to the development of an office force stratified both by class and by sex.

The typewriter was invented in 1873. The office rapidly became divided into lower-paid clerical and secretarial functions, increasingly held by women, and the better-paid accountant and semi-managerial jobs, held by men (many of whom had earlier been clerks). Compulsory public education created a large pool of literate women ready to enter the expanding office workforce. As new categories of jobs were created—for instance, by the invention of the telephone—it was women who were recruited into them: By 1902 the Bell system had 37,000 women operators, but only 2,500 men.

The proportion of women in a number of clerical occupations has increased steadily since the 1870s. While women made up only 2 percent of bookkeepers, accountants, and cashiers in 1870, by 1940 they were 51 percent (Davies 1974: 22), and by 1973 they were 88.3 percent of all bookkeepers and 86.7 percent of all cashiers (U.S. Dept. of Labor, Women's Bureau 1975: 89). A decade later the percentage was even higher.

The image of the woman office worker in 1900 was that she was a daughter of the middle class. Whatever the proportion of middle class literate women entering the office labor force was, they were accompanied by large numbers of daughters of farmers and blue-collar workers. By the turn of the century, the cities were beginning to be inundated with rural women who had come to find work, many in factories, but many others in offices. According to Benét, the hotels operated by the YWCA, WCTU, and other welfare organizations were one result of this. World War I and the Depression of the 1930s further increased the demand for secretarial and other office workers as government employment increased, and with it the flood of paperwork associated with the modern bureaucracy, and the need for cheap office labor.

By World War I, scientific management had been introduced into office work in the United States. The office hierarchy gradually became transformed:

> A new, male managerial stratum took over the quasi-managerial activities of the clerks, leaving the detail work to the now predominantly female office staffs. . . . Two distinct occupational hierarchies evolved: a male one, made up of many layers of managers, and a female one of file clerks, typists, stenographers, clerical supervisors and secretaries. (Glenn and Feldberg 1977: 54–55).

This was not simply the spontaneous by-product of increased mechanization. The Taylorization of the office was carried through in accordance with carefully laid plans; in Germany Frederick Taylor's missionary, Frank Gilbreth, pioneered "touch-typing" and the typing "pool" during World War I (before U.S. involvement) and later designed desks along "scientific," rational lines so as to maximize output (by minimizing superfluous motions). He was responsible for the idea of having a delivery person take mail to desks rather than having each employee pick up his or her own materials (Lorentz 1981: 117ff.). The standardization of typing, including the form letter, soon made many kinds of secretaries obsolete, and at the same time drastically curtailed opportunities for advancement in the office, since the newer clerk-typists needed far less education and hence were unqualified for promotion into managerial-level jobs. These innovations were not unresisted either by the workers or by management, however. Secretaries resented standardization and employers found that the saving in wages was offset by the cost of more intense supervision. The result was more careful screening of potential employees through the medium of commercial-secretarial schools, which became the entry route into clerical jobs (Lorentz 1981: 126–27). This gradual process of rationalization resulted, says Lorentz—in agreement with many other observers—in the "dequalification" of women's work: Women were reduced to machine-tending, without advancement opportunities.

The rationalization of office work was accompanied by the development of ideologies to justify the monotony and the stress. All sorts of moral messages were delivered by employers, accompanied by secondary rewards such as candy and jewelry at Christmas (Glenn and Feldberg 1977). Identification not only with the firm but with society at large was stressed: "Is not your work also valuable in the service of Society?" asked a typist's magazine (Lorentz 1981: 151). Youth, and sex appeal, were advantages in employment (and still are); the office became a "sexual arena" (Benét 1972: 83) at the same time it began to approximate factory-like conditions.

As the industrial revolution sent women from farm and domestic servitude into the modern factory, the factory in turn created the technology that was to pull still more rural, middle class, and blue collar women into the lower strata of office life. At the same time, in both industry and the office, women came to constitute a "reserve army" in that their relative presence or absence (in the form of unemployment) reflected the current state of the economy—needed in wartime, excess baggage in times of recession, women bore the brunt of scientific management's zeal to rationalize the office, a zeal always closely correlated with the need to cut costs in bad times. Occasionally the drive toward rationalization benefited younger, less-qualified women, who were hired or kept on to replace older, more-qualified (and higher-paid) men; but in general women were disproportionately the victims of economic crisis (Lorentz 1981: 57–102).

At the level of culture, the stratification system of the factory and the office, as both Davies and Benét argue, reflected the patriarchal relations of family life. Typically,

five or six typists, stenographers, or file clerks would be directly ac-
countable to one supervisor. And if that supervisor was a man (as was
generally the case in the early twentieth century) and those clerical workers were women, it is easy to see how patriarchal patterns of male-female
relations would reinforce the office hierarchy. (Davies 1974: 21)

At the upper level of secretarial life—the realm of the "personal secretary"—the upper class male was able to recreate a rapidly dying Victo-
rian system in which men were allegedly (if not in actuality) masters: In
addition to his wife, the man now had a secretary to minister to his
needs—and even to assume the role of real powerbroker at the micro
(office) level.

The growth of the services sector, including the public sector, with
its insatiable demand for lower-level office skills, explains the present
large number of women office workers, made available by the growth
of public education and the historical sex-stereotyping of office jobs.
But not only office jobs in the services sector are sex-stereotyped:
Since the 1940s some 60 percent of all services sector workers have
been women; 60 percent of workers in education are women as are 75
percent of workers in the medical and health-care fields, and in personal services. "Many jobs in the service industry can be described,"
Waldman and McEaddy point out, "as extensions of what women do as
homemakers—teach children and young adults, nurse the sick, pre-
pare food" (1974: 3)—and, we should add, jobs that are reinterpreta-
tions of the traditional homemaking support functions such as cleaning
up, preparing tools and meals, and laying out clothes. Those tasks are
also performed by many secretaries for their bosses.

The sex stereotyping that has developed over time is reinforced by
the economic pressure on the services sector (especially the public
sector) to keep wages in these relatively labor-intensive fields down
relative to total costs. Discriminatory practices against women, which
keep their labor cheaper than that of men (even in similar to identical
jobs), is therefore "functional" to the economic health of a particular
firm or agency. These practices not only involve outright personal
discrimination, but are institutionalized. They also involve longer-term
structural factors such as differences in socialization and education,
career training, and social expectations, including career interruption
to have children. Studies differ as to what proportion of the differences
in earnings between men and women can be accounted for by outright,
as against institutional, sexism, especially since many do not precisely

define "discrimination," but there is no doubt that the gap persists for persons of different genders in similar jobs with similar educational backgrounds (Suter and Miller 1973; Fuchs 1974; Featherman and Hauser 1976). In fact, the overall gap between male and female clerical salaries has increased over time (Wharton and Burris 1983).

One argument that has been made to account for income differences between men and women is that women have higher turnover rates— they engage in more job-hopping or leave the labor force (e.g., to have children) more than men do (Simpson and Simpson 1969). This argument has been extended to explain why women might sometimes be less likely to join unions, which limits their ability to protest poor working conditions, low wages, or the ravages of workforce erosion by automation (Seligman 1970). These arguments have recently been seriously challenged, however. While women do indeed leave the labor force altogether in somewhat higher proportions than men, and job-hop, these rates are cyclical, and are closely correlated with the unemployment rate. In 1955, for instance, women clerical quit rates were identical to those of men; in 1961 the quit rate was about 20 percent higher—but so was the unemployment rate. In periods of higher unemployment, however, fewer people quit overall, so that the proportion of women who quit goes up (cf. Matilla 1974). (However, it is true that "the occupational careers of women are not continuous as their labor force participation is geared to the family life cycle" [V. Oppenheimer 1968]. In jobs where seniority leads to higher pay, as in government, interrupted careers lead to lower wages relative to those of men.)

The assumption that women are less likely to join unions than are men must also be modified. As early as 1969, data on a series of union elections among white collar workers indicated that women did not differ significantly from men in their votes (Dewey 1971), while in a 1977 Quality of Employment Survey, more women than men indicated they would vote for a union given the opportunity (Kistler 1984: 99). The growth of unions in just those services (such as health care) in which women predominate also seems to refute the idea that women lag behind in joining unions.

In the public sector, where a large percentage of the labor force is white collar, the phenomenon of women office workers is even more significant than in the private sector. In 1979, 7.3 million of the nearly 16 million government workers were women (U.S. Department of Labor, Bureau of Labor Statistics 1980: Tables 77, 100). Here too,

Table 6-5. *Employment Grade and Percentage of Women in Grade in Full-Time Federal Employment, 1973*

Grade	Percentage women
1	68.5
2	77.2
3	77.2
4	74.5
5	56.2
6	24.4
7	41.6
8	35.1
9	28.5
10	18.3
11	13.8
12	8.1
13	5.1
14	4.1
15	3.9

SOURCE: U.S. Department of Labor, Women's Bureau, *Handbook on Women Workers*, Bulletin 297 (Washington, D.C.: GPO, 1975), p. 117.

women are concentrated at the lower levels. In federal employment, according to a 1973 study, women accounted for 47 percent of General Schedule Grades 1–6, only 23 percent of Grades 7–12, and only 4.5 percent of Grade 13 and higher (See Table 6-5). In addition, the proportion of women in government employment has steadily increased. In the federal service, for instance, it grew from 19 percent in 1939 to a high of 37 percent during World War II, then dropped back to 24 percent in 1947, and has been climbing gradually since that time. Overall women comprised about 34 percent of federal service workers in 1973.

The sex stereotyping of office jobs has been carried over to the new technology, and the new, computerized office. Men maintain a monopoly over the better-paid and more skilled computer jobs, just as they did over office manager jobs in the old-style office, while women find themselves once again locked into the lower-level jobs. They have more limited training in computer skills, and quickly reach the top of their promotion ladders and remain there. Productivity gains obtained through the use of computers are not passed on to clerical workers; in several highly automated industries wages are actually lower than the national average (Wharton and Burris 1983).

The elimination of the traditional office is not without its problems. Managers (males) lose perquisites, while employees—especially secretaries—resent the impersonality. A conflict has developed between patriarchy and capitalist rationalization, between male perquisites and the modern office. Yet both sides of the conflict enforce the feminization of the office workforce and its domination by men.

Consciousness

The classical Marxian tradition would argue that these kinds of conditions should lead to worker dissatisfaction and, thus, to trade unionization—as a first step in the direction of further radicalization. Indeed, as *Business Week* reported (28 April 1980),

> The message is clear: office workers are no longer decorously quiet. They are campaigning to upgrade their jobs through higher wages, improved benefits and promotion opportunities, and more of that elusive commodity known as respect. Since one-third of today's 42 million working women are clerical workers, the potential impact is enormous.

There are two research approaches that support the general idea that there is considerable dissatisfaction at the lower—and primarily female—levels of white collar employment: job satisfaction studies, and studies that attempt to measure women's commitments to work versus family and home. The overall picture was described in the previous chapter. Later surveys, which ask somewhat different questions, indicate a deeper level of dissatisfaction than seemed to be the case in the 1960s and early 1970s: In 1978, for instance, 40 percent of the secretaries surveyed said they would quit if they could afford it; 21 percent (including some overlap) said outright that they disliked their jobs. Among secretaries who were college graduates, one out of three said they disliked their jobs. The main areas of complaint were low pay, boring and undemanding work, sex discrimination, lack of leisure, lack of help at home, and lack of opportunity to train for a better job (NCWW 1978; also see Howe 1977).

Similar results have been reported in both academic and business studies. Grandjean and Taylor (1980), in a survey of employees in a federal agency (most of whom had at least a high school education), cited lack of opportunity for advancement and lack of sense of accomplishment as the main areas of complaint. *Office Administration and Automation* (March 1983) reported on a series of management studies (including a survey of 1,263 secretaries) that indicated a widespread desire by clericals to have more say in the purchase of equipment. The majority felt they were not consulted (and 68 percent of those using text-editing equipment believe its use could result in health problems).

Another group of studies compares women's commitment to their work with their commitment to family and home. The respondents were asked whether they "would work if they could," "actually plan to work," or are "working now and plan to continue," depending on various circumstances. Safilios-Rothschild (1971), for example, finds that low work commitment is related to less meaningful jobs (as measured by low degree of skills, responsibility, and prestige). Haller and Rosenmayr (1971) report that white collar women are more likely to work, even without financial need, than blue collar women (as measured by their current jobs). A Finnish study found, however, that work is rarely the central source of satisfaction for men or women (except unmarried women) in any occupation (Haavio-Mannila 1971). This corresponds to a finding by Blake that most women in the Western world continue to see employment as a secondary goal: "Survey data," she claims, "show no vast discontent among women" (1974: 144). A more accurate statement, probably, would be that women are probably no more, but possibly slightly less, discontented than men. The question is, in what dimension of life? To this, Fuchs (1971) replies that women with low work satisfaction are also dissatisfied with family life, and with their wife-mother roles, and that the reverse is also true: high satisfaction in one dimension is correlated with high satisfaction in the other.

In short, there is a delicate network of variables involved in the desire to work, including occupation, motherhood, financial need, work satisfaction, and family satisfaction. Good work experiences seem to lead to a greater desire to work, just as good family experiences seem to lead to a greater commitment to family. But the actual percentage figures for any one group's satisfaction or commitment to anything lack meaning in the abstract, unless we know "relative to what." Most surveys, as we pointed out earlier, do not present their subjects with alternative social arrangements to choose from, so that the resulting satisfaction, or lack of discontent, may tell us only that there are no perceived alternatives, and that, given this circumstance, life is adequate.

In one of the few follow-up studies, done by Social Research, Inc., for the publishers of *True Story* and other magazines (MacFadden-Bartell Corp., which had sponsored the study *Workingman's Wife* [Rainwater 1959]), the research team concluded that "most housewives in our study are unready to reject homemaking, embrace a career, and fend for themselves . . . [but] in the meantime they are using the [women's liberation] movement to support their wish to be more independent." As contrasted to the earlier surveys done by this group, women in 1972 were less homebound and more active in community affairs. Middle class (i.e., white collar, as measured by husband's occupation) wives saw white collar work as work they could do as readily as their husbands, while blue collar wives were less likely to perceive job equality with their husbands as a real prospect. White collar wives were more likely to support women's liberation, a finding that might have been related to the fact that the great majority are at least high school graduates. Unfortunately, the study gives virtually no comparative figures from one period to the next (Social Research, Inc. 1973).

The question of consciousness or attitude is obviously highly complex but four issues at least can be raised here: (1) As many observers of the political socialization literature have pointed out, what surveys reveal today does not necessarily show how people will behave tomorrow. External factors, particularly the economic crunch that is hitting white collar workers for the first time since the 1930s (and in the case of many clerical wives, hitting their blue collar operative husbands particularly hard), may be altering presumed middle class or conservative attitudes. (2) White collar workers are not alone in their middle class aspirations (e.g., to consumerism). These appear to be shared by many strata of the labor force, including blue collar workers. Such aspirations do not make them any less workers. On the other hand, as Hamilton (1972) has pointed out, the "line" dividing the strata on many political issues appears to put white collar workers, especially clericals ("lower non-manuals," as he calls them), more into agreement with blue collar workers than with the more conservative upper nonmanuals. (3) If trade unionization is taken as one index, even though a minimal one, of at least the beginnings of a working class consciousness, which is what most Marxists would argue (although Ollman [1972] expresses some reservations), then recent trends suggest that women office workers, though they may lag behind blue collar men, cannot be discounted (see below, and chapter 8). (4) Finally, and perhaps most important of all, overt measurements do not reveal many other layers of consciousness—but this is another issue that deserves more space and will be raised again in chapter 9.

Women and Unions

The feminist movement has led women office workers to a growing awareness that the conditions they face in the office need not be tolerated. At the same time, many unions have become aware that they must organize white collar workers in order to survive. The result has been a dramatic increase in unionization among clerical and sales workers (see chapter 8). In 1952 women constituted 18.1 percent of all union members (2.9 million women); by 1972 this had risen to 21.7 percent (4.2 million), and by 1980 to a remarkable 30.1 percent (over 6 million). Women made up 30 percent of the total increase in union membership in the decade from 1958 to 1968, and their entry rate since then has more and more closely approximated their proportion in the labor force (Dewey 1971; Bergquist 1974; Gifford 1982). Yet only 15.9 percent of employed women (at all levels) were organized in 1980, a slight increase from 13.9 percent in 1973 but still significantly below the overall figures of 23 percent.

As with unionization in general, growth of union membership among women workers is closely associated with the growth of the white collar labor force and the public sector. Women union members are clustered in a relative handful of unions associated with the kinds of both blue and white collar labor associated with "women's work." Three-fourths of all women unionists belonged to only twenty-one unions in 1968 (the AFL-CIO has about one hundred federated member unions); 25 percent of unions had no women at all. By 1972 only twenty-four unions included 50,000 or more women members each (see Table 6-6). That year six large unions had majority female memberships: the Amalgamated Clothing Workers, the International Ladies' Garment Workers, the Retail Clerks, the Communications Workers (which includes telephone workers), the American Federation of Teachers, and the smaller Office and Professional Employees. The National Education Association also has a female majority, as do several other smaller professional associations that function like unions.

Although the majority of unionized women continue to be found in

Table 6-6.   *Women Membership in Unions with*
50,000 Women Members or More, 1952 and 1972
(Top Twelve in 1972 Only Listed and Ranked)

Union	1952	1972
1. Ladies' Garment	292,500	342,400
2. Retail Clerks	125,000	316,600
3. Electrical (IBEW)	150,000	287,000
4. Clothing Workers	261,800	273,800
5. Teamsters	n.a.*	255,000†
6. Communications Workers	n.a.	230,500
7. State, County, & Municipal Workers	n.a.	195,700
8. Auto Workers	118,400	195,100
9. Steelworkers	80,000	175,000
10. Service Employees	55,500	145,200
11. Teachers	37,500	129,200
12. Electrical Workers (IUE)	n.a.	116,000

SOURCE: Based on Virginia Bergquist, "Women's Participation in Labor Organizations," *Monthly Labor Review*, October 1974, Table 3, p. 6.
*Not available.
†Figure is for 1970.

predominantly blue collar unions (in the clothing industry, in retail trade, and in a few manufacturing areas, such as auto and steel), growth of union membership is largely in white collar unions, especially in the public sector.

For instance, the American Federation of State, County, and Municipal Employees (AFSCME), which has been the fastest growing union in the AFL-CIO, began to face a membership decline due to shrinking public employment in the face of fiscal crisis. Women became the union's top organizing priority (*Business Week*, 23 June 1980). Early in 1981, in another indication of the trade union movement's growing awareness of the necessity of organizing female clericals, Working Women–National Association of Office Workers, itself an outgrowth of such local groups as Boston's "9 to 5," merged with the Service Employees International Union (the Boston group had already become Local 925). Total membership was about 660,000 (*New York Times*, 29 March 1981). Nevertheless, only half a dozen unions represent about half of all unionized clerical workers—three of them government.

Although union membership among women has increased rapidly, even dramatically, the increasing numbers of nonunionized women entering the labor force has kept the proportion of unionized women down. Why has it been so difficult for unions to recruit new white collar women? After all, union workers earn more than nonunion workers, and male-female wage differentials in unionized enterprises are less than in nonunion organizations, so unions apparently help to equalize women's chances (Gunderson 1974). Both of these should be powerful arguments for joining unions.

First, as Bergquist points out, part-time employees probably feel less of an incentive to participate in the union movement due to their "frequent entry into and exit from the labor market" (1974). Second, despite the trade unions' gradual acknowledgement of the special needs of women, women continue to be discriminated against in union leadership (although this is less true of white collar unions in which there are large proportions of women members, especially the government unions).

Recently, however, a number of unions have been holding conferences oriented to women's needs. In March 1974, the Coalition of Labor Union Women (CLUW) was established at a conference in Chicago, attended by 3,200 delegates from 58 unions. Since CLUW was open only to union women, a struggle ensued between CLUW leaders who were union officials—and who wanted the organization to proceed within traditional channels of trade union practices and demands—and those women unionists who sought a more open membership (including housewives) and a less traditional approach to union goals. The latter group lost the battle and CLUW has maintained a moderate stance.

At the local level a series of women's groups, some affiliated with CLUW and some more independent and radical, sprang up in the late 1960s and early 1970s. They include Women Employed in Chicago; Women Act to Gain Equality on the West Coast; Women Office Workers (WOW) in New York; and "9 to 5," which was originally the title of a newsletter in Boston. These groups were all feminist—often more feminist than unionist, at least at first; and while their total membership was minuscule compared with their "target population," this did suggest what could happen when the feminist alumnae of the new left entered the office workforce.

Over the years this movement has grown. By 1979 there were, in addition to Boston, Chicago, and New York, groups of the "9 to 5" kind in a dozen cities.

Despite the increasing fragmentation of clerical work (implying increasing discontent), and the growing presence of feminist-oriented union organizing, there is no reason for great optimism. Management appears well aware of the "dangers" of white collar unionization (*Business Week*, 2 May 1983) and is taking countermeasures, ranging from decentralized, less alienating office structures to hiring union-busting "consultants" to undermine organizing efforts. The move to place terminals in women's homes is also a threat to organizing efforts, while the persistence of somewhat higher turnover rates among women and the ideology of identifying with the prestige of the (male) boss provide further obstacles. The suburbanization of many white collar firms—for example, in the insurance field—which removes clerical workers from traditional working class urban centers, insulates them also from union activity.

Nevertheless, a considerable pro-union—or at least antimanagement—sentiment exists in many offices. When a word-processing clerk in a New York City law office shot and killed one of her bosses in December 1982 because of dissatisfaction with her Christmas bonus, the incident became the subject of a good deal of washroom conversation and subdued cheering.

The Impact of Feminism

The basic questions concerning the relationship between feminism and developments in the labor force have not changed in the past decade. Is feminism the logical outgrowth of the increasing number of women in the paid labor force, or do women enter the labor force because they have "liberated" themselves? There is little doubt that some relationship between the two phenomena exists, but specifying exactly what it is has plagued unionists, feminists, and radicals for some time. Moreover, despite what might seem to be similar interests, there have been conflicts between feminists and the labor movement, just as there have been conflicts between feminists and socialists, and trade unionists and socialists. What, then, is the likelihood of a more permanent alliance between trade unions and feminist groups, one that goes beyond such short-term issues as equal employment opportunity and equal pay for equal work?

One view is that aside from these short-term alliances, the women's movement is unlikely to gain a significant following among women workers, especially blue collar women. This is because there is a certain amount of mutual distrust: "Liberation" issues are trivial to many lower income women, while the unions themselves are considered discriminatory by many women's groups. In the past decade, hundreds of women union members have filed discrimination charges against unions with the federal Equal Employment Opportunities Commission—500 in 1970 alone. One result is that parts of the women's liberation movement have come to perceive unions *in toto* as foes, which does not help them in reaching women union members. At the same time, although unions are increasingly building women's issues into their negotiating demands, the trade union movement continues to be very slow in integrating women into real leadership positions. Even female organizers, on the front lines of what unions need most to do, report continued discrimination from their own unions. Moreover, many male trade unionists remain suspicious of feminism on the ground that it constitutes a threat to the stable family, a belief used by the political right to undermine trade union organizing (in the same way that racism is used to divide workers and prevent unionization).

Part of the problem on both sides has been differing definitions of what women's roles are supposed to be. Harris and Silverman (1973) point to two contradictions, or strains, in the position of women: First, the fact that they are an increasing proportion of the labor force—that they play a significant role in the economic structure—runs counter to a more traditional ideology that excludes them from that structure and tries to confine them (by means of socialization plus discrimination) to family and home. Second, the family itself is under stress. The traditional form of the family is confronted by a rapidly changing economic reality: The woman enters the labor force partly as a result of—and partly resulting in—the smaller role the family plays in socializing children into future work roles. The "typical" family—husband, wife, and their children living in a first marriage with only the man employed—is now the exception rather than the rule. Virtually everyone is confronted with serious dilemmas concerning family versus work priorities. Furthermore, the idea of perpetual upward mobility (particularly for the college-educated), which helped to justify the distribution of power and wealth within the family, is now undermined by the reality of a relatively dead-end work life (and even unemployment) for many white collar workers. Economic reality, changing family structures, and new forms of socialization are challenging the conceptions women once had of their role in society, and younger people are finding that they have different values from those of their parents.

What is the likely outcome of this crisis, particularly among white collar workers? For one thing, workplace organizing, particularly trade unionization, may grow with or without the input of feminism. But trade unionization is not synonymous with "class consciousness," and even if it were (or to the degree that it is) it does not necessarily lead to radical consciousness. On the contrary, if unions are able to secure minimal gains for their members, as they have in the past, they may be able to channel women workers into fairly narrow "bread-and-butter" interest-group (as contrasted to classwide) politics.

A more complex outcome would be based on the assumption of a deeper economic crisis, and a deeper crisis in the entire culture, so that trade unionism by itself would not be an adequate solution for the problems of women workers. In this context, feminism, as well as other forms of radicalism, might play a larger role at the workplace than is presently the case.

Superimposed on either situation is the possibility, suggested by Blake (1974), that there may be an upper limit to the employment of women, particularly when jobs are in short supply, so that the number and proportion of women workers, office and otherwise, may not grow, though the profile may change as a result of technological change. Nevertheless, there remains a vast reservoir of potential union members in the clerical and sales strata. Whether that reservoir can be tapped for membership, and whether that membership will become more politically volatile, remains to be seen.

Conclusion

In summary, then, the woman office worker is a proletarian: by her position as a wage earner, her status as a direct or indirect contributor to the generation of surplus value, the conditions of her servitude in the modern office-factory (including her vulnerability to the fluctuations of the labor market), the actions she takes to protect her status at the workplace, and, at least to some degree, her relationship to other sectors of the working class through her family ties. Her status as a woman introduces a second oppressive condition that overlays her first exploited one. The feminist movement expresses the sense of that oppression.

The main index of consciousness of membership in the working class, on the other hand, continues to be trade unionization. While women office workers are unionizing (and at a more rapid rate than many other sectors of the labor force), growth is nevertheless slow. In any case, trade unionization may lead not to consciousness of class, but to consciousness of the need to develop interest-group political clout, a development that can inhibit class consciousness. But a larger crisis in the culture, of which feminism is one symptom, today coincides with a deeper economic crisis. Such a coincidence may produce a radicalization that goes beyond interest-group politics, in the direction of a socialist or a social-democratic political awareness.

7
The Professions:
The Great Schism

What is true of white collar workers in general can be seen most explicitly in the ranks of those occupations labeled "professional": Two opposing trends are at work, putting professionals into several sets of contradictory class locations, and in turn making their political ideologies most problematic.

As we saw in chapter 3, no grouping of occupations has been assigned so many contradictory functions, political missions, and cultural outlooks. From "new class" to "lackeys of capital," from leaders of a "service society" to misleaders of a dismal bureaucratic future—all these functions and many more have been laid at the doorstep of this ill-defined agglomeration of occupations. As in the case of "white collar," the expression "professional" serves to mask a host of contradictory phenomena, and glosses over fundamental class divisions—and within classes, important fractional distinctions. Above all, the term falsely unifies people in occupations (and parts of occupations) whose working conditions are improving, people who are gaining control, knowledge, and power, with those who are becoming de-skilled and proletarianized.

The growth of "the professions," both in the number of jobs that are defined as professional and in the number of persons and proportion of the labor force, is widely assumed to be a major index of industrial development. Indeed, critics of modernity see this as one of the few positive features in an otherwise dismal picture (T. J. Johnson 1972: chap. 1). This is because even they view professionals as making a contribution to their particular mission. To the aristocrats, professions represent a bulwark against mass society. To the modern bourgeoisie, on the other hand, they are allies against superstition and monarchistic conservatism; to liberals they are aids in countering selfish bourgeois interests, and to radicals, particularly those in national independence movements, they are part of the anti-imperialist bloc.

Yet from the first appearance of professional ideologies in precapitalist times, there were tensions between two types of professionals: those involved in "basic" research and those in "applied" fields, whom they saw as below themselves. "The medical profession was organized in a hierarchy with the physician at the top and below, in descending order of prestige . . . surgeons, apothecaries and even druggists" (Carr-Saunders and Wilson 1933, quoted by Johnson 1972: 73). These tensions—for example, between CPAs and other accountants, between physicians and pharmacists or nurses—preceded modern capitalism, but capitalism continues to find these divisions functional. Thus professions rooted in medieval patronage systems carry their ideologies over into contemporary patronage systems—into the corporations, and into bureaucracies more generally.

Historically, as Larson (1977) states, the development of the professions came in spurts, in response not only to changes in technology but also to the creation of markets—the populations needing professional services. These markets grew rapidly during the industrial revolution, and outstripped the traditional markets created by earlier aristocracies and national bourgeoisies. The distinction between "old" professions, such as the ministry, medicine, and law (the traditional occupations Larson terms *ancien regime* professions "dependent on aristocratic sources of legitimation" [1977: 4]), and the newer professions and semi-professions such as engineering, linked to the rise of modern capitalist enterprise and the modern state, is related to the development of such markets.

In the United States, although most older—and even some newer—professions were established by the Jacksonian era, the major expansion came after the Civil War. By the 1830s, attending medical school was clearly the only legitimate way to a career as a doctor (Larson 1977: 129). But it took another sixty years for the American Medical Association (founded in 1847) to drive competing health "sects," such as homeopathy, out of business. (The struggle of osteopaths and chiropractors to establish, or reestablish, their legitimacy continues.)

Between 1860 and 1890 over one hundred engineering schools were established (Noble 1977: 24). By the late 1890s the corporations were moving to set up standards for engineering education (an effort that led to the founding of the American Management Association, in order to

coordinate industry's campaign), and the exchange of personnel between corporations and engineering schools (including their heads)
presaged the development of placement services, testing programs,
and uniform curricula so as to establish "effective" personnel training
for industry. The first head of the American Council on Education
(ACE) was an engineer; ACE later on set up what is today the Educational Testing Service as a continuation of these early management
efforts (ibid.: 255).

The development of the teaching profession was somewhat more
complex. Sherry Gorelick describes it thus:

> Teaching expanded because schooling expanded, and schooling expanded
> because of the development of capitalism and class conflict. Workers
> demanded compulsory schooling and prohibition of child labor. Capital-
> ists promoted schools to control and socialize the children of labor . . .
> substituting publicly taught skill training for union-controlled apprentice-
> ship. . . . These forces . . . vastly increased the need for teachers.
> (Gorelick, 1982: 204)

Despite a rapid increase in number, "normal schools" were soon
supplanted by college departments of education such as Teachers College, Columbia University, founded and controlled by New York City
financiers, including the Vanderbilt family, in the 1870s. It was in such
graduate institutions for the training of teachers that a professional
ideology was developed and inculcated. The middle class teachers
trained at Columbia and elsewhere became the school system's administrators, who later feminized the teaching workforce, centralized
it, and created an educational content responsive to the needs of businessmen, although not without opposition. By 1900 the Ph.D. degree
had become standard for many university teaching positions. In 1910
the Flexner Report on medical education laid the foundation for uniform medical school standards (see Larson 1977: 37). By that time
graduate schools, the first of which was founded at Johns Hopkins
University in 1876, had become part of most larger universities (ibid.:
151). Larson describes the critical variable in this development: the
"massive availability of surplus capital" by the mid-1890s that enabled
the rise of the modern system of higher education, unifying training
and research, and resolving many of the ideological issues that had
divided professionals prior to that time (ibid.: 136). The development
of a national ruling class, the bureaucratization of organizational life,
the ideology of efficiency, the growth of scientific management, and of

course the precipitous decline of small entrepreneurship as a political and ideological force all combined to launch professional occupations on an ever-upward trajectory. Today there are 17 million "professionals" in the U.S. labor force (nearly a 100 percent increase in the past twenty years), of whom fewer than 2 million are self-employed (ibid.: 250; see also Table 5-1).

What Are the "Professions"?

The professions include, depending on authority, governmental classification system, time, and place, every occupation from upper-level manager to store-front lawyer; from surgeon and priest to student nurse and computer programming coder; from astronaut, athlete, and author to technician, therapist, and veterinarian. Historically, quite obviously, the professions range in time and place from those mentioned in the Old Testament (if we limit ourselves only to Western literature) to occupational titles that appeared virtually yesterday. National norms affect not only definitions but also behavior, both required and proscribed. Many occupations considered professions in the United States are part of an apprenticeship system in another country, such as opticians in Germany and Belgium, or accountants in England (Orzack 1974). What a professional can do in one country may be illegal in another: In the European Economic Community opticians are considered technicians, not medical practitioners, and may not touch the eye with light, instrument, or drug; in France, chiropractic is illegal. The functional place of professionals also varies widely: In Germany, 80 percent of veterinarians are in agriculture on a private basis; in the Netherlands, a state veterinary service supplies virtually all veterinarians (ibid.).

The term "professional" is a reification: The label is not a neutral, objective description of a particular reality, but a function of a specific social context that in turn promotes definitions that become part of, and help define, social reality. As Lasch puts it:

> Recent studies of "professionalization" by historians have shown that professionalism did not emerge, in the nineteenth and early twentieth centuries, in response to clearly defined social needs. Instead, the new professions themselves invented many of the needs they claimed to satisfy. They played on public fears of disorder and disease, adopted a deliberately mystifying jargon, ridiculed popular traditions of self-help as backward and unscientific, and in this way created . . . a demand for their own services. (1977: 16–17)

The point is underlined by Larson (1977: 14), with her concept of the "market," the need for "commodities" created by professionals (even if fictional), the prime example being modern medicine. She sets forth a series of "conditions" that help to establish this commodity as needed, and to create markets for it. The less visible the service, the more esoteric or "scientific" its cognitive basis, the closer to the dominant ideology, the better for the professional. Lasch emphasizes this latter issue and attacks several studies that do not take managerial (capitalist) ideology into consideration, charging them with

> ignoring the connection between the rise of modern professionalism and the rise of industrial management. . . . The new historians of professionalism, by treating professionals as a separate class with their own interests and identity, repeat the mistake made by earlier students of the "managerial revolution," who argued that managers constitute a "new class." In reality, both the growth of management and the proliferation of professions represent new forms of capitalist control. (1977: 17)

In contrast with Larson's and Lasch's point of view, most sociological discussions define professionals by criteria that are narrowly historically determined, in part by the professionals themselves: A profession is an occupational grouping that defines itself as a profession, declares membership limited to those meeting qualifications set by itself (including educational levels and certification), creates for itself a "rationale," that is, a code of ethics or behavior, and develops an argot that in turn further excludes nonmembers. The outside world then accepts this set of (self) definitions: The label comes to be part of reality as the rest of society finds itself excluded from the knowledge over which the profession has declared a monopoly.

The rationale for this monopoly of knowledge is often said to be the "knowledge explosion," which theoretically forces specialization and prevents the "layperson" from commanding the details of *any* profession (except perhaps the one he or she belongs to). Not incidentally, the monopolization of an area of knowledge or technology protects that particular labor market in a guild-like fashion. So long as the supply of labor can be regulated by the guild itself, the price of labor (especially in those remaining areas that are self-employed) can be kept relatively high. As Larson puts it, the profession's system of credentialing "functions more as an implicit justification for the price of the professional commodity . . . than as the actual quantitative translation of 'average socially necessary labor time' into market value" (1977: 212) simply because a monopoly over the training process can put the price of labor outside of normal market determinations. The credential, the degree, creates the *appearance* of the measurability of the commodity, which is then legitimized in the public mind and in turn becomes integrated into the commodity. The doctor's service is not purchased; rather, the degree hanging on the wall is.

This brings us to the question of how some occupations are able to redefine themselves as professions while others are not. One of the key variables in this process is that of "higher education." Here there appears to be a "halo effect" at work: Certain occupations define higher education as one of their characteristics; as this occurs in more and more professions, it becomes an assumption of the society that all educated people (meaning university-trained and certified people) are per se professionals, so that anything they do is therefore "professional." If, for example, all city planners are college-educated, it quickly becomes a social definition that planning is a "profession" *because* (in part) they are college-educated. Planners then accept this label, incorporate it into their self-concept, and define planning as a profession (including in that definition not only college education but also a variety of other "requirements" without which one might be, say, a sociologist, a community organizer, or a draftsperson, but not a professional planner). On the other end of the decision-making process, city management could hardly accept plans from "mere" engineers or community organizers, especially those without college degrees. The existence of a "planning profession" thereby legitimizes management's exclusion of socially undesirable (namely, working class and minority) elements from decision-making processes with the rationale that they are not professional.

Society has come to define professional jobs as desirable. For example, in an oft-cited 1963 National Opinion Research Center poll on "what jobs are desirable," respondents ranking ninety job titles placed "professional" titles in all of the first thirty "most desirable" jobs. Only thirteen of the next thirty job titles were professional, and none of the bottom thirty titles were (Sennett and Cobb 1972).

This should not be surprising, for professional work is, in fact, craft-like (or at least more so than "nonprofessional" work). It does, for whatever historical reasons, involve more autonomy, more self-direction, less hierarchical interference. It appears to satisfy some aspects of what Veblen termed the "instinct of wokmanship," a component of doing a job well and taking satisfaction from it that repeatedly appears as one of the more desirable or sought-after features of work. It is logical, then, that professionals attempt to protect this status. Paradoxically, even the unionization of professionals—which, on the surface, appears to be a move toward proletarianization—is at the same moment an attempt to protect traditional (and positive) work conditions.

Conversely, those in occupations that are not officially labeled professional but in which the workers take some measure of pride (that is, see themselves as doing a professional job, meaning an expert job not readily done by people outside the field of engineering, baseball, or even killing) seek to "professionalize" by emulating existing professions. They organize, publish journals (there is, for instance, a journal for mercenaries or professional soldiers), and create structures for admission and certification. This is known as "upgrading" the occupation. Thus social workers are actively seeking to be licensed by the state: Some of them believe licensing will exclude nonprofessionals and will legitimize those passing the examination. The American Nurses' Association (founded in 1911) has for decades pushed for professional nurses' training leading to a Bachelor of Nursing Science degree in the attempt to make nursing more "respectable," with the consequence of inculcating a more professional ideology that sometimes has inhibited unionization and segmented the health-care workforce by separating some nurses from those "below" them (*Dollars & Sense* 1978). Within the field of sociology a new specialty, "clinical sociology" (i.e., sociology applied in action settings such as therapy, planning, and law enforcement so that it overlaps—and challenges—those professions presently licensed to practice in those fields), is seeking governmental licensing so that it can effectively compete for professional jobs now monopolized by social workers, clinical psychologists, lawyers, planners, engineers, etc.

Whatever the short- or long-term payoffs of such processes for either workers or management, the concept of professional as applied to any particular occupation or set of occupations is a *process:* Occupations come and go, they are nonprofessional today, semiprofessional the day after. Other professions, meanwhile, lose ground, become more fragmented so that their lower layers now "require" less training or education (a Bachelor's degree in social work rather than a Master's for lower levels of state employment, at cheaper wages), the result of other processes at work in the society.

Professions do exist; they are real enough and can therefore be described, sociologically, in ideal-typical terms. Professional has come to mean work involving discretion and judgment, so that it cannot be standardized or mechanized, work in which the worker produces an entire product, be it a painting, a surgical operation, a book, a bridge, or an idea; where the worker's pace, workplace conditions, the product and its use and even to a degree its price, are largely determined by the worker; where the source of income is an individually regulated sale of a product or service under fairly loose market conditions established by face-to-face bargaining rather than the sale of labor time in advance of the creation of anything; and where the bulk of the income goes to the worker without any bureaucratic intermediary except perhaps an agent (as in the case of an artist). Finally, it is work involving high degrees of training, apprenticeship, or other forms of formalized education.

Consequently, the term implies the existence of its opposite, which can also be described in ideal-typical terms. This is the "proletarianized" worker for whom an extensive division of labor exists. He or she typically performs only one, or a small number, of tasks in a total process. The pace of work, the characteristics of the workplace, the nature of the product, the uses to which it is put, and its market conditions are determined not by the worker but by higher authorities (private or public). The worker's primary source of income is a wage, which is determined by large-scale market conditions and economic processes (not excluding collective bargaining). The worker, in order to defend this situation from the deterioration of living standards or working conditions, often moves toward some form of union.

Since professions are the products of specific historic processes, these same processes can also have de-professionalization as their consequence. This is where professions move away from the ideal-typical conditions described above toward their opposite, toward conditions typical of the classical working class. Note that I say *toward*. This does not mean that there are professions that have become synonymous with blue collar labor, or that there are not fluctuations, or that, like other forms of labor, the professions do not attempt to frustrate this process, often successfully. It is only to say that this is a process, at work at the moment, and that it is happening with increasing frequency (sometimes within a single firm some professionals may be undergoing de-professionalization, while others are gaining in those aspects of work life that are professional in nature). The fragmentation of a set of occupations such that some are in the process of becoming

proletarianized while others are moving "upward" is a serious obstacle
to considering them as a unity.

If both tendencies are underway within even a single profession,
how does this work? What is the process by which those at the bottom
may find themselves de-skilled and proletarianized while those at the
top find their professional skills being transformed into administrative
ones?

In computer programming, the number of computer specialists increased an astonishing 41.1 percent in the six years from 1970 to 1976,
compared with an overall employment increase of 11.3 percent. However, there was a more than 100 percent increase in computer capacity
in that period, implying that employment does not increase at the
same rate as production—that what increases is the productivity per
computer specialist. What is the price of this increase in productivity?
Kraft informs us that "the development of structured programming . . .
indicate[s] that the period of relative openness and high levels of occupational mobility is about to come to an end" (1979: 16). What is
happening is rapid routinization and de-skilling of programming—and
with it the appearance of large numbers of women, largely at the lower
skill levels. In an earlier work, Kraft describes this routinization historically. In sum, over the years there has been an extensive division of
labor in programming, undermining the generalist and creating separate educational tracks leading, specifically, to careers in systems analysis, programming, and coding (the last-named being at the bottom).
"Programmers," says Kraft, "have not been reduced to quite the same
level of fragmented activity as autoworkers. . . . But the social and
individual consequences have been remarkably similar" (1977: 61).

Managers, in turn, are drawn from the upper levels of the computer
field, from those trained more generally in "software sciences." "Crea-
tive" work becomes separated from the increasingly detailed labor at
the bottom, and is used to control that labor—a situation reflected in
salaries, so that managers may earn seven times as much as the lowest-
level nonmanagerial computer specialist. Moreover, it is at the managerial level that salary increases accrue at the fastest rate; as Kraft and
Dubnoff put it, "the key to financial success in software is not to
specialize and not to get too technical. . . . What the best-paid people
spend most of their time doing is making general decisions . . . planning the direction of their department or organization, and in other
traditional managerial roles" (1984: 9–10).

A similar picture has developed in pharmacy. In 1970 there were 19,820 small independent retail pharmacies in the United States, most operated by professional pharmacists. This number had been cut by two-thirds by 1980 (Birenbaum 1982:873). The pressure of large chains, combined with changes in the manufacture and dispensing of drugs, has made the traditional independent pharmacist obsolete, although employment opportunities in hospitals and nursing homes have expanded. Some pharmacists have sought to become upgraded in order to maintain their prerogatives, particularly those honorific ones associated with being a professional. In an attempt to share authority with doctors, they strive to obtain a Pharm.D. degree for themselves—still a relative rarity. The field, Birenbaum predicts, will become segmented between that group, largely supervising others and in charge of the standards of the profession, and the many licensed bachelor's degree pharmacists whose main job, regardless of professional rhetoric about providing an essential service, will be to move drugs from a larger to a smaller container and type a label.

Similarly, the segmentation of nursing is leading to a situation in which "upward mobility" within the field is dependent on obtaining the Bachelor of Science in Nursing (BSN), a degree that involves less clinical experience than the traditional Diploma Nurse. Yet the BSN is increasingly necessary to obtain administrative nursing work in a hospital, and this is seen as upward mobility—getting off the floor and into the office. The rest of the nursing profession is further segmented between Diploma nurses, those with Associate (community college) degrees (all of whom can be Registered Nurses), and, below them, Licensed Practical Nurses. Somewhere between are the (predominantly male) Physicians' Assistants (PAs), who also have college degrees. The PA is licensed in some dozen states to prescribe drugs and earns, on the average, considerably more than an RN, yet has only two years of medical training as part of the college degree program, a situation that has led to considerable resentment on the part of the often better trained nurses.

The social work profession is increasingly segmented. The Master's in Social Work (MSW) is widely regarded as the prerequisite for a supervisory position, while state licensing serves to prevent non-MSW's and others untrained in professional argot from attaining upper-level jobs. Many social workers working at lower-level semiclerical jobs, as in public assistance, have only an Associate degree: The segmentation of public sector social work into those who determine eligibility for public assistance and those who do home visits or deal with clients face-to-face enables the state to settle for a less-educated employee who earns, correspondingly, less pay. The MSW, on the other hand, is eligible for a supervisory role, and for the kind of social work practice that pays well—private clinical practice, state-licensed.

Are Professionals a Class?

Like other occupational groupings, professionals are subject to the dynamic of capitalism, which tends to drive some of them toward proletarian conditions of existence while others are upgraded into the ranks of management and the bourgeoisie, while still others are part of past class relations (small proprietors such as pharmacists, privately practicing professionals such as some attorneys and social workers, and many artists). Thus many professionals are constantly in the process of changing their objective class positions, of joining some other class (for example, hungry artists who are forced to work for advertising agencies, or who eke out an existence through part-time teaching).

Professionals as a group are therefore not a class—new, old, middle, or any other. The various fractions of the professional stratum, insofar as they can be identified, either belong to a vestigial class formation (the petty bourgeoisie) or are marginal to one of the major classes, or even both of them, depending on their function within the capitalist mode of production at any given moment—a moment that is constantly in motion, so that the situation of a given fraction of the professions, or of a profession, is "normally" contradictory, ambiguous, mystified. Their lack of political cohesion, worldwide, suggests that we must look more carefully at their workplace conditions so as to ascertain why these conditions have not pushed them more unambiguously toward socialist politics.

One method of attempting to measure the class location of a particular occupation is, to follow Wright, its degree of autonomy. This would seem an especially important measure for the professions, inasmuch as this is how many of them establish that they *are* professions. At one extreme, as Wright points out, every worker has at least some limited, narrow control over the workplace, formal or informal. At the other, virtually no one has total autonomy in today's marketplace. The semi-autonomous employee—e.g., the research scientist—thus occupies a "contradictory location" between the traditional petty bourgeoisie and the modern proletariat, sharing some of the characteristics of each.

Using a series of criteria, Wright places from 5 percent to 11 percent of the labor force in this classification. Similarly, many professionals who occupy jobs in management and administration ("technocrats") are in a contradictory location between the big bourgeoisie and the proletariat. Wright suggests that about 12 percent of the labor force can be classified as being in this top- and middle-management group (1978: 84).

Following Wright's logic, we can try to locate the various strata of professionals along the dimension of power. While all occupy contradictory locations between the bourgeoisie and the proletariat, it is clear that the uppermost stratum is most closely involved in the control aspects of the capitalist system. Professionals at the second echelon of authority are also involved in a set of oppressive and exploitative relations, but they are in a far more dependent position and find themselves under more direct pressure from their subordinates; they suffer most from their contradictory location between management and employee.

The third stratum of professionals and semiprofessionals (social workers, teachers, librarians, nurses, writers, and others who actually carry out the designated task of the organization) suffers a different kind of contradiction, that between pride in craft and skill on the one hand, and the requirements of working in a bureaucracy (public or private) that is both oppressive to its workers and functions to oppress people in the society in general. It is in this stratum that deprofessionalization, insofar as it exists, will be most pronounced. It is here that unemployment will take most of its toll, and here that unionization appears as a defense against deteriorating conditions. (Table 7-1 illustrates the distinctions between these strata.)

In addition, it is well to remember that professionals are segmented *vertically* as well as horizontally, that is, by the kind of work they do as well as by their place in a hierarchy. Thus they will be affected differentially by such processes as automation. There is, moreover, considerable overlap between level 2 and level 3; moreover, income differences between these levels may not be significant, so that a perceived community of interest between them, based on their common identity as professionals, can develop.

Basically there are three types of professionals, divided vertically. *Technicians* are defined as experts who plan and make technical decisions based on managerial or governmental directives from above (systems analysts, computer programmers, engineers, laboratory research-

Table 7-1.   *Power Strata among Professionals*

Private sector	Public sector
(1)	*Policymaking (direct)*
Upper and middle management	Top political appointees; commissioners; heads of agencies
(2)	*Policymaking (indirect, through manipulation of bureaucratic processes; carrying out of policy by commanding subordinates)*
Administrators, supervisors, lower management	Assistants to heads of agencies; subagency heads; supervisors of large numbers of personnel
(3)	*Policy carrying out (almost no influence over policy; vulnerable to termination for insubordination)*
Semi-autonomous employees (scientific and technical personnel; legal departments; researchers; personnel who personally deliver services, i.e., social workers, teachers, advertising department writers, news writers, computer programmers, etc.)	

ers, and other personnel identified with the "hard sciences"). *Service professionals* are those engaged in the delivery of such services as education, social work, and the like. Functionally, under capitalism, technicians (who work mainly in the private sector) participate directly in the planning and production of a commodity, and in some cases in its sale and distribution (e.g., advertising), that is, the generation and realization of surplus value in the Marxist sense. Service professionals, on the other hand, tend to be more involved in the reproduction of the labor force (teachers, for example) and in the reproduction of the relations of production (the social relations of the system, super/subordinate relations) (teachers, social workers, clergy). *Social control professionals* are those primarily engaged (through the state) in what functionalist sociologists call "boundary maintenance," that is, keeping undesirable elements of the population (criminals, deviants, the unruly poor, the insane, the politically dangerous) under some form of lock and key. This includes primarily the employees of the so-called criminal justice system, but also overlaps with such service professions as social work, law, psychiatry, etc. Workers in this category are chiefly engaged in "reproducing the social relations" of capitalism, but more by demonstrating what happens when one deviates than by teaching proper behavior directly. In short, they perform a deterrent function. It can be seen, therefore, that the different sets of professions and professionals vary in a number of significant ways: in level of authority or access to power, in the kinds of contradictions they confront in the workplace, and in the function they perform within the mode of production. These real differences in the way professional work is organized help to separate one set of professionals from another, and prevent their coalescing into anything resembling an independent class.

Are Professionals Becoming Proletarian?

Contemporary authors differ widely as to the likely future for professionals. Eliot Freidson states:

> It seems to be implicit in discussions of the prototypical worker of the postindustrial society that knowledge-based work, the work of middle-class experts, professionals, and technicians, is by its very nature *not* amenable to the mechanization and rationalization which industrial production and commerce have undergone over the past century. (Freidson 1973: 55)

Haug, on the other hand, argues that "deprofessionalization, rather than professionalization, is the trend of the future" (1973: 197).

The fact is that little overall research has been done to establish one or the other argument as "the truth." Total de-skilling, in the Braverman sense (1974), is clearly not taking place, nor, for many professionals, will it ever dominate their work. Many professionals below management ranks continue to have a great deal of autonomy over technical aspects of their work, although their control over the general conditions of employment has deteriorated. It is therefore useful to distinguish between "ideological proletarianization"—the loss of control over the *uses* of one's work—and "technical proletarianization"— the loss of control over decisions as to how to do the job (Derber 1982: 169). While many industrial workers are proletarianized in both senses, most professionals have suffered loss of control only over the first of these, although there are some signs that the second is also deteriorating as austerity hits public sector professionals. College professors, for example, continue to control most of the content of their curricula ("academic freedom"), although their managerial functions in such areas as personnel decisions and budget have become largely fictional.

However, if a given field becomes horizontally segmented so that the upper layers retain their professional status while the lower ones are relabeled and downgraded, the overall result will be that significant segments—even numerically the bulk—of a former single profession will be proletarianized in both ways. For example, tenured university professors may retain relative technical autonomy, but if the bulk of university teaching is relegated to teaching assistants and co-adjunct instructors who have no autonomy and who are proletarianized both ideologically and technically, focusing on the tenured professors misses the point. The case is similar in the field of computer programming. Moreover, computers themselves, in whatever field, may provide the basis for shifting control of knowledge from practitioners to management, and for standardizing a vast array of formerly individualized professional services, from teaching to law to physicians' treatment procedures. All of this is underlined by the increasingly weak bargaining position in which many professionals find themselves, as universities produce an excess of some kinds of professional workers in a time of diminishing demand and shrinking public budgets.

Some professions are undergoing ideological proletarianization, sometimes as only the first step, with technical proletarianization following soon after. Other professions are undergoing horizontal segmentation, with the lower segment proletarianizing in the dual sense. In either case, the whole notion of what professional life is supposedly about is being undermined.

What are the larger causes for these proletarianizing processes? Three phenomena can be identified as being critical: the development of modern bureaucracy, the growth of the public sector, and the economic "recession" with the resulting financial crisis of the public sector.

All three have as their historical common denominator the industrial revolution and the rise of capitalism in the West. Although there have been precapitalist bureaucracies and public sectors (one thinks of Sumer, Egypt, and the civilizations of the Mayas and Incas, to cite but a few), and although bureaucracy is hardly limited to capitalism in the contemporary world, it can nevertheless be argued that our particular brands of these three phenomena cannot be adequately understood without reference to the rise of capitalism (Clawson 1980).

The first phenomenon refers to the fact that the formerly independent professional, such as the small-town doctor or attorney, the journalist-newspaper publisher, the inventor, even the artist, today finds himself or herself absorbed into large-scale organizations with an extensive division of labor (specialization of skills), so that his or her job is linked in a planned way to the jobs of many others. Under these conditions such an individual is no longer able to work at a self-determined pace, or to determine the use of his or her talents or product, or their price, or in fact much of anything about the workplace, the owners or controllers of which are often far removed, both physically and in terms of social standing.

More and more professionals find themselves working in such bureaucratic organizational settings, characterized by fixed jurisdictions, rules established top down, hierarchical command systems, and job entry, promotion, and tenure based on uniform performance in tasks, examinations, certification or "degrees," or longevity. Work tends to become broken down into specialized units.

Bureaucratization has become a basic tendency throughout the technologically advanced world and in all professions. Perucci and Gerstl, in a study of American engineers, observe: "Clearly for engineers the overwhelming pattern is not only employment in organizational settings, but employment in organizations containing thousands of employees" (1969: 181). Likewise, whether we are talking about law, medicine, or the ministry, the trend is toward specialization within a "group practice," work in larger firms or organizations with a concomitant division of labor and/or work in the public sector, where the merit system has always fostered very specific and specialized job descriptions and boundaries. The urban hospital, law firm, or denominational headquarters is as different from the practice of the small-town general practitioner, lawyer, or minister as the agribusiness is from the family farm.

Such an organizational context undermines many of the characteristics traditionally associated with professional life, particularly the factor of discretion or judgment. Job satisfaction deteriorates because it is so closely connected to autonomy or decision making in one's job.

But bureaucratization by itself is insufficient to explain these proletarianizing tendencies. It is the growth of the public sector (the state) in all capitalist countries that has made bureaucracy virtually synonymous with organization. In the private sector, even in manufacturing (the sector with the largest establishments in terms of number of workers), about 25 percent of all workers are in organizations with fewer than 100 employees and nearly 75 percent in establishments with fewer than 1,000. In the growing services sector, over 65 percent of all workers are in organizations with fewer than 100 people (see Granovetter 1984). By contrast, in 1983 2.8 million people worked in the executive branch of the U.S. federal government (over 1 million civilians in the Defense Department alone).

The growth of the state sector in the United States is largely attributable to the special role of the state in the world capitalist system, a role discussed in some detail in chapter 2. The "defense" of capital on a world scale against the encroachments of competing capitals, and of revolutionary movements, has come to require an enormous outlay of funds and recruitment of personnel. The development of infrastructure domestically, including the growth of the educational establishment, and the requirements of social control have added still more millions of workers to the state payroll. By 1980, for example, close to 4 percent of the labor force was involved in education, with some 7.5 percent of gross national product being spent in that one area alone. The regulation of intracapitalist and interclass social conflicts, the ensuring of a technically appropriate workforce, and the need to control surplus populations and "fend off . . . a legitimization crisis" have, in all capitalist countries, led to growing proportions of the labor force being employed by the state (O'Connor 1973: 69).

State sector workers, subjected to the discipline of large-scale bureaucracy, have always been vulnerable to proletarianizing trends, and indeed at the lower levels are indistinguishable from other blue and white collar workers in every important respect. Today, however, this trend has become critical in its proportions as the state has been increasingly unable to generate revenues to meet its expenditures. This inability is related to the state of the entire economy, which as it deteriorates produces fewer taxes, both corporate and individual, at least in real dollars. As real income decreases with increasing unemployment and underemployment, plant closings, and the like, the public reaction is to resist taxation, which leads to legislators' calling for balanced budgets, the introduction of accountability measures, and the demand for more productivity. The impact on the working conditions of state workers has been enormous as they confront layoffs, speedups, "givebacks" of fringe benefits, and as the quality of the services they provide consequently deteriorates.

Two further factors have affected the fiscal crisis of the state, although they did not cause it: the post–World War II and post-Sputnik educational explosions, and a subsequent reduction in the birth rate. Education came to be regarded as a major source of employment, and massive numbers of better-educated people entered the labor force expecting jobs commensurate with their education, including in the field of education itself. However, by 1968 the number of births was declining, and declines in elementary school and high school enrollments soon followed. Suddenly there was a "surplus" of the college-educated, and educational "experts" were calling for cutbacks at the university level. Competition for a number of kinds of professional jobs, especially in teaching, became fierce. Other Western countries also reported unprecedented unemployment rates for trained teachers, as well as other college-educated people, as public expenditures began to slow down (Leventman 1981: 230).

Another factor that adds to the problem of the general fiscal crisis is the "normal" problem of economic cycles and shifts in government spending, particularly in the "defense" area. Every two to four years business publications switch their predictions as to engineering manpower needs—for example, from glut to critical shortage—with rosy predictions often based on the assumption that the public sector (especially the Defense Department) will at some time in the near future pick up the slack of a temporary economic downturn.

These cycles and shifts, as the Germans seem to understand better than the Americans do, in turn trigger predictions that themselves affect later cycles: A shortage in any particular field causes an expansion of recruiting into the educational areas required for that field, but there is a delay in filling the demand equivalent to the time required to complete the education. By the time that manpower becomes available, industry and government have adjusted to the shortage of manpower, for example, by upgrading lower-level technicians or by breaking professional tasks down into smaller units that can be handled by less-educated people. If, on top of this, courses of instruction have been shortened to meet the "emergency" manpower need, the labor market may suddenly be swamped by professional graduates entering a field in which yesterday's shortage abruptly becomes today's surplus. Educational policy then swiftly changes gears, and closes out programs because graduates cannot get jobs, and the cycle begins again. Meanwhile, unemployment hits older professionals, overspecialized employees whose retraining would be expensive, and of course the upgraded, less-educated technicians, who can now be displaced by better-trained people (sometimes at equally low wages). Or, the technicians are retained because they are cheaper, and the professionals enter the ranks of blue-collar labor.

But it should be remembered that a business cycle, or a shift in government spending (which may be in response to the cycle), is only a marginal phenomenon: It does not constitute a long-range, structural crisis such as that which now confronts business and government. It accounts for zigs and zags in employment, but not for long-term, creeping trends around which the zigs and zags take place. Whether short- or long-term, two forces contribute further to undermining some professionals' traditional independence and job security: the development of a "two-tier" professional labor force (not to be confused with the two-tier labor force concept associated with dual labor market theory), and the "bumping-up" versus "bumping-down" problem.

Older, technologically more obsolescent workers become less employable in professional-technical jobs, as younger, more up-to-date (and cheaper) workers enter the labor force. The younger tier is therefore relatively more advantaged. At the same time, the younger worker is entering a situation in which he or she is likely to be overeducated for jobs that are becoming more segmented, less autonomous and professional. The likely payoff is that both tiers move toward unionization in order to deal with their respective problems—though younger workers will be more likely to emphasize issues related to on-the-job decision making and pay, while older workers will be more concerned with job security, pensions, etc.

The bumping problem involves two contradictory tendencies: better-qualified individuals displacing the less qualified as larger numbers of them are produced by the universities, so that in a period of labor surplus they will work at wages previously paid to the lesser degreed; or, contrariwise, less-qualified, lower-paid individuals (e.g., paraprofessionals) displacing better-qualified individuals in order to cut labor costs. In the field of social work, for example, both phenomena are taking place—bumping up tends to take place in public welfare and bumping down in private agencies, such as those involved in family counseling. Again, the victims of bumping up and bumping down both move toward unionization in order to protect their job security, with the less-qualified making the claim that the credential is a false and discriminatory device (hence arguing, perhaps, for a substitution of some form of community accountability for professional accountability) while the better-qualified will claim to be upgrading services by requiring ever more credentials.

Management's response (both in the public and private sector) to recessionist economic conditions is to *increase* professional jobs at the supervisory and administrative level, while calling for more and more accountability and measures of productivity. Sometimes these supervisory efforts are a response to pressures from outside funding agencies, foundations, etc. On July 1, 1980, the U.S. Office of Management and Budget, for example, established new criteria for determining the cost of grants and for the first time required detailed "time-and-effort" activity reports from researchers. At one university the administration felt it necessary to organize workshops so that professors might be familiarized with the new record-keeping systems. At another, more prestigious, university, researchers refused to go along, with the argument that, quite apart from the time wasted on such paperwork, their work could not be arbitrarily measured in numerical terms.

Pressures toward increasing accountability and productivity in the professions are ubiquitous despite the fact that measuring productivity in the services sector is notoriously difficult. How, after all, can one measure the "soft" services, those that primarily involve relationships, counseling, education, and other informal processes? The answer seems to be that whatever can be measured, is: numbers, dollars, cases closed, students in classes, their grades, their examination scores (before and after). This means that administrators put into operation rules and regulations that have the effect of turning professional work into measurable units, thereby eliminating or undermining the professional dimension of that work. The official rationalization is as follows:

> The current crisis in social services is a crisis of credibility based on an inadequate system of accountability. Social programs are in trouble because they focus on processes and not results. . . . With respect to the "soft" services—those that primarily involve relationships, counseling, and process technologies—it is difficult to attribute changes in the individual's status to the service activity. (Newman and Turem 1974: 15)

Few would argue that accountability for "results" is bad. The issue, rather, is accountability to whom, and productivity of what? Current pressures do not come from client populations and are not likely to improve the *quality* of a product or service. Instead they come from employers, administrators, and politicians and are calculated simply to cut costs, either in terms of overall budgets and/or in terms of per-unit costs, whatever that unit may be. In the soft services, cutting per-unit costs does not by itself lead to a better-quality product; on the contrary, it often leads to a worse one.

One effect of the financial pressures on government is that some wages will contractually be tied to improvements in productivity. For example, pay increases are tied to costs saved by working harder. While this is sometimes good, it does not help save jobs, and it makes for contrived statistics about improving services—there is an incentive, for example, to close welfare cases sooner than is warranted, and to exaggerate the amount of bureaucratic activity in general. In New York City, 16 agencies set 300 "productivity targets." But many of these targets were in terms of sheer numbers. The number of times a hospital room is visited tells us nothing about what goes on inside that room.

Many people believe that those who work for government in general, and for education in particular, do not work very hard for their money and that there is a great deal of waste. This makes it easier to increase workload pressures, and to insist that measurable indices be devised. In education this means students per teacher—and in universities, it means that departments begin to compete for students in order to increase class enrollments so that jobs can be protected or a request for a new position justified. The potential for pandering to current fads is easy to visualize.

A second effect of financial pressure on government (and private management) is that administrators increasingly "stonewall" on wage demands, asking instead for givebacks. In many cases management refuses to bargain in good faith with unions of professionals. The phenomenon of union-busting, in the form of management-instigated decertification efforts, is becoming common.

Conclusion

The proletarianization of working conditions is only one aspect of what de-professionalization is about. Another is the deterioration of earnings. Actually, many professionals had relatively low wages to begin with: In 1970, over 50 percent had earnings of less than $9,000, when craftsmen were averaging $9,253; over 30 percent were earning under $7,000, less than the average pay of service workers. The high-paying and prestigious professions of doctor, lawyer, architect, engineer, college professor, scientist, or computer system analyst made up only 29 percent of those in the professional category (Dicesare 1975; Sommers 1974).

Until recently, however, male professionals were earning, on the average, $4,500 more than the average for all males in the labor force; self-employed professionals, twice as much. But many professionals are doing poorly relative to the rate of inflation. University professors' real wages, for example, declined by about 1 percent per year throughout the 1970s, and are increasing now at the rate of only about 1 percent per year.

The incomes of the employed tell us little of the increasingly sad lot of the unemployed professional, or of the professional who is forced to make a living at lower skill levels than those for which he or she has been trained. While unemployment rates for professional occupations continue to be significantly lower than overall rates, the upturn of all of these rates, not only in the United States but also in a number of other Western countries, suggests that something more than cyclical unemployment is going on.

How do professionals react to the combined pressures and threats of proletarianization, including deteriorating standards of living and the dangers of under- and unemployment, or employment outside their fields? Here we discuss only one aspect of this issue—what might be called work alienation. The other two major aspects—trade unionization and political behavior—will be discussed in more detail in chapters 8 and 9.

The literature on professional alienation is considerable and need not be reviewed here. However, the trend toward ideological proletarianization is generally not considered in such studies. Social dynamics, particularly those rooted in capitalist economic relations, are widely ignored by conventional sociologists.

Derber suggests two types of reaction to ideological proletarianization. First, there is "ideological desensitization," a process whereby "workers disassociate themselves from the ideological context of their work and disclaim either interest or responsibility for the social uses to which their work is put" (1982: 180). They deny that what they do has any value or significance; they refuse to admit that their work serves the interests of particular social groups. This attitude is reflected in studies of medical students, dental students, nursing students, etc., whose relatively high early idealism declines the longer they are in school. This acquiescence to loss of power is rationalized by the intrinsically interesting nature of the work itself. Quoting Schevitz (1979), Derber notes that defense work is considered very interesting because it involves highly sophisticated engineering systems.

The second form of reaction, according to Derber, is "ideological co-optation." The professional accepts and identifies with organizational—as distinct from professional—interests. It is plausible, says Derber, to maintain professional identity yet serve a bureaucracy, because the professional identity is often based purely on technical expertise, and not on distinct values and moral objectives, which, if the profession ever claimed them, were probably long ago relegated to the archives (1982: 185ff.). Today most professional groups do not have special moral purposes but emphasize skills that are consistent with organizational goals. Those professions that are historically most dependent on organizational employment, like engineering, are most ideologically co-opted. In social work, the clinical model itself served to redirect "the moral and social concerns of practitioners toward individual therapeutic rehabilitation, rather than social or political change" (ibid.: 187). And in many professions it can be argued that there was nothing to co-opt in the first place.

Both ideological desensitization and ideological co-optation are rooted in continuing control over the technical aspects of the job. Either the purposes of the organization or the values of the profession are irrelevant. What is real is day-to-day technical practice, which continues to be seen as the monopoly of the professional practitioner. It separates him or her from both clients and other professionals, none of whom have the right to share in decision making or knowledge. This continues to segregate the professional from potential allies and from a viable political base of support. The segmentation of professional life in all the ways that have been detailed here functions, in the final analysis, as an obstacle to both professional unity and unity between proletarianizing professionals and other workers. Overcoming that obstacle politically is a formidable task, to say the least.

8
White Collar Unions:
Consciousness for What?

Introduction

Both conventional theorists of the labor movement and radicals share a certain less-than-flattering view of U.S. trade unions: that they are limited to trying to obtain for their memberships certain basic "economistic" or bread-and-butter demands. In the words of Sam Gompers, what they want is "more"; their social rhetoric, their claims to a wider social purpose, as well as their appeals to solidarity, are secondary. To the degree that bread-and-butter demands, however liberally defined, are successfully attained, say these theorists, unions function to integrate the working class into the capitalist mode of production so that the labor movement's politics will remain wedded to the assumptions of private property, economic gain, and the welfare of the union's own membership—if necessary, at the expense of other workers and the public. For conventional theorists (such as those discussed in chapter 2), the integrative function of unions is a positive contribution to a smoothly operating society, although when union gains come at the expense of the "public," this smooth operation may occasionally malfunction. Legal measures must then be taken to get the unions back into line. For radicals, on the other hand, the integrative function of unions represents an obstacle to a more revolutionary politics oriented to fundamental social change.

At the same time, trade union consciousness—that is, a commitment on the part of a worker to that form of collective action called trade unionism—is generally believed by radicals to be a necessary though not sufficient step toward the development of a radical consciousness, for it marks a departure from the view that gains can be made, or protected, only by individual action. Commitment to a labor union implies an acknowledgement that individual action is not sufficient, that only collective action can protect—and advance—the individual worker. But this phenomenon is admittedly contradictory: While on the one hand the union represents a tremendous step in the direction of a political commitment to the collectivity, its very success encapsulates political struggle within the legalistic structure of collective bargaining. Trade union successes in the past have often led to complacency, to the institutionalization and bureaucratization of the union, and to the gradual separation of the union leadership from the rank and file.

Radicals in the trade union movement sometimes argue that despite their shortcomings (such as a commitment to narrow economic self-interest, a tendency to put union ahead of the collective labor movement, bureaucratization, corruption), unions function to provide previously oppressed groups with a sense of self-worth and dignity, without which consciousness that the world can be changed cannot take place. While this view may hold in certain less-skilled or traditionally blue collar occupations, where unionization has literally meant the difference between poverty and basic dignity in everyday standards of living, it is questionable in the newer white collar occupations, particularly in the professions. The latter hold a rather high view of their calling to begin with; it requires a sense of real deprivation for professionals to see themselves as workers, sharing a proletarian lot. It is at least arguable that successful collective bargaining among professionals and semiprofessionals will sustain a self-image that inhibits, rather than encourages, solidarity with other working class people, and that narrow interest-group protectionism will prevail over a more "social" form of unionism.

The elevation of the professions over other occupations (and the larger problem of the segmentation of the labor force in general) is mirrored in the structure of the labor movement, which replicates many of the schisms within the working class (particularly that between the more skilled and the less skilled). As chapter 2 noted, this schism was partially created by employers in their attempt to structure the workplace so as to keep labor divided and cheap. Employers try to exploit not only the segmentation of the labor force in the workplace, but also the separation of workers in a particular firm within different unions, by playing one union off against another, or even one local of the same union against another local.

Similar actions take place in government employment, where, according to Aronowitz, "management is distributing benefits unequally among various sectors of public bureaucracies in the hope of splitting off certain sections of the labor force from other sections in order to hold down costs and maintain control" (1973: 321). Unions have developed an unconscious partnership with management to keep the workforce divided by virtue of union structures—there are some sixty unions representing public employees, and in a single enterprise of any size, public or private, there may be a dozen, including several different locals of the same national union.

Within the general context of these kinds of divisions, there is a series of problems specific to the public sector, the major area of white collar unionization. Many public sector unions came into being without struggles or strikes, by administrative or executive order or through an arrangement between union and management to keep out a more militant union. Workers in such units tend to be less union-conscious. Moreover, they, together with most other white collar trade unionists, lack the historical traditions of the older unions in the manufacturing sector because they do not live in working class "urban villages" as their parents may have done. Scattered in the suburbs, they do not have the time to attend to union business, especially if they are women. Finally, the tax-paying public often views public sector unions as antithetical to the "public interest." Partly in consequence, they are denied many of the rights of other unions, including the closed shop, the union shop, and in some places even the agency shop (where nonmembers pay a fee for union services and are covered by a collective bargaining agreement). Generally, too, strikes are *de facto* or *de jure* outlawed. At another level, white collar workers often feel that their work is cleaner, more prestigious, and provides them with more autonomy than blue collar work, so that they tend to identify less as workers (Mercer and Weir 1983: 260) and are less dissatisfied with their working conditions. All of these factors have been viewed by observers of the white collar union scene as obstacles to unionization. As one observer noted a quarter of a century ago, the labor movement will have only token success in this area because white collar workers consider it beneath their dignity—because they feel they differ from blue collar workers in job and status, because they do not want to hurt their chances for advancement, and because the labor movement seems to them crude and exploitative (see Bruner 1958). Yet white collar workers do belong to unions in ever-larger numbers and as an increasing proportion of all U.S. union members. A brief review of the history of white collar unionization, not only in the United States but in some other Western nations, makes it clear that despite the obstacles, pessimism concerning white collar unionization was never fully warranted.

History: An Overview

The history of white collar trade unionism varies widely from country to country, but the widest variation, at least in the early years, exists between the United States on the one hand and Canada and Western European countries on the other. Western white collar organizations do share one characteristic: Their growth is directly related to the growth of the services sector. Since the manufacturing sector antedates these by several decades, so that the development of modern industry comes to full flower (in any given country) at a time when the services sector is relatively small, the lag between blue and white collar organizing should not be surprising.

The chief difference between the United States and other countries with regard to white collar organizing is that the proportion of unionized white collar workers is far lower in the United States, a situation largely attributable to the overall differences between the U.S. labor movement and the labor movements of all other nations in the past—the causes of which were discussed in chapter 2. While less than 16 percent of white collar workers in the United States are organized, in Sweden, which has the highest proportion of unionized workers in the Western world, a quite opposite situation pertains. There, some 70 percent of all white collar workers, including doctors, lawyers, army officers, clergymen, and many layers of management, are organized. As early as 1930, 65 percent of state employees were organized, although they did not yet have union contracts (Adams 1976: 368ff.).

In Germany, white collar employees' organizing efforts were closely integrated with the work of the Social-Democratic Party and began earlier than in Sweden. In 1887, under Social-Democratic Party sponsorship, a union of shop assistants and helpers was formed, with 255 members. By 1914 it had 26,000 members, and after some mergers, it had a membership of 400,000 in 1920 (Kadritzke 1975: 209). The first white collar strike in Germany appears to have taken place under this union's auspices in 1903 in Berlin, in a firm doing mailings (and addressing them by hand). A year later a technical and supervisory officials' union, the Butib, was formed. It grew from 1,638 to 20,452 members by 1920.

There is an immense literature on the subsequent development of German white collar unions because of the significance of white collar politics during the rise of Hitler (see chapter 9). The period of the German revolution (1918–1919) saw a significant thrust leftward by white collar groups such as the Butib, whose members joined with the Kiel sailors in the series of strikes and protest actions that triggered the revolt that led to the downfall of the Kaiser and the end of World War I (Kadritzke 1975: 265ff.). White collar unions were involved in a vast wave of strikes in department stores, banks, insurance companies, and manufacturing concerns from December 1918 to April 1919 (in some cases a majority of the strikers were women). Thousands upon thousands of them demanded workers' councils and other measures of self-determination at the workplace—hardly a symptom of the "middle class" consciousness of the lower-level white collar employee. In early 1919 the defense minister forbade public meetings—including a rally of some 20,000 striking bank employees—and in response the *Angestellte* in Berlin called for a general strike (ibid.: 302). A wave of strikes resulted, and yielded a co-determination law that was institutionalized in West German practice after 1945, having been abrogated by the Hitler regime. However, despite the pleas of such theorists as Lederer (discussed in chapter 4), the Communist and Socialist left was unable to extend its influence further over the lower ranks of white collar employees. In fact, the Social Democratic–oriented white collar union federation, the A.f.A., lost strength to unions influenced by more conservative ideologies (Kocka 1980: 29). "In Germany," Kocka tells us, "bureaucratic tradition, law, and consistently conservative governments before the First World War had made it impossible for lower and middle level officials to ally with a labor movement that was defined as a public enemy" (ibid.: 273).

Today most white collar workers in West Germany belong to the same federation as blue collar workers, although there is also a separate white collar federation. About 24 percent of all white collar employees are in these two federations.

In France, on the other hand, white collar employees solidly supported the socialist-oriented labor movement. The militant history of this group began in the 1850s, following the appearance of the first department stores in Paris. Working conditions were deplorable and mutual-aid societies were formed by their workers. Masonic, repub-

Table 8-1.   Membership in the Three Major Federations of
White Collar Associations in Germany, 1920–1930

	1920	1925	1930
AFA (social democrat)	690,000	428,000	480,000
Gedag (nationalist)	463,000	411,000	592,000
GDA (center-liberal)	300,000	313,000	385,000
Total	1,453,000	1,152,000	1,457,000

SOURCE: Jügen Kocka, *White Collar Workers in America 1890–1940* (Beverley Hills, CA: Sage Publications, 1980).

lican, anarchist, and Marxist influences coincided to assist these early organizing attempts. By 1900 a large mass of civil servants, especially postal employees and teachers (mainly outside Paris), had formed several associations that participated in the general strike of 1909 (Crozier 1971: chap. 3). White collar employees also played a large role in the wave of strikes that shook France in 1919 and 1920. In May and June 1919, department stores and, for the first time, banks were closed down.

But in the early 1920s, a period of retreat ensued in France, as elsewhere in Western Europe. Nevertheless, by June 1936, white collar strikers had joined their blue collar colleagues in support of the Popular Front against fascism, and again put a halt to the activities of most Parisian department stores, insurance companies, commercial firms, and many manufacturing firms. Within the largest labor federation, the Confédération Générale du Travail (CGT), white collar workers (including civil service employees) constituted 35 percent of the membership. The Parisian Regional Chamber of Employees (primarily white collar) had more than 100,000 members (30,000 in department stores, and 20,000 each in banks and insurance companies), and the National Federation of Employees had 300,000.

The labor movement in France split after World War II as a result of the "cold war," with social democrats on one side, and Communists (in the CGT) on the other. Despite this division, "the greatest social disturbance of the entire period, the general strike of civil servants of August 1953 was launched by militants in the postal and telecommunications services" (Crozier 1971: 51). By 1965 about 40 percent of all civil service employees were unionized in France, as compared with only 15 percent in the private sector; however, these civil service

unionists were subdivided among more than 400 national organizations, constituting a "mosaic" of groups that still managed, in moments
of crisis, to come down on the side of the workers (ibid.: 61). In the
uprisings of May 1968, for instance, white collar workers joined with
their blue collar colleagues (as well as with students, many of whom
considered themselves future white collar proletarians) in making
some rather revolutionary demands (Kocka 1980: 274). French white
collar unionists feel much closer to blue collar union members than do
their German counterparts.

English white collar workers also began organizing in the 1880s, but
the process was slower. By 1914 there were still only fourteen white
collar unions affiliated with the Trades Union Congress (TUC), the
main British labor federation with 196 member unions. As in other
countries, the 1920s marked a period of general union decline—but in
Britain the white collar unions continued to grow. A nonmanual section
of the TUC was formed in 1924 and a year later there were 25 TUC-
affiliated white collar unions, with that many again outside the federation (Jenkins and Sherman 1979: 28–29). While the Depression led to
an overall decline, World War II marked a period of new growth,
especially in the public sector. By the 1950s there were white collar
unions in the fields of banking, railroads (by now in the public sector),
insurance, engineering, the postal service, health, and of course
among clerical employees in general. Supervisory and managerial personnel also had unions. By 1978 there were 44 primarily white collar
unions with about 3.3 million members; if white collar workers in
manual workers' unions are included, there were some 4.6 million
white collarites in 75 different unions, or about 43 percent of all white
collar workers (Price 1983: 151). The spectacular increase of the white
collar proportion of union membership in Britain (2.5 million of the
TUC's 3.6 million new members in the 1957–1977 decades were white
collar workers) is attributable to the affiliation with the TUC of former
independent unions and "professional" associations; to the growth of
large public and private bureaucracies; and to the relative decline of
traditional private sector industries, probably more marked in Britain
than in other Western countries up to that time. Jenkins and Sherman
predict that this trend will continue.

The integration of white collar unions within the main body of trade
unionism puts British white collar unions closer to the French than to
the more segregated German or Swedish models (Kocka 1980: 271).
Some of the newer British unions have, moreover, developed new

tactics to cope with the deterioration of their living standards, with some success. In a civil service strike involving two unions (300,000 members) in early 1979, only 1,300 workers were actually called out on strike (to maximize disruption and minimize pay losses). They included computer operators and foreign service code clerks, resulting in the shutdown of all government computer operations including billings for taxes, defense contract payments, and all routine communications with British embassies abroad (*New York Times,* 27 February 1979).

There are significant differences among Western European countries when it comes to white collar unionization, ranging from proportions organized to union structure to relationship with blue collar unions and parties of the political left. These differences could be extended were further examples from other Western European countries, or from Canada, included in this discussion. Nevertheless, until recently, differences between the U.S. white collar union situation and that in all other Western nations were still greater than the differences among the other nations and might help account for the relatively slow rate of growth of white collar unions to date. However, an examination of the history of white collar union development in the United States shows that this apparently overarching difference has been exaggerated, and that even if it existed at one time, it may now be less important.

White Collar Unions in the United States

White collar unions have a long tradition in the United States too. At least one group of white collar workers, the retail clerks, can trace the origins of their present union back to the Retail Clerks' National Protective Association, founded in 1888 and affiliated with the American Federation of Labor (AFL) from its inception (Kocka 1980). Local associations devoted to the improvement of the clerical lot existed as early as 1820. However, white collar unionism in the United States grew very slowly: The National Society of Marine Draftsmen was organized in 1913–1914 and eventually affiliated with the AFL; local bookkeepers and stenographers' unions participated in AFL conventions, but the AFL refused them a national chapter; an insurance union struck the Prudential Insurance Company in 1916, but was not allowed into the AFL either. Only the Post Office Clerks, which had been in the AFL since 1906, and which had grown significantly (ibid.: 164), engaged in job actions against the government in 1915. The Railway Clerks, formed in 1899, affiliated with the AFL in 1908, and, together with the Railroad Telegraphers, joined other railroad unions in the AFL's narrow form of craft unionism. A handful of other unions, including the American Federation of Teachers (AFT) (which joined the AFL in 1916), were also predominantly white collar.

In 1916, dissatisfaction with working conditions in the federal civil service was serious enough for employees to form an AFL-affiliated union, the National Federation of Federal Employees (NFFE). The immediate impetus was an amendment attached to a House of Representatives appropriations bill increasing the workday for all government employees from seven to eight hours without a proportionate pay increase. The AFL lobbied extensively against this amendment, which was defeated. The union accepted both white and blue collar workers, regardless of craft. In its early years it militantly supported other white collar unions and their strikes, including a department store clerk struggle in Washington, D.C., to obtain Saturday half-days during the summertime. From an initial 10,000 members, the NFFE grew to 50,000 by June 1919 (Dopkins 1983). The American Federation of Government Employees (AFGE), which is today the largest union in the federal service, traces its history back to the NFFE, from which it had seceded: the NFFE quit the AFL in 1932 and the AFGE became the AFL—later AFL-CIO—affiliate.

Despite such activity, by 1935 only about 5 percent of white collar workers belonged to unions in the United States; percentages in other Western countries were much higher, close to one-third in both Germany and Sweden. Kocka lists some 26 white collar unions with 588,000 members in the United States in 1935. They ranged from the National Association of Master Mechanics and Foremen of Naval Yards and Naval Stations (AFL), with 250 members, to the Brotherhood of Railway and Steamship Clerks, Freight Handlers, Express and Station Employees (AFL), with 135,000. They included such professional occupations as airline pilots, actors, artists, architects, engineers, chemists, musicians, newspaper journalists, teachers, and postmasters. But there were relatively few unions with large clerical memberships, an exception being the American Federation of Government Employees (Kocka 1980: 207).

When the Congress of Industrial Organizations (CIO) was formed in 1935–1936 (primarily to organize workers across industries rather than by craft), a number of the AFL's white collar unions seceded to become part of the new structure. New York retail clerks formed the United

Retail and Wholesale Employees and by 1938 had more members than the Retail Clerks from which it had split—some 40,000. The Newspaper Guild and the Federation of Architects, Engineers, Chemists, and Technicians also went over to the CIO. A number of the CIO's industrial unions, including the United Automobile Workers (UAW), advocated mixed blue and white collar unions based on the firm, not on the job, consistent with the CIO's philosophy of organizing workers by company rather than by craft. At the same time, general unions for white collar workers were established, both in the CIO and in the AFL. One of the first was the CIO's United Office and Professional Workers, which was expelled for alleged Communist affiliation in 1949.

In the United States, there are four different kinds of white collar unions, as Kocka recapitulates: those that replicated the traditional AFL craft approach; those that united blue and white collar workers in a CIO-type industrial union; unions that transcended occupational boundaries and united many kinds of professional or other white collar workers; and those that were limited to single firms (sometimes to keep nationwide unions out).

There was considerable growth in white collar unionism between 1935 and 1948, and by the latter date some 16 percent of all white collar workers belonged to one or another type of union (Mills 1951: 302). Yet by 1956 this had slipped to 12.8 percent and by 1968 to 11.2 percent, even while white collar members as a proportion of all union members increased from 13.4 percent in 1956 to 16.1 percent in 1968 (Blum 1971: 7). Much of this slippage was due to the failure to win members among clerks, and for long periods unions lost elections in shops where there were large numbers of female clericals.

During the early 1970s, white collar workers accounted for half or more of all new union members. This big surge came, of course, in the founding years of the many white collar unions, when a number of them showed between 50 percent and 350 percent increase in a decade. Contrary to the expectation of several experts, the growth of white collar unionism has not tapered off. White collar membership as a percentage of total union membership climbed dramatically, from 23.8 percent in 1973 to 34.9 percent in 1980, and in numbers from 4.3 million to 7.01 million. These figures include such non–AFL-CIO associations as the American Nurses' Association, the National Education Association (NEA), and the American Association of University Professors, which perform many if not all of the functions of the traditional trade union. Still, only 15.3 percent of all white collar employees were

Table 8-2.   Growth of Unions with Large Proportions of
White Collar Members, 1964–1981

	1964	1968	1972	1976	1981
Retail Clerks	428,000	552,000	633,000	699,000	(merged)
AFSCME	235,000	364,000	529,000	750,000	957,000
AFGE	139,000	295,000	293,000	260,000	223,000
Communications Workers	288,000	348,000	438,000	478,000	526,000
Retail, Wholesale Workers	167,000	175,000	198,000	200,000	(merged)
Postal Workers	139,000	166,000	249,000	252,000	249,000
Amer. Fed. Teachers	100,000	165,000	249,000	446,000	461,000

SOURCES: U.S. Department of Commerce, Bureau of the Census, *Statistical Abstract of the United States* (Washington, D.C.: GPO, 1970, 1978); Courtney D. Gifford, ed., *Directory of U.S. Labor Organizations* (Washington, D.C.: Bureau of National Affairs, 1982).

organized by 1980, compared with 32.3 percent of workers in manufacturing, and unionization rates among professional and technical workers continued to outstrip those among clericals (Wharton and Burris 1983).

Of the five largest AFL-CIO unions in 1981, three were heavily white collar (the merged United Food and Commercial Workers with over 1 million members; the Service Employees International Union and the Retail, Wholesale and Department Store Union, also a merger, with 910,000; and the American Federation of State, County, and Municipal Employees, with 957,000). The National Education Association, an independent organization, had 1.7 million school employees on its rolls that year—almost as many members as the powerful Teamsters (*New York Times*, 19 April 1981). On the other hand, white collar workers were heavily concentrated in only a few unions: three, each with 75 percent or more of their members working for the state, accounted for 42 percent of all clerical union members in 1978 (U.S. Department of Labor 1979; Gifford 1982). (Table 8-2 shows the growth of U.S. unions with large proportions of white collar workers).

The apparently dramatic increase in the proportion of white collar union members compared with all union members is due primarily to the overall decline in union membership in other sectors. High-tech jobs are displacing manufacturing jobs. Unions are trying to compensate by organizing high-tech workers. Coalitions of unions in Massachusetts and California now organize technicians, and are taking advantage of the layoffs that have undermined management credibility to recruit lower-level employees as well (*Business Week*, 11 April 1983).

The increase in white collar unionization has been even more impressive outside the United States. In Sweden, the largest white collar union federation increased its membership 17.2 percent from 1955 to 1975; in Britain, white collar union membership increased 83 percent from 1948 to 1974; in Denmark, the largest white collar affiliate of the Federation of Trade unions grew by 18.4 percent from 1955 to 1975; in West Germany, the number of unionized white collar workers went up by 104 percent in the same twenty years; in Austria, 67 percent. In each case the white collar rate of growth was at least twice—and often up to five times—the blue collar rate. While this may mean that blue collar organization has reached its limits, it also suggests that aggressive organizing efforts among white collar workers do pay off (Kassalow 1977).

Public Sector Unions

The federal service has been among the most successful hunting grounds for white collar unions. Following President Kennedy's signing of Executive Order 10988 in January 1962 giving federal employees the right to bargain collectively, there was a tremendous increase in employees covered by collective bargaining agreements, and unions recognized by the government. (See Table 8-3 for a listing of the largest public sector unions.) White collar unions added over 250,000 members from December 1962 to November 1967. Yet even this did not keep up with the rapid growth of the white collar labor force, and the percentage of workers in the federal workforce already covered by contracts declined.

One difference between public sector workers in the United States and those in Western Europe that helps explain the different rates of unionism in the two areas is that government unions in the United States operate under a series of legal handicaps. Strikes are illegal and/ or subject to court injunction in all but eight states. In 1974, the AFL-CIO set up a 24-union Public Employee Department, parallel to its Industrial Union Department, to try to cope with some of the problems faced by their (then 2 million) public sector members (including, of course, blue and gray collar workers, e.g., police, sanitation, etc.). Since that time, the fiscal crisis has led to a deterioration in working

Table 8-3   *Largest Government Collective Bargaining Agents, 1978*

National Education Association	1,700,000
Am. Fed. of State, County, & Municipal Employees	957,000
Am. Fed. of Teachers	461,000
Am. Fed. of Government Employees	223,000
Am. Postal Workers Union	249,000
Natl. Ass'n. of Letter Carriers	151,000
Service Employees Intl. Union (excluding private employees)	219,000

SOURCES: U.S. Department of Labor, *Directory of National Unions* (Washington, D.C.: GPO, 1979); *New York Times*, 16 August 1981; Courtney D. Gifford, ed., *Directory of U.S. Labor Organizations* (Washington, D.C.: Bureau of National Affairs, 1982).

conditions. Nevertheless, or perhaps correspondingly, public sector strikes not only take place, but their number is increasing (1976—378; 1977—413; 1978—481; 1979—593; 1980—536). In 1980, 2.4 million work days were lost by strikes, about 25 percent in the public schools (*Business Week*, 27 April 1981)—this despite their illegal status.

Not only are unions in the public sector limited in the kind of power they can use to enforce their demands, but the courts have also restricted the matters on which they can bargain. For example, in New Jersey teacher transfers are not bargainable because a negotiated agreement would "significantly interfere with the exercise of inherent management prerogatives" (*Ridgefield Park Education Association* vs. *Ridgefield Park Board of Education* 1977). And a 1980 Supreme Court decision in the case of Yeshiva University, as well as a 1984 administrative court decision in the case of Boston University (still being appealed), stated that faculty, because of their participation in university governance, were part of management and were therefore not protected by the National Labor Relations Board (NLRB) and did not have automatic bargaining rights. In short, insofar as faculty in private institutions retain, or obtain, access to decision making over their conditions of work, they may lose their right to have a union, the very instrument that can protect that power.

Another weapon currently aimed at public sector unions is the legal challenge to the "agency shop" that is underwritten by the conservative National Right to Work Committee and its local chapters. This challenge can cripple a union by limiting its income to members' dues only. Nonmembers can have the benefits of collective bargaining and "ride free." Finally, union members in the public sector are often in the paradoxical situation of having to pay their own attorneys' fees, and then, as taxpayers, having to pay their employers' attorneys' fees as well. In addition, the experience of many public sector unions is that the courts, too, are hostile. In short, the state has most of the weapons on its side. This is a major reason why public sector unions are paying more attention to legislative relations as a path to protecting and improving their members' benefits.

Unions of Professionals

All professionals are, by definition, organized, but few are organized into trade unions. Indeed, many professional organizations have traditionally fought bitterly against unionization on the grounds that professional standards are undermined by organizations with "outside" interests, and collective bargaining as such undermines individual rights, including the professional's right to autonomy over the service being rendered. In the United States, by the mid-1930s, only

> a minority of technical employees, journalists, and pilots—teachers, musicians, and actors might also be mentioned—found that professional identity was not an obstacle to trade union organization. The great majority . . . did not follow this course. (Kocka 1980: 233)

Yet, today, professionals are proportionally more unionized than other white collar strata. And that minority has been far from insignificant; both old and newer professions had organized early in the century. The AFL chartered its first actors' union, the Actors' National Protective Union, in 1896. In 1919 the AFL set up an umbrella group for all actors' unions, the Associated Actors and Artistes of America, which included the successor to the Protective Union, Actors' Equity Association (1919); the Screen Actors' Guild (which joined the AFL in 1934); the American Federation of Radio (now Television and Radio) Artists, organized in 1937; and several other specialized actors' groups. The Writers' Guild of America (Independent) traces its history to the Screen Writers' Guild (1938) and the Authors' League of America (1912) (Fink 1977).

Actors' Equity has engaged in a number of strikes. In 1919, in its fight to obtain recognition, it closed theaters in eight cities, and with the help of other unions in the entertainment field—notably the Musicians—won. In 1947 it ordered a successful boycott of the National Theatre in Washington, D.C., which it accused of practicing racial discrimination. It won contracts in New York that pioneered nondiscrimination clauses. Following the collapse of a Hollywood strike in 1929, it gave that jurisdiction up to the Screen Actors' Guild, which won a closed "guild shop" provision in 1937. The Screen Actors' Guild can claim the distinction of being the only union to have had one of its presidents become a president of the United States.

Technicians were the first of the "new" technical professions to organize: In the United States the National Society of Marine Draftsmen was founded in 1913 and later affiliated with the AFL (Kocka 1980: 161). Airline pilots secretly organized a union in 1930, then went public with the AFL in 1931 (as late as 1942 its constitution contained a clause limiting membership to "white males of good character") (Nielsen 1982: xv). Women professionals organized their first union when the Air Line Stewardesses Association was founded in 1945; it was recognized by United Airlines a year later. Today called the Association of Flight Attendants, it is loosely affiliated with the Air Line Pilots' Association of the AFL-CIO. It remains the only predominantly female union that was both organized by women and has consistently been led by women.

The late 1960s and early 1970s saw an upsurge of unionization among professionals. A number of previously anti-union professional organizations, including the NEA, became quasi-bargaining agents or outright unions, partly to prevent a mass exodus of their membership into the AFL-CIO. Today, the NEA is more militant (on such issues as peace and minority rights) than the older AFT.

In 1970 the AFL-CIO formed the Council of Unions for Professional Employees, which by 1974 included unions representing more than a million members; the Conference Board of New York estimated that by 1976, some 40 percent of salaried professionals were represented in collective bargaining units—a rate considerably in excess of the overall unionization rate of 20–25 percent. (Table 8-4 lists the top AFL-CIO unions with predominantly professional memberships.)

One of the first physicians' unions to organize (in defiance of the American Medical Association's [AMA] open opposition to collective bargaining) was the Committee of Interns and Residents in New York City, which signed its first contracts in 1970. It was responsible for the first doctors' strike in the United States five years later. Oddly, the AMA supported the strike, calling it a strike for better patient care. Hospital management struck back by getting the NLRB to declare residents and interns students and therefore not entitled to the right to

Table 8-4.   Membership in Selected AFL-CIO Unions with Predominantly
Professional Memberships August 1981

Am. Fed. of Teachers	461,000
Communications Workers of America (prof. only)	263,000
Am. Fed. of Musicians	206,000
Associated Actors & Artistes (includes Actors' Equity, Am. Fed. of TV & Radio Artists, etc.)	89,000
Air Line Pilots Assn. (includes Flight Attendants)	57,000
Newspaper Guild	25,000
Inter. Fed. of Prof. & Technical Engineers	16,000
Nat. Assn. of Broadcast Employees & Technicians (NABET)	10,000
Inter. Org. of Masters, Mates, & Pilots (Inter. Longshoremen's Assn.)	9,000
Am. Fed. of School Administrators	9,000

SOURCE: Courtney D. Gifford, ed., *Directory of U.S. Labor Organizations* (Washington, D.C.: Bureau of National Affairs, 1982).

negotiate, but a number of the doctors' demands were met, including an eighty-hour week with no more than fifteen consecutive hours on duty.

The AFL-CIO had moved into the doctors' field already by recognizing the Nevada Physicians Union as an affiliate (*New York Times*, 18 June 1972), even though George Meany, then president of the AFL-CIO, had declared that there was "no place" for doctors in the federation (*New York Times*, Editorial, 22 March 1975). By 1975, the AFL-CIO had ten physicians' locals. In Jersey City, New Jersey, ninety-five staff physicians at the Medical Center voted for the AFL-CIO as their bargaining agent that December. In 1973, the American Federation of Physicians and Dentists (Independent) was organized for collective bargaining purposes, and claimed a membership of 10,000 (Bognanno 1975: 33). Two years later, by the time of the New York strike, the national affiliates of the New York doctors' group, the Physicians Housestaff Association, claimed 20,000 members. In March 1981, 2,000 New York doctors struck seven municipal and two private hospitals again, mainly to protest conditions they thought dangerous to patients, but they were taken to court and fined $175,000 for violation of court injunctions to return to work, and gave up the strike. Said the *New York Times* (10 May 1981), "More than six weeks after the strike ended there are still no signs that the conditions cited by the doctors have improved significantly." Despite this local setback, it had by then become clear that the unionization of that most elite of all professions, doctors, was under way.

A seemingly endless stream of professional occupations became involved in unions in the 1970s. Although the proportion of the labor force that was unionized declined between 1960 and 1980, the proportion of professionals in unions increased. In places where the quasi-union tactics of professional organizations did not seem sufficient, there were formal moves into unions. By 1971, the American Association of University Professors, which had traditionally opposed collective bargaining, had contracts at seven campuses; by 1982, 60 percent of its membership was in collective bargaining chapters. Overall, faculty union membership grew from about 3,000 in 1966 to 82,000 in 1973 to about 130,000 in 1980—but still comprised less than 25 percent of all full-time college and university faculty (*Academe,* September-October 1982). In New Jersey, in 1972, professors at the eight-college state system voted out an affiliate of the National Education Association and voted in the American Federation of Teachers (AFL-CIO). In New York State, the NEA and AFT merged. In the fall 1972 semester alone, union elections were held at thirty-eight colleges and universities, and in only four cases were unions rejected.

In New York City in the single year of 1973 there were strikes by Legal Aid attorneys; musicians at the New York City Opera, the New York Philharmonic, the New York City Ballet; workers at the Museum of Modern Art and, in March 1974, at the Brooklyn Museum. In the 1974–1975 and 1975–1976 seasons, classical musicians went on strike in Dallas, Denver, Detroit, Omaha, Pittsburgh, Kansas City, and New Jersey (*New York Times,* 21 December 1975). In 1970 investment brokers began to talk union and were, in Chicago, in contact with the Teamsters and with the AFL-CIO; New York brokers followed suit two years later. In April 1974, unaffiliated translators at the United Nations staged a sick-out protesting workloads. In the same year, an independent union struck Harper & Row, the publisher, over wages and profit-sharing, and members of Local 153, Office and Professional Employees (AFL-CIO) picketed Macmillan Publishing Company protesting lay-offs, which the union said had come "in response to our union organizing drive and to a discrimination suit filed against Macmillan by women and minority workers" (*Guardian,* 30 October 1974.)

Professional sports have had a notable though not well-reported history of union activity. The first job action by professional baseball players seems to have been in 1912, when the Detroit team refused to play because Ty Cobb had been suspended. A scab team was hastily put together, and badly beaten. The current baseball union, now famous for its strikes, dates back to 1946 (Fink 1977). The National Football League Players Association, also representing some of the aristocrats of American labor, has struck from time to time, most notably in 1970, 1974, and 1982, virtually wiping out the season altogether in 1982. Union efforts among professional sports players met with fierce opposition from owners, partly because the very notion of players' unions undermines management's ability to treat players as tradeable commodities, partly because of the authoritarian structure of professional sports, and partly, perhaps, because many of the more militant union activists are black, thus illuminating the racist structure of much of professional sports in the United States (Hoch 1972).

A traditional area of professional union strength is the newspaper field. Until recently it has been divided among a number of unions, many of which are in trouble, as owners merge and technological change eliminates jobs. The American Newspaper Guild, founded in the mid-1930s for reporters and other white collar editorial workers, had 29,000 members in 1982 and was talking about a possible merger with the International Typographical Union. Neither this nor several other merger possibilities among smaller noneditorial unions in the printing field have come to pass, but such mergers seem one of the few ways to retain power in the face of mergers by publishers (*Business Week,* 22 November 1982). Workers in the publishing industry, many of whom are professionals, are perhaps even more likely than others to find themselves redundant as computerized technologies are introduced or as corporations merge.

The early generation of professional unions, in such industries as airlines, entertainment, sports, and publishing, sought to obtain decent working conditions for people who saw themselves as downtrodden professionals. The generation of the 1960s and early 1970s, on the other hand, organized in response to the "proletarianizing" trend discussed in the previous chapter. These professionals want to protect certain prerogatives that their more traditional professional associations are unable to defend because they refuse to bargain collectively or to strike. A comment by the president of the Union of American Physicians, a 2,800-member group in California, is indicative of this trend:

> We're not just a bunch of rich doctors merely trying to get richer. We're trying to prevent the regimentation and nationalization stemming from

socio-economic changes in medicine from reducing the doctor to the functionary level of the postman and school teacher. (*New York Times,* 18 June 1972)

The contradiction confronting unionized professionals is stated here in a nutshell: In the effort to maintain professional standards based on earlier—and often outdated—technologies and social relations, a profession is being forced to use modern organizational forms that in turn threaten those standards by the use of collective bargaining. Union activity comes about due to a fiscal crisis that has led to pressures to rationalize the field; the threat of reduced real incomes and unemployment; a political backlash threatening some professions, such as librarians and college professors, with political repression and firings; demonstration effect as nonprofessional (generally white collar) employees in the same firm accept unions; and the influence of black and women's caucuses demanding some organized way of obtaining equality on the job.

Nevertheless, unionization leads to the negotiation of items that many professionals would prefer left to individual decision making. The American Federation of Teachers, for example, negotiates such items (at the college level) as maximum teaching loads, advising loads, committee assignments, office space, use of audiovisual equipment, travel time between campuses, and even the requirement that there be seats for students and lecterns and blackboards for teachers—all matters that the traditional professor preferred to assume and not have codified. The 1981 collective bargaining agreement between the National Association of Broadcast Employees and Technicians (AFL-CIO) and the American Broadcasting Company consisted of a 329-page book (excluding index and table of contents) covering everything from meal periods ("A meal period not to exceed one hour shall be taken as near the middle of the shift as possible except in case of emergency or when a skeleton force is operating") to grievance procedures and the appointment of safety committees (*NABET-ABC Master Agreement* 1977–1981: 30).

Once professional matters become rationalized and legislated, nothing remains sacred or exempt from codification except those items that the courts have already taken away from practitioners and given to administrators. The interstices of worklife that have always been the mark of professionalism because they are determined autonomously no longer exist.

Most professional unions have toed the mark and stuck to noncontroversial issues, such as wages and insurance policies (where these are not automatically set, as in some state sectors). The process of having to win a collective bargaining election tends to exclude serious (hence controversial) discussion of more basic challenges to work rules, while the day-to-day process of negotiating contracts, processing grievances, or litigating a case forces attention to organizational details such as membership drives and fund raising that tend to put larger issues on the back burner. Particularly in a time of job shortage, professionals, like other workers, protect themselves first and worry about social vision afterward. Such a "protectionist" approach is then exploited by administrators, especially in the public sector, who are quick to point out the discrepancy between the professionals' alleged commitment to the public good and their actual demands at the bargaining table. The result is that unions become weakened and even destroyed as they lose the support of the public. The further consequence is that with weak unions, working conditions deteriorate and the quality of services becomes poorer.

So far, signs of moving beyond "bread-and-butter" unionism have been few and far between. For a short time in the late 1960s and early 1970s, when veterans of the student, civil rights, and antiwar movements were entering professional life, radical, minority, and feminist caucuses made a considerable stir within professional academic associations, and even in such professional unions as the American Federation of Teachers. The issue of the professional's ethical obligation to service as opposed to his or her job within modern (oppressive) bureaucracies came briefly to the fore. This movement has declined, however, perhaps due to the general decline of the left following the end of the Vietnam War. In any case, with the exception of "9 to 5," discussed in chapter 6, the caucuses have not been able to develop into a nationwide political movement, although a few caucuses still exist. To the extent that radicals, professional or otherwise, do work within the trade union movement, they have found themselves in the classic dilemma: Effective organizing is possible only around immediate issues, yet organizing around immediate issues involves bureaucratic processes in which long-term radical goals become lost, all the more so in a period of sharp economic cutbacks, during which radicals, minorities, and women find it increasingly difficult to retain their jobs at all. The defense of the job relegates all other tasks to the sidelines, and the issues of meaningful work, autonomy, service to clients, and self-determination are less and less clearly articulated. With few exceptions, professional unions are unions in the American style (that is, economistic) first, and concerned with professional issues second, if at all.

A well-known instance of what can happen when a professional union is concerned almost exclusively with economic issues is that of the Professional Air Traffic Controllers (PATCO). Among the aristocrats of labor, air traffic controllers made an average annual salary of $30,000 in 1981. The union had about 12,000 members when their strike began on August 3 of that year. Technically they are in the public sector, since the federal government operates air traffic control facilities, thereby "socializing" (and centralizing) this service on behalf of the many airlines. PATCO members overwhelmingly rejected a new contract with the Federal Aviation Administration, and embarked on an illegal strike. President Reagan then began steps to have the union decertified, and its leaders fined and jailed. The administration warned that striking controllers would in effect be blacklisted from all future federal employment.

The union sought help from the AFL-CIO, which offered to mediate with President Reagan—after all, both PATCO and the Air Line Pilots had supported him in the 1980 election—but these efforts met with no response from Washington. Aside from that, along with a good deal of rhetoric about solidarity and some money to aid the families of the fired controllers, little real help was forthcoming from the AFL-CIO or from other unions in the airlines industry. For one thing, PATCO had a reputation of not consulting with the AFL-CIO before it took action, and had not done so in this case; for another, it had not helped other airlines workers in the past, particularly the Air Line Pilots.

PATCO wage demands did not generate much sympathy from the public, despite the fact that a number of other demands were clearly safety-related. In addition, it was relatively easy for management to engage in what has become known as "technological scabbing"; supervisors took over in this case in conjunction with Air Force controllers. The union was decertified on October 22 and, when the government refused to rehire most of the strikers, a rationalization of air traffic labor ensued, giving the government an opportunity to engage in "productivity improvements" and make do with perhaps 25 percent fewer controllers.

PATCO's traditional business union approach led to its inability to obtain any real support from the trade union movement, much less from other unions within the industry. The public was in fact hostile to the union. In the context of a government committed to labor control, PATCO was, in *Business Week*'s words (16 November 1981), "out of luck." The effect of President Reagan's action was not dissimilar to Polish-style martial law: Union leaders faced jail, militants were barred from employment in their profession, and the union was made illegal.

The lesson was not lost on other unions in the airlines industry and in the public sector. The Air Line Pilots' pleas for support from other unions in an attempted boycott of nonunion New York Air failed, and it was forced into a series of givebacks during its own contract talks. Postal employees, who were voting on a contract at about the time the PATCO strike began, quickly settled.

An Ambiguous Future

The ambiguous future of blue collar trade unionism in the United States is replicated in the white collar field, with certain important differences. While blue collar workers are decreasing as a proportion of the labor force, and while the old manufacturing centers are in decay, white collar workers are increasing proportionally, with continuing relative growth in the services. The result is that blue collar unions are increasingly in jeopardy, as white collar unions become more significant.

But the increase in the absolute number of white collar unionists, including professionals, is offset by the failure of unions to keep up with the even larger overall shift from blue to white collar work, so that even though white collar union membership makes up a larger propor- tion of total union membership, that total membership is at best re- maining stable and may even be declining slightly as a proportion of all workers.

Further, white collar unions, with few exceptions, have failed to move beyond the business unionism of their blue collar counterparts. Even those white collar and/or public sector unions that have included more "social" issues in their bargaining demands have not been able to convince the public (and in some cases not even other unions) that these client-oriented demands (smaller classes, fewer patients per floor nurse or clients per social worker) are seriously meant. The public continues to perceive unions in general as selfish interest groups, no worse, perhaps, but no better than other pressure groups—as Mills put it long ago (1951: 319). A large part of this perception is based on the fact that unions, especially in the state sector, often pit their members against clients and taxpayers; the immediate victims of wage demands are not private owners and profits, but the public at large. When a strike takes place, it is the public and clients who are inconvenienced first, whether they are students and parents, travelers, or baseball fans. Yet unions in those sectors of the economy that are defined as providing services to the public (not only the public sector strictly speaking) have failed to develop alternative tactics that would give them power without hurting client populations, and, even more important, have failed to come up with strategies that would enlist the public's sympathy.

The strike, taken over from the manufacturing sector (where it may make sense as a weapon against private owners), is the easiest form of job action to organize in that it involves a simple withdrawal of work. Alternative job actions that might be less inconveniencing, such as slowdowns, "work-to-the rule" strikes, sit-ins, or other tactics that challenge management prerogatives (for example, by having workers continue to perform work and indeed perform it better without administrators) are more difficult to organize and require more involvement on the part of the members. Tactics such as spreading work (and income) to keep on laid-off employees undermine already deteriorating standards of living and are in any case thwarted by tax laws. Task forces that will examine alternatives to strikes (especially in the public sector where they are often illegal and where unions can be broken by fines and decertification) are urgent, yet do not exist. No union has actively sought out the tacticians of the civil rights and antiwar movements in such a venture (while the latter have not done much to "sell" nonviolent alternative tactics to unions).

White collar unions have been no better at dealing with the current economic crisis—particularly unemployment—than their blue collar counterparts. They too are faced with wage freezes and other forms of givebacks, which are often applauded (in the state sector, at least) by other workers, who see them as leading to lower or stable taxes, enabling state administrators once again to play the public off against the government workers.

With a few notable exceptions, unions have not challenged management arguments that workplace reorganization will be cheaper for the taxpayer, or will provide better services. They have by and large failed to demonstrate better ways to save tax funds than to lay off workers and/or segment jobs further. One exception is a union-initiated worksite committee system in three San Francisco agencies: Productivity gains due to these labor-management joint committees are used to improve public services. However, most other departures from conventional bureaucratic organization do not go beyond flexible work schedules—"flextime"—or, at best, "Quality Circles." Moreover, these schemes are rarely initiated by unions (Martin 1983: 22).

The role of unions—including white collar unions—in Western society continues to be ambiguous. They are instruments for integrating the workforce into the present economic system, despite their links to left-oriented parties in Western Europe. At the same time, they must necessarily act to defend workers' rights and protect and improve workers' living conditions, if for no other reason than to assure the loyalty of their members and the survival of the union as an institution. This is no less the case in Western Europe or Canada than in the United States. Although unions continue to be less accepted in the United States than in most other Western nations, virtually every union in democratic, industrialized nations is likely to face less favorable labor market conditions in the future. The services sector generally, and the public sector in particular, must, in all countries, become a growing proportion of the labor movement if unions are to keep pace with the changing nature of their economies, including the decline of manufacturing.

Important differences between the U.S. labor movement and that of other Western nations continue to exist, but they have become differences in emphasis rather than in fundamental outlook. Most Western European unions, for example, place a far higher priority on worker participation, or co-determination, than do U.S. unions. Work-sharing and reduction of work time are also more common demands. If anything, unions in Western Europe are more closely integrated into the social system than those in the United States because they have had more political clout and therefore have more input into state policy. U.S. and other Western union movements diverge in their histories, but converge in their day-to-day task, which is to obtain the best possible deal under the given circumstances.

In all Western nations the problem is similar: In periods of economic stagnation, cutbacks in state expenditures, and challenges to those social programs traditionally supported by all unions, what programs can be developed that will enable unions to grow? How will the division between union members and other workers be overcome? How can the perception that unions are just another selfish interest group—now not so unusual in Europe either—be changed? In the public sector, how can unions convince taxpayers and clients that what is good for the one can be good for the others? How can new forms of work organization that fragment and de-skill workers, and undermine the quality of services, be fought successfully? Whether unions will develop answers to these kinds of questions—perhaps with the help of their counterparts in other countries—will determine their relevance to progressive change in the future.

9
White Collar Politics:
Class, Identity, and Party

Trade unionism constitutes one possible index of class consciousness, but a majority of U.S. workers—and an even larger majority of white collar workers—are not union members. Do these people lack class consciousness, or are they not workers at all? Theoretically, as discussed in chapter 1, members of a social class cluster around some set of objective attributes (approximating a "normal" or bell-shaped curve). It should follow that at the subjective level classes will approximate the same kind of curve for a set of relevant political attitudes and behavior. This curve will differ for each class, as with objective attributes, even though the curves may overlap somewhat. Sharing important objective and even subjective attributes is not, however, synonymous with class awareness, which is the outcome of political and economic struggle. In other words, the ideological location of a given class, or fraction of a class, is not precisely correlated with objective reality. Nevertheless, in Marxist theory the two are never totally at odds with one another, and the clustering of a group around some important subjective indices ought to provide important clues about the political development of that group.

Earlier it was posited that the white collar grouping does not constitute a single class, but that the different occupations that come under the white collar label are parts of different classes, and—complicating the picture even further—that many white collar people are in contradictory class locations, between several classes or belonging to more than one class. If this is so, it should follow that there will be no coherent and identifiable political mode for white collar workers as a whole. The data will lead to a confusing or inconclusive picture with, for example, alignment with the upper class on some issues and the working class on others. If, on the other hand, the white collar strata together in fact constitute a new class, they should share a common consciousness, distinctly different (with the exception of some overlap at the outer edges of the normal curve) from that of other classes.

To test these hypotheses concerning the class nature of the white collar strata, it is necessary to identify a set of relevant ideological indices and then see whether these take a coherent shape when compared with those of other classes.

There are, however, some important qualifications to keep in mind when looking at any measure of consciousness. First, social scientists rarely use comparable data. Indices of class and stratum, as well as ways of measuring what people think, differ markedly from one situation to the next. Second, what people say and do today is not necessarily what they will say and do tomorrow; nor can it be determined what one group of people will do later on the basis of what another—and supposedly similar group—did at another time in another country. In other words, future behavior is hard to predict with any precision on the basis of current responses to questionnaires or current voting behavior. Class consciousness is a fluid process. This is particularly true in times of rapid change and social dislocation—for example, when white collar workers suffer serious rates of unemployment as they are now, for the first time in recent memory.

A further qualification is that class consciousness cannot be equated with radicalism or socialist ideology, as radical social scientists often do. If class consciousness is a fluid process, then it should not be surprising that some workers can be class-aware on some issues and nationalist, racist, xenophobic, and hostile to civil liberties on others. In such a case, although the potential for socialism may exist, fascism is just as likely a voting choice. Elementary class consciousness may not be sufficient to overcome other factors.

It is frequently assumed that a radical consciousness develops in the following order: (1) an elementary class consciousness, a sense of "us" against "them," based on some rough economic calculation; (2) union consciousness; (3) a social-democratic consciousness, leading to a political affiliation with very general socialist ideology; (4) a revolutionary consciousness, a commitment to fundamental (although not necessarily violent) change in the social order. But in fact workers have moved from (1) to (4) or from (3) to (4) and "back" to (1) under demoralizing circumstances. This underlines the extent to which consciousness can be altered.

The political "arms" of classes, including parties that strive to educate in the direction of "raising" consciousness (that is, enabling the historical subject to become more aware, and thereby act to change the situation), are important factors in shaping such developments.

Class Identification

One of the few things that can be said with certainty about the political behavior of the white collar strata is that nothing certain can be said about the *whole* group, as we shall see. What "they" will do (including responses to questionnaires) varies with stratum, income level, ethnic and religious identification, and time and place. Empirically, "they" have done many different things politically.

Two indices of class-related political behavior are often cited: class identification (what class or stratum the individual believes himself or herself to be in), and political party preference (on the assumption that some parties appear to represent class interests, or to draw the votes of people who think these parties represent their interests). If large numbers of certain socioeconomic strata say they belong to a particular class, they are said to be more "class conscious"; similarly, if they vote for a particular party, they are said to be voting "along class lines."

Although there does seem to have been a correlation between socioeconomic status and voting behavior this correlation appears to have weakened since the end of World War II (Lipset 1981b). It can be hypothesized that this is due to the very success of workers' parties in achieving reform and higher living standards. Improvements in living standards may have contributed to a decline in class voting.

Yet this apparent weakening of identification leaves several questions unanswered. First, many relatively better-off manual workers continue to identify with the working class and the parties claiming to represent it, including the British Labour Party and the Democratic Party in the United States (Goldthorpe 1968; Hamilton 1975). Second, the gradual decline in the proportion of blue collar workers voting for social-democratic, Communist, or other parties traditionally identified as having working class bases (in the United States this would include the Democratic Party) may not be the result of voters no longer seeing themselves as workers but the result of their no longer seeing the parties as "theirs." Most social-democratic parties, the U.S. Democratic Party, and even some Western European Communist parties have waffled rightward as they have tried to attract what they believe to be the less radical white collar vote. Class identification may thus be stable but without an existing political structure through which to express it. Still another way of looking at this issue would be to argue that working class cannot be equated with blue collar alone. If many lower-stratum white collar workers are indeed workers, then the decline in working class votes for parties based on the working class is spurious: Large numbers of white collar workers also vote for them.

Whether class voting has declined or not, the fact remains that working class–based parties have become more reluctant to advertise themselves as "parties of working people," while their programs have become more conservative. As often as not, when they constitute the government, or are partners in it, they urge workers and their unions to surrender the gains of the past decades. Parties that once boasted a significant output of theory, as well as ardent campaigning for the unity of blue and white collar workers, have virtually given up their educational mission. Blue collar workers make up only some 20 percent of the German Social Democratic Party, as compared with over 50 percent thirty years ago, and the party puts out only one daily newspaper and one theoretical organ. In fact, there is little in the way of popular left media in any Western country—either a reflection of, or a contributing cause to, the apparent decline in class voting.

The assumption that political parties must move rightward in order to attract white collar voters is based on the idea that white collarites have significantly different values from their blue collar counterparts. These values are said to reflect either the "new class" nature of the white collar occupations or the "middle class values" of the white collar worker. This is in turn attributed to the white collar workers' "sensitivity," which leads to a desire to be apart from the blue collar group (e.g., Presthus 1964). But more careful analysis, at least of U.S. data, suggests that lower-level white collar workers differ from their blue collar colleagues more in degree than in kind (Hamilton 1972, 1975). As Hamilton notes, "None of the salaried groups have that kind of monolithic identification with the middle class (or avoidance of the working class label)" (Hamilton 1975: 105).

Numerous studies support this point. Hamilton reviews surveys from 1956 to 1968. In 1968 about half of clerical and sales workers identified with the working class, compared with 75 percent of manual workers. The responses correlated closely with income, except for high-income manual workers, who continue, as Goldthorpe found in Britain, to identify with the working class. Even among high-income managers and officials, some 20 percent identify themselves as working class. In the aggregate (though this may be misleading because it once more lumps all white collar occupations together), between one-quarter and one-third of "middle class" people call themselves workers. Of course, the other side to this is that between two-thirds and three-fourths of the lower white collar group do *not* identify themselves as workers; 75 percent of salaried professionals identify with the middle class.

In general, income level turns out to be the most important determinant of class identification; the lower the income, the higher the level of identification with the working class, according to Hamilton. But religious affiliation and ethnicity have been shown to be significant. Generally, "White Protestants at any given class level are more conservative than are equivalent Catholics, Jews, or Negroes" (Hamilton 1975: 123; see also Leggett 1968). Family background counts, too: "lower non-manuals" from working class and farm backgrounds are less likely to consider themselves middle class than those from nonmanual backgrounds (Hamilton 1972: 345).

Other studies have been concerned with attitudes toward economic issues such as property rights and social reform programs, civil liberties, and civil rights. Brint (1981) examined the difference between "new class" members (as defined by four different authors and more or less synonymous with professionals) and high-income owners and blue collar workers. On almost every economic issue (including, for example, government spending on social programs) the new class scored *between* the business group and the blue collar group.

Burris summarizes a similar series of opinion studies as follows:

> In terms of class formation, the basic cleavage between salaried position is thus one which places manual workers . . . and routine nonmanual workers firmly on one side, with either or both of the two remaining class fractions (managers/supervisors and professionals/technicians) on the other. . . . This class antagonism is confirmed by the consistency with which managers and supervisors occupy opposing positions to other salaried employees on a wide range of political issues. (1981: 30–31)

It is often assumed that insecure, status-sensitive white collar workers will be more authoritarian—hence more right wing—than better off upper-class people (see the discussion of the Nazi vote, below). But this is not the case. Numerous studies of the United States (summarized by Hamilton 1972) indicate that the most "tolerant" (of deviant opinions, hence protective of the Bill of Rights) occupational group is professionals, followed by proprietors, managers, and officials, and then by clerical and sales people. Trailing these are manual workers and farmers. However, the responses vary according to the question asked, and the surveys were done during the McCarthy period and tend to equate dissidence with communism alone. On racial issues, lower nonmanuals are somewhat more tolerant than upper nonmanuals. On anti-Semitism, the higher the income, the more anti-Semitic the attitude. In summary, as Hamilton puts it, "The major division in political outlook is between the upper class and the upper-middle class, on the one hand, and everyone else . . . on the other. . . . The white Protestant upper-middle class (and also the equivalent upper class) form an 'isolated mass'" (Hamilton 1972: 507).

Class Voting

There are of course hundreds of voting studies, in many nations— some three dozen for the last years of Weimar Germany alone (see Hamilton 1982: 37). While most attempt to correlate voting behavior with some measure of stratification, few of these are useful because they use various definitions of class, stratum, and occupational grouping. As pointed out earlier, occupational labeling differs from one country to the next, so that the term "middle class" can involve quite different sets of categories. We will thus limit the discussion to a few indicative studies, all in the United States, focusing on the perennial question of whether it was among the lower levels of the middle classes, and especially among white collar employees, that demagogues of the populist right found their mass base, as Crozier (1971: 26), echoing many other political observers, has argued.

The first case is that of Senator Joseph McCarthy. When all the evidence is in, it appears that McCarthy's greatest support came from among upper-class and upper-middle-class voters (Hamilton 1972), the people whose educational levels are supposed to make them the protectors of public virtue (including civil liberties). The working class, on the other hand, despite less tolerant responses on many attitude surveys, supported liberal candidates.

The case of Governor George Wallace of Alabama is even more instructive, since he ran three times in the presidential primaries and once (1968) in the general election. Carlson (1981) has mustered the available data in a very thorough treatment of the Wallace campaigns.

In a June 1964 Gallup poll giving respondents a choice between Wallace, Lyndon Johnson, and Barry Goldwater, 18.7 percent of Wallace's supporters were "white collar," as compared with 17.9 percent of Johnson's and 25.9 percent of Goldwater's. Among professionals—a separate category from white collar—5.8 percent of Wallace supporters, compared with 10 percent of Johnson's and 10.9 percent of Goldwater's were in that stratum. In terms of party identification, Michigan Survey Research Center data showed that non-South lower-middle-class voters identified heavily with the Democratic Party (Hamilton 1975).

Michigan data for the general election year 1968 show that Nixon supporters had the highest percentage of middle and high socioeconomic statuses (58.5 percent), Wallace supporters were next with 44.7 percent, and Humphrey supporters last with 26.2 percent. Insofar as downwardly mobile (and hence insecure) voters are concerned, Wallace supporters more frequently reported themselves as *gaining* status than did either Humphrey or Nixon supporters (Carlson 1981: 105). There appeared to be no significant difference in the proportion of self-employed versus wage earners supporting each candidate. Hamilton's analysis of voting in 1968 agrees with that of Carlson: "The basic finding . . . is the absence of differentiation by class. Nine percent of the non-South manuals voted for Wallace as opposed to 8 percent of the non-manuals." In the South, according to Survey Research Center polls, nearly twice as many manuals voted for Wallace as did nonmanuals (42 percent vs. 23 percent) (Hamilton 1972: 460).

In the 1972 Florida primary, Knight Newspaper Survey results confirmed earlier findings: The same proportion of supporters of all major candidates were in the middle- and upper-income third of the population (Carlson 1981: 166).

By 1976, Wallace appeared finished politically. An assassination attempt had left him a cripple, and was followed by a divorce. Nevertheless, he entered the Florida Democratic primary, losing to Jimmy Carter. According to CBS/New York Times polls based on nationwide samples, which included a number of occupational classifications, the bulk (59 percent) of Wallace supporters in February 1976 were blue collar; 27 percent were professionals, and 3 percent were clerical and sales people. By April, 48 percent were manuals, 21 percent professionals, and 11 percent lower nonmanuals. There was very little difference in the occupational-group support of any of the candidates: No group—including white collar workers—disproportionally supported the candidate of the "powerless" (Carlson 1981: 238). While this may or may not be an argument for the decline of the significance of class in voting, it clearly undermines the thesis that white collar voters are the bastion of right-wing populism, or proto-fascism.

The voting behavior of the white collar strata in Europe after World War II is even less supportive of this proposition. France is perhaps the best case for the counterargument, namely that white collarites, as proletarians-to-be (or as members of a new working class), vote left, but not as left as the traditional blue collar working class. French white collarites have always demonstrated leftward tendencies, participating in strikes as early as 1869, and again during the turmoil of 1919–1920, 1936, and 1968. Further, white collar workers supported the antifascist popular front of 1936 (Kocka 1980: 274).

The postwar situation has been similar. In the 1958 elections analyzed by Lipset, 26 percent of white collar voters opted for the Communist or Socialist parties and another 10 percent for other leftist groups, while about 30 percent voted conservative (Lipset 1981a: 164). Hamilton, analyzing a series of elections in postwar France, concluded that white collar voters generally supported moderate left and other parties oriented toward social reform. A strong minority (up to 16 percent in these immediate postwar years) voted Communist (Hamilton 1967: 42).

No extensive discussion of white collar political behavior in the third world will be attempted here. This is a complex topic beyond the scope of this book. However, one brief observation, no doubt subject to many exceptions, will be made with regard to the political situation of salaried employees in such third world areas as Latin America. First, unlike their peers in North America and Europe, a much higher proportion of these employees work for the state, live in urban areas, and are well educated. In the absence of large-scale local industry, they are often limited to state employment: The state's beneficence stands as a bulwark between them and poverty. They thus tend to be loyal to their employers and to fear fundamental change, especially revolutionary change that would restructure the state and force them to share their small powers (and benefits) with other workers and peasants. Open, multiparty elections that might truly test their political affiliations are rare. In many of these countries, class issues are fought out inside the ruling party, rather than among competing parties at general elections. Elections, such as that in Chile before the counterrevolution, do suggest that the middle strata support the more conservative side of the political continuum (though students may be an exception). In short, white collar politics in the "developed world" is rather different from that in the third world.

The Nazis

The pivotal question with regard to the political affinities of the "lower middle class" (which includes clerical and sales people, lower-level professionals, semiprofessionals, and the traditional small-business petty bourgeoisie) is in the degree of their support for the National Socialist German Workers' Party (NSDAP—the Nazis) prior to January 1933. The prevalent thesis, shared by many students of white collar political behavior (and/or Nazism), is that as the relative position of a stratum declines, loss of status results in anxiety, making such a stratum vulnerable to reactionary and authoritarian movements. The middle class is said to be particularly vulnerable to this threat of downward mobility, or "skidding," in a period of economic crisis, and is therefore especially open to ultra-rightist appeals, such as fascism. It is likely to become involved in conservative politics, movements, and parties because it values what it has lost, or is about to lose, and rationalizes its failure by identifying with the higher origins and more conservative ideologies of the upper class. Moreover, the middle class refuses to align with such collectivist ideologies as trade unionism because it resists making common cause with its new, "lower"-status peers. Lipset summarizes the prewar European situation thus:

> Fascist parties found disproportionate support from segments of the middle class displaced or threatened by the emergence of centralized, large-scale industry and the growing power and status of organized labor. . . . Small entrepreneurs, small farm owners, and other insecure members of the middle strata were particularly prone to mobilization by fascist movements opposing both big labor and big capital. (1981a: 489)

Let us first of all dispose of the question of the composition of the Nazi Party. Lerner (1951) took a sample of 410 Nazi Party members from the 1934 *Fuehrerlexicon,* a "who's who" put out by the party. This volume included many prestigious names, at least some of whom were not particularly active Nazis so that the upper strata of occupations are probably overrepresented. The largest occupational groupings in the sample were civil servants, professionals, business people, and func-tionaries. Without comparative figures from the leadership cadres of other parties, we cannot tell if this is unusual or not. It stands to reason, however, as Hamilton (1982) argues, that party leaders are usually better educated and disproportionately represent the upper layers of society. In any case, the *Fuehrerlexicon* does not support the "insecure middle class" thesis. The argument made by Lasswell (1952: 35) that at least one subsample is "plebeian" because only 43.1 percent had attended some form of post–high school institution is not convincing and does not alter the basic picture of a party led by relatively well-educated, economically secure people.

Gerth (1940) found that while only 21.1 percent of the party's membership in 1933 was white collar (compared with 31.5 percent manual workers and 17.6 percent independent professionals, merchants, etc.), when these data are compared with the proportion of these occupational groups among all employed persons, manual workers were underrepresented by 14.8 percent, white-collar employees overrepresented by 8.6 percent, and independents and civil servants overrepresented to an even greater extent (in Lipset 1981a: 147). Again, we have no comparative figures for the other parties.

In Abel's study (1938), which is based on volunteered autobiographical essays, 35 percent of his 600 life histories were from workers, 51 percent from the lower middle class, 7 percent from the upper middle class and aristocracy, and 7 percent from peasants. However, while these autobiographies give valuable insights as to why individuals from various classes might have wanted to join the Nazis, these volunteers, many of whom were militant Brown Shirts, are not necessarily representative of the party as a whole. In 1945 Peak did a population survey and found that membership was reported to have been highest among executives and managers, followed by professionals, farmers, small businessmen, office workers, skilled workers, semi- and unskilled workers, and the unemployed, in that order (1945: 13, 14). This too contradicts the lower-middle-class thesis.

In summary, all the analyses of Nazi Party membership either contradict the lower-middle-class argument or provide only weak support for it. What really counted in Weimar Germany was popular support, or votes. From May 1924 until November 1932—the last parliamentary election before Hitler was appointed chancellor on January 30, 1933—the NSDAP increased its proportion of the vote from 6.5 percent to a high of 37.3 percent (in July 1932). And although support for Hitler actually decreased in the last free election, held in November 1932, in the July election 13.74 million Germans voted for Hitler. Even the data provided by the proponents of the lower-middle-class thesis only minimally support their position. For instance, Pratt (1948) shows a positive correlation between Nazi support and upper-middle and lower-middle-class occupations, and a negative correlation in proletarian districts. He found virtually no difference between upper- and lower-middle-class groups except in large cities, where the uppers (usually considered more secure) had a higher positive correlation. Lipset (1981a) reviews a number of election studies for the period 1928 to 1932 and concludes that the greatest amount of Nazi support came from small proprietors, including farmers (except in Catholic Bavaria), not the lower-level white collar employees.

In a study of fourteen of Germany's largest cities, Hamilton (1982) attempts to correlate the class composition of a city district with its voting record. No district was homogeneous. Even middle class districts (which included managers and other upper class elements) had some blue collar workers, and districts with proletarian majorities had some upper-middle-class elements. However, it was possible to demonstrate that the higher the proportion of upper-middle-class people, the greater the support for the Nazis. In Berlin, for example, four of the five most upper-middle-class districts consistently gave the Nazis a higher proportion of their vote than did the city as a whole. Of the five districts with the greatest Nazi support, four had the largest homes—and the highest proportion of domestic servants—in the city.

Overall, Hamilton estimated that the differences in Nazi support between blue collar and white collar workers (particularly those among the latter who lived in working class districts) was small. About 25 percent of each group probably supported Hitler in 1932, while the remainder voted for some party of the left. Differences between predominantly middle class districts (including both upper and lower strata) and those that were predominantly working class were larger, the average for the middle class districts in July 1932 being 35.1 percent and for working class districts 26 percent (1982: 78).

Hamilton's studies of other cities show the same pattern.

Support for the National Socialists in most cities varied directly with the class level of the district. The "best districts" gave Hitler and his party the strongest support. In the few cities where this was not the case . . . the tendency was either one of no difference among the non-manual districts, or . . . of a below average level of support in the best-off districts of the city, with the other well-off districts being generally above the city average. In *no* city did the results show the expected pattern of a pronounced and distinctive National Socialist tendency in the mixed districts, those with large middle-class populations. (1982: 421)

Utilizing a sample of about 200 cities with populations of 15,000 and up, Childers came to a similar conclusion: "Before the September election of 1930 less than 20 percent of the variance [in liberal, conservative, and leftist votes] can be explained by such structural variables" as class and religion (1976: 18–19). Further, "despite widespread unemployment among white collar workers in early 1924, for example, the non-manual variable remained a weak predictor of the Nazi vote before 1930" (ibid.: 22). Nazi gains after the onset of the Great Depression were disproportionately bourgeois and Protestant: "The self-employed variable [became] a significantly more powerful predictor in 1930 and 1932," and, though the Nazis attracted white collar voters in increasing numbers, this variable continued to lag behind others as a predictor (ibid.: 27). Civil servants supported the Nazis more than did other white collar employees, but they enjoyed greater job security and possessed a high educational level, hardly evidence for the insecure lower-middle-class thesis.

Voting data are also available from elections to workers' councils *(Betriebsraete)* and to salaried employees' *(Angestellte)* insurance boards. Kadritzke shows that social-democratic and other republican (as opposed to Nazi and conservative-national) candidates regularly obtained between 65 percent and 100 percent of the vote. These workplace elections, Kadritzke argues, showed "a widespread immunity among *Angestellte* wage-earners, in workplace relations, to the ideological and political program . . . of the NSDAP" (1975: 131).

Conclusion

Readers may find the discussion of the class base of the Nazi party esoteric, coming fifty years after Hitler's rise to power. But it is relevant to the discussion of white collar politics for several reasons. First, the analyses of voting patterns during Germany's Weimar years constitute the largest available body of literature on the question of the class basis of fascism. These data provide us with one of the few studies of the relationship of the white collar strata to populist-rightist political parties. Second, this research appears to lay to rest once and for all the idea that middle class, lower middle class, and white collar people are uniquely susceptible to fascist appeals. Theories of "status panic," whether put forward by left theoreticians or by conservatives, do not hold up under scrutiny. Third, the case study provides ammunition for the argument that the white collar middle class does not exist as a single class "for itself" but is instead stratified and divided among several classes, as is reflected in their voting.

Finally, and most important, the German case demonstrates that while middle class support for populist reaction is always possible, it is not inevitable. Economic catastrophe has led to different political allegiances in different countries: In some cases some of the white collar strata have moved left; in others they have voted for the "out" party (as during the New Deal in the United States); in still others, they have voted for fascism. This means that the possibilities are many—and must be understood and utilized.

Why then is it still widely assumed that white collar workers form the mass base for conservative or fascist movements? As Burris (1982) has argued, it is in part because vested political interests require that theory. Social democrats cite the alleged conservatism of the middle strata to support their own move rightward, away from revolutionary programs toward parliamentary responsibility and moderation—a position that undergirds their role as caretakers of capital. The ultra-left, still wedded to antiquated notions of the purity of industrial workers, view white collar workers as adjuncts of the bourgeoisie. Conservative and neoconservative thinkers put "lower-middles" into various mass "revolutionary" camps, not excluding the Communist one, to shift responsibility for fascism from the capitalists, and/or to scapegoat middle class intellectuals for being responsible for world revolution.

The data presented in this chapter indicate that the real mass base for conservative, ultra-right, or fascist movements consists of people from a number of different social classes; the upper middle and upper classes, which disproportionately support such movements, are not sufficient to constitute the "masses." Where such movements attain a significant following among white and blue collar working people, it is an indication of the failure of the socialist movement to pose alternatives that can capture the imagination and engage the commitment of enough people to thwart the demagogy promoted by the Old Order in its efforts to keep itself in power. One source of such a failure may be the inability of the left to understand the changes occurring in work, in class structure, and in social relations among the many fractions of the working class, both blue and white collar, old and new.

10
Contradictory Locations, Contradictory Consciousness: A Summation

It has been argued throughout this book that the white collar strata constitute a set of class fractions that are constantly in motion as a result of the pressures of economic change. Individual members of these strata thus often find themselves in contradictory locations, straddling more than one fraction within a class, and sometimes even more than one class.

As was discussed in chapter 9, such a situation inevitably contributes to contradictions in consciousness as well, and these have political repercussions. In the past, writers have assigned the white collar population every conceivable political task, based on many different interpretations of the role they played in society. C. Wright Mills, writing at mid-century, proposed a list of interpretations and political missions not much different from that presented by observers at the turn of the century, or one that might be presented today. Although many thinkers lean to some version of the "lower middle class as supporters of the right" thesis, this view, as we saw in chapter 9, has never gone unchallenged. Marxists such as Corey are bolstered by the empirical work of scholars such as Hamilton in their argument that lower-level white collar workers, at any rate, have the potential for moving in a socialist direction.

If there is an "openness of the historical possibilities" so that, as Hamilton argues, widely varying developments may occur in the politics of the white collar strata (1982: 443), it is important to explore the probable conditions that will move larger fractions of white collar people in a more progressive, rather than in a more reactionary, direction. How can progressive political movements understand these conditions and use that understanding to gain the allegiance not only of the majority of the (shrinking) traditional working class but of those white collar workers who are partially or wholly working class because of the nature of their working conditions and lives?

In trying to answer these questions, we first need to summarize the empirical realities concerning the white collar strata as they have emerged in this book:

1. With rare exceptions, the white collar (and/or middle) strata have not been independent political actors on the historical stage. They are too heterogenous to develop their own politics. One important reason for this heterogeneity is that within a single occupational grouping, upgrading and downgrading, "professionalization" and "proletarianization," are going on simultaneously, thereby further splitting one group of workers from another in terms of their working conditions.

2. The upper layers of the white collar occupations constitute elites, or portions of elites, but are not necessarily part of a ruling upper class (though some may be). Being a member of the elite is not synonymous with being a member of the ruling class (at least in capitalist societies).

3. The heterogeneous and often internally contradictory nature of the middle strata can make them a force for either stability or change. More specifically, some strata may be forces for stability, while others are oriented to change.

4. Mills's belief (1951: 352) that white collar workers "can only derive their strength from 'business' or from 'labor,'" and that they are the dependent variable, the so-called "tail-enders" in the struggle for political power, must be revised: The white collar population has in the past allied itself with not one but several other classes. Different fractions of the white collar grouping have aligned with different classes, as Corey (1935) predicted long ago, but these alignments have differed from country to country, and from time to time.

The fact that members of the white collar strata are located in several classes, or in different fractions of one class (so that it is impossible to identify a single "white collar" political thrust), is, particularly in the United States, related to the fact that the entire working class is broken into fractions. One of the major tenets of the theory of "American exceptionalism" is that of the extensive segmentation of the working class, not only by occupation, skill level, gender, and ethnicity, but also between the private and public sectors, and by the tendency for working conditions to improve for some and decline for others. These segmentations overlap so that, for instance, women tend to be at the lower, proletarianizing levels of white collar work, while men are at the upper, professionalizing levels. The white collar category as a whole is even more fractionalized than other parts of the labor force since white collar occupations (as defined by the government) can be placed in at least three different classes—the bourgeoisie, the petty bourgeoisie, and the working class—with many on the margins and others in over-lapping (and contradictory) circumstances. This is clearly a problem when it comes to developing a political program that will gain the allegiance of white collar people. An approach that appeals to the interests of one class alone will not suffice: Appeals based on working class interests, for instance, can be made only to some white collar workers. Although these may be numerically significant, the persis-tence of a "middle class" identity among such "proto-workers" has, in the past, made working class appeals a weak strategy, something that Hitler grasped better than did his leftist opponents. When social democrats in Western Europe finally understood this, they threw out the class approach altogether—thereby ironically losing strength among their traditional working class allies. The classic dilemma for socialists continues to be how to retain the support of the traditional blue collar working class while at the same time attracting sufficient white collar support not only to win elections but to move nations toward a socialist reconstruction of society.

The major tenet of the theory of American exceptionalism is that the working class is becoming embourgeoisified. The extraordinary hori-zontal mobility (from blue collar to white collar) of many working class families is perceived as a step upward, into the middle class, even when that assertion is subject to many qualifications. Indeed, mobility in the United States is no more noteworthy than that in several other industrial countries. Nevertheless, accompanied by an ideological patina that has been inculcated from the cradle, the perception of mobility has had real—and basically conservative—consequences. Both blue and white collar Americans are thus steeped in an ideology that is an obstacle to looking at the world in class-oriented political terms. Celebrants of the status quo, of course, salute this state of affairs. It is good, they say, that Americans have not succumbed to the European disease of class conflict; lack of class politics means political moderation. Indeed, in this view, moderation shows that classes do not in fact exist, and conflicts have been solved. But we must always re-member that although class politics may be notable for their absence, this does not mean that classes do not exist, or that class issues have dissolved.

Given the extensive fragmentation of the U.S. working class, and the continuing widespread perception of mobility, how can a progressive alliance between the working class fractions of the white collar strata and the blue collar working class be created? How can a class-conscious social movement that transcends single-issue reforms be brought about?

First, the trade union movement must organize among white collar workers, women workers of all collar colors, workers in smaller firms (an expensive proposition), new immigrants (including undocumented immigrants), and runaway firms wherever they are located. It must develop imaginative new programs that will attract workers, particularly in the services sector and among professionals, who have been slow to join unions. Many white collar workers, especially professionals, do not see wages as the only bargaining issue: "Service" and professional pride are often equally important, and rightfully so. Unions must learn more about how to translate these concerns into contract demands. Worker participation is an issue closely related to professional self-regulation and self-determination; employee participation systems must be a priority lest management turn them into token "co-determination" programs. To overcome public hostility, unions must play a larger role in seeing to it that quality services are delivered. The rhetoric of professional service often does not extend to working class and/or nonpaying "recipients."

The union movement must forge alliances with unions in other countries on a truly international basis. In embryonic form, such international cooperation (among a few unions in similar industries) already exists, but such efforts are not the priority they must become if the trade unions are to deal effectively with multinational corporations. It must also dramatically change its foreign policy, opposing the United States's authoritarian allies, if only on the self-interested ground that authoritarian governments suppress labor, cheapen it, and thereby undermine employment and standards of living in the United States. Military spending, the collapse of détente, interventionism in Central America or the Middle East, and war—all of which affect labor—must become central concerns within all trade unions.

This is a large task, with many obstacles. U.S. unions appear to be determinedly economistic. In addition, there is no organized left to help develop strategies: Radical unionists work in isolation, and usually find themselves immersed in union logistics, to the detriment of the development of long-range strategies for the growth of the trade union movement, and for its turn toward becoming a significant force for change.

On the other hand, there are signs of change. The feminist movement, notably in the white collar field, has contributed new dimensions of thought and program, and is certainly more oriented to change and readier to challenge conventional union wisdom than many union leaders would like. Further, black workers, who are "overrepresented" in both blue and white collar unions, are also active in the black community and in civil-rights related campaigns: Women and blacks in unions may help make possible the convergence of working class and sectoral issues. A growing number of rank-and-file groups exist within many unions (mostly in the blue collar and service field). Many, influenced by socialist activists, are pushing the leadership to make substantive changes. Reform-oriented leaders, where they exist, are sometimes able to raise important public issues and organize educational campaigns around them.

But the trade union movement cannot by itself either overcome the fragmentation of the working class or create a class-conscious movement for fundamental change, no matter how enlightened it may be. Its primary function, as we saw in chapter 8, is a contradictory one: defense of its members but in the context of integration into the capitalist framework. To challenge that framework implies a politicization of trade unionism that is unlikely in the foreseeable future, especially in the absence of either a labor party or a mass socialist movement.

A trade union strategy must therefore be accompanied by the creation of a significant organized left in the United States. Although several small socialist and Communist groups exist, as do some nonsocialist but radical parties (such as the Citizens' Party) and some independent newspapers (such as *In These Times* and the *Guardian*), in no way do any of these, singly or in combination, constitute even the beginnings of a movement.

Beyond the organized left there are perhaps 5 million Americans who have had "movement" experience in civil rights, antiwar, student, feminist, gay, antinuclear, prison reform, tenants' rights, ecological, health-care reform, and similar contexts. Many are now over forty and are located disproportionately in the professions and semiprofessions and in white collar occupations as a whole. They are often isolated and in many cases suffer from the frustrations that come from trying to do political work in an era of conservative retreat. Many are not unionized, although they could be. Many would—and do—become involved in short-term projects and reforms, but may also be open to working on more specifically socialist issues, and for a socialist movement were one to emerge. Avowed socialists have been elected to several city councils and in a few cases have become mayors. While campaigns of this kind are often limited to calls for "clean government" and "clean air," they have nevertheless begun to make it possible to talk politically about socialism in America.

The obstacles to the emergence of a significant socialist movement in the United States are considerable. First, existing organizations of the socialist and Communist left have developed ideological and organizational rigidities that make outreach difficult, and the surrender of their identities for the sake of unification within a larger organization perhaps impossible. Second, there are real differences of political strategy that impede unity. The issue of whether to work within the Democratic Party or to take independent political action, for example, remains unresolved. Many unaffiliated veterans of the new-left movements will continue to prefer to work on local and/or reform issues rather than expend energy on explicitly socialist organizational work. This is a "Catch-22" situation: Movement activists will not join a socialist organization until a significant, unified one emerges—yet it will not emerge until they join.

The purpose of a unified, significant socialist organization should be to provide the trade union movement with a vehicle that can provide help in developing an independent political program. Such a program would begin to cope with the fragmentation of the working class. But a modern socialist movement must provide a milieu in which its own many sectoral interests can overcome their isolation from one another and create common programs across lines not dissimilar to those that fragment the working class as a whole: race, gender, class fraction, cultural orientation, and of course the question of which issues should have priority in the socialist program.

It should be clear by now that the blue collar working class alone (including its unions) is at an impasse. It is too weak to devise and implement social policies to protect itself; only in alliance with other fractions of the working class (especially white collar workers) and with some elements of other classes (such as the remnants of the petty bourgeoisie, including small-holding farmers) can it obtain the kind of power required to protect and humanize jobs and maintain, much less extend, standards of living. The converse is equally true: White collar workers alone are helpless, and small businesspeople and farmers even more so. Working people have made gains only where they have created a political party that has been able to attract support from other classes or fractions of classes. In Sweden, for instance, political power for the working class has traditionally been based on an alliance with the petty bourgeoisie of tradesmen and farmers. Although that petty bourgeoisie has largely been destroyed by the march of economic events, Sweden's working class has been able to defend its position by substituting the support of the emerging white collar working class. In West Germany, on the other hand, where such support has been less effectively secured, or in the United States, where a party that could create such a strategy does not exist, the working class has lost ground (on this issue for Europe, see Esping-Anderson and Friedland 1982).

In the past it was the social-democratic parties of Western Europe and Canada that were closely related to trade unionism, and that were supported by large segments of the "old" working class. In most cases they were able to attract some "new" white collar and some middle class elements as well. One could find, in these parties, lively political debate and a rich cultural life. They sponsored extensive economic and social institutions, such as cooperatives, theaters, and publishing houses. Any party engaged in the job outlined above—and seeking to attract militant unionists and activists in peace, ecology, feminist, anti-racist, and community movements—will without question be social democratic (that is, reform and electorally oriented) in its general character. This is inevitable because its program must advocate a wide-ranging set of reforms in order to obtain a significant following from among blue and white collar workers, and from among activists who are in touch with the issues troubling working class communities, as well as other communities of the oppressed, such as racial and ethnic minorities.

The social-democratic organizational framework is the one inside of which socialist issues, including the failings of social-democratic policy itself, can be confronted and debated, and from which socialist alternatives can be presented to a wider audience. Such a framework would represent an immense step forward for U.S. politics. It is a necessary (if hardly sufficient) prerequisite to the revitalization of the labor movement and the linking of labor to other issues of the day.

But a word of caution is in order. If such an organization is to emerge and attract a significant following, it must be true to the original conception of social democracy—of which the Socialist Party of Eugene

Victor Debs was a fairly good example—rather than to the social democracy we see today in the Western European social-democratic and labor parties. These parties have, over the years, become bureaucraticized and elitist. The political debate and cultural life so essential to attracting an active membership have deteriorated, while programs that cope with the economic crisis—historically their strongest propaganda weapon—have failed. And the kind of international cooperation and solidarity required to deal with those economic problems, as well as with the urgent problem of world peace, does not exist.

A social-democratic formation in the United States cannot emerge unless it is open to many kinds of people, many different ideas. It must be tolerant of internal debate and dissension. It must foster a cultural life and nonelitist social relations. It must be internationalist. And once it is established as a political force, it must avoid bureaucratization. This is a very difficult—perhaps impossible—agenda.

But what is the alternative? The fact is that we live in an era of ongoing crisis. Even if the current economic depression is overcome for some, it will leave a residue of permanently scarred and poor people, while imperialism and war, racism and sexism, remain rooted in the capitalist system. Failing the development of a viable left movement and culture, how will these evils be confronted? Reaction in every form thrives in a milieu where people cannot account for their troubles. Scapegoats are being—and will be—found; demagogues will manipulate fear to support adventures abroad and repression at home: of blacks, of the poor, of "deviants" of all sorts. Anti-Semitism, fueled by economic insecurity, may once again appear in overt form.

So we must accept the difficult agenda. We must work to create a serious, critical, political counterculture out of the materials at hand: reality, dualities of consciousness, existing movements, the strengths and weaknesses of our own veterans of the left, the available theoretical handles, and, of course, the ultimate fact that people who are exploited and oppressed feel it and know it. This political counterculture must develop strategies that will maximize the likelihood of alliances between the lower and middle white collar strata, including many professionals, and the "old" working class in a vast social movement that will solve the crises of "our" society, and ultimately do away with the rule of capital altogether.

Bibliography

Abel, Theodore. 1965. *Why Hitler Came Into Power.* Englewood Cliffs, NJ: Prentice-Hall. (Orig. pub. 1938.)

Acker, Joan. 1973. "Women and Social Stratification: A Case of Intellectual Sexism." *American J. Sociology* 78, no. 4 (January): 936–45.

Adams, Roy J. 1976. "White-Collar Union Growth: The Case of Sweden." In Donald Bogue and Stanley G. Hudson, eds., *Personnel Management of White-Collar Employees.* Community and Family Study Center, Univ. of Chicago Press. (Orig. pub. in *Industrial Rel.* 13 [May 1974]: 164–76).

Althusser, Louis. 1971. *Lenin and Philosophy.* New York: Monthly Review Press.

Anderson, Charles H. 1974. *The Political Economy of Social Class.* Englewood Cliffs, NJ: Prentice-Hall.

Andrisani, Paul J. et al. 1977. *Work Attitudes and Labor Market Experience.* Center for Labor and Human Resources Studies, Temple University, Philadelphia.

Anyon, Jean. 1979. "Ideology and U.S. History Textbooks." *Harvard Ed. Review* 49, no. 3: 361–86.

Aronowitz, Stanley. 1973. *False Promises.* McGraw-Hill.

———. 1979. "The Professional-Managerial Class or Middle Strata." In Pat Walker, ed., *Between Labor and Capital.* Boston: South End Press.

Baltzell, E. Dibgy. 1964. *The Protestant Establishment.* New York: Random House.

Bazelon, David. 1967. *Power in America: The Politics of the New Class.* New York: New American Library.

Becker, James F. 1973. "Class Structure and Conflict in the Managerial Phase." *Science & Society* 37 (Fall): 259–377.

Bell, Daniel. 1960. *The End of Ideology.* New York: Free Press.

———. 1979. "The New Class: A Muddled Concept." In B. Bruce-Briggs, ed.,

204   *White Collar Politics*

The New Class? New Brunswick, NJ: Transaction Books.

Bellamy, Edward. 1888. *Looking Backward.* New York: Ticknor & Co.

Belleville, Pierre. 1963. *Une Nouvelle Classe Ouvrière.* Paris: R. Julliard.

Benét, Mary Kathleen. 1972. *The Secretarial Ghetto.* New York: McGraw-Hill.

Benson, Susan Porter. 1983. "'The Customer Ain't God': . . . Department Store Saleswomen, 1890–1940." In Michael H. Frisch and Daniel J. Walkowitz, eds., *Working-Class America.* Champaign: Univ. of Illinois Press.

Berger, Henry. 1979. "Organized Labor and American Foreign Policy." In Irving Louis Horowitz, John C. Leggett, and Martin Oppenheimer, eds., *The American Working Class: Prospects for the 1980s.* New Brunswick, NJ: Transaction Books.

Bergquist, Virginia A. 1974. "Women's Participation in Labor Organizations." *Monthly Labor Review* (October): 3–9.

Bingham, Alfred M. 1935. *Insurgent America.* New York: Harper.

Birenbaum, Arnold. 1982. "Reprofessionalization in Pharmacy." *Social Science Medicine* 16:871–78.

Birnbaum, Norman. 1969. *The Crisis of Industrial Society.* New York: Oxford Univ. Press.

Blake, Judith. 1974. "The Changing Status of Women in Developed Countries." *Scientific American* (September): 136–47.

Blum, Albert A. 1971. "The Office Employee." In Albert A. Blum et al., eds., *White-Collar Workers.* New York: Random House.

Bognanno, Mario F., Dworkin, James B., and Fashoyin, Omotoyo. 1975. "Physicians' and Dentists' Bargaining Organizations: A Preliminary Look." *Monthly Labor Review* (June 1975): 33–35.

Brandt, Willy. 1982. *Erinnerungen.* Pt. I in *Der Spiegel,* September 6.

Braun, Siegfried. 1964. *Zur Soziologie der Angestellten. Veröffentlichungen zu Politik, Wirtschaft, Soziologie u. Geschichte.* Bd. 25.

Braverman, Harry. 1974. *Labor and Monopoly Capital.* New York: Monthly Review Press.

Brecher, Jeremy. 1972. *Strike!* San Francisco, CA: Straight Arrow Books.

Brint, S. 1981. "Is There a New Class Ideology?" Paper presented at the Annual Meeting of the Eastern Sociological Society, March.

Brody, David. 1960. *Steelworkers in America.* Cambridge, MA: Harvard Univ. Press.

Bruce-Briggs, B. 1979. "An Introduction to the Idea of the New Class." In B. Bruce-Briggs, ed., *The New Class?* New Brunswick, NJ: Transaction Books.

Bruner, Dick. 1958. "Why White Collar Workers Can't Be Organized." *Harpers Magazine* (August): 21–27.

Burris, Val. 1980a. "Capital Accumulation and the Rise of the New Middle Class." *Rev. Radical Polit. Econ.* 12 (Spring): 17–34.

———. 1980b. "Class Formation and Transformation in Advanced Capitalist Societies: A Comparative Analysis." *Social Praxis* 7:147–79.

————. 1981. "Class Structure and Political Ideology." Paper presented at the Annual Meeting of the Pacific Sociological Association, March.

Byrne, Harriet Anne. 1932. "Women Office Workers in Philadelphia." *U.S. Women's Bureau Bull.* 96.

————. 1935. "Women Who Work in Offices." *U.S. Women's Bureau Bull.* 132.

Carlson, Jody. 1981. *George C. Wallace and the Politics of Powerlessness.* New Brunswick, NJ: Transaction Books.

Carr-Saunders, A. M. and P. A. Wilson. 1933. *The Professions.* New York: Oxford University Press.

Childers, Thomas. 1976. "The Social Bases of the National Socialist Vote." *J. Contemp. History* 11, no. 4, (October 1976): 17–42.

Clawson, Dan. 1980. *Bureaucracy and the Labor Process.* New York: Monthly Review Press.

Corey, Lewis. 1935. *The Crisis of the Middle Class.* New York: Covici, Friede.

Croner, Fritz. 1937. *The White Collar Movement in Germany Since the Monetary Stabilization.* Trans. from *Archiv für Sozialwissenschaft u. Sozialpolitik* 60 (1928). Columbia Univ.: N.Y. State Dept. of Social Welfare & Columbia Univ. Dept. of Social Science.

Crozier, Michael. 1971. *The World of the Office Worker.* Chicago: Univ. of Chicago Press.

Davies, Margery. 1974. "Women's Place Is at the Typewriter: The Feminization of the Clerical Labor Force." *Radical America* 8, no. 4 (July–August): 1–28.

Davis, Mike. 1980. "Why the U.S. Working Class Is Different." *New Left Review* 123 (September–October): 3–44.

deKadt, Maarten. 1979. "Insurance: A Clerical Work Factory." In Andrew Zimbalist, ed., *Case Studies on the Labor Process.* New York: Monthly Review Press.

Derber, Charles, ed. 1982. *Professionals as Workers: Mental Labor in Advanced Capitalism.* Boston: G. K. Hall.

Dewey, Lucretia M. 1971. "Women in Labor Unions." *Monthly Labor Review* (February): 42–48.

Dicesare, Constance B. 1975. "Changes in the Occupational Structure of U.S. Jobs." *Monthly Labor Review* (March): 24–34.

Djilas, Milovan. 1957. *The New Class.* New York: Frederick A. Praeger.

Dollars & Sense. 1978. "Professional 'Upgrading' Hits Nursing." November: 6–8.

Dopkins, Laurie Beth. 1983. *"Labor Relations in the State Bureaucracy."* Ph.D. diss. Rutgers Univ.

Ehrenreich, John and Barbara Ehrenreich. 1979. "The Professional-Managerial Class." In Pat Walker, ed., *Between Labor and Capital.* Boston: South End Press.

Elsner, Henry, Jr. 1967. *The Technocrats.* Syracuse, NY: Syracuse Univ. Press.

Engelhard, Erich. 1939. "The Salaried Employee." Trans. from *Kölner Viertel-jahrshefte für Soziologie,* 1932. Columbia Univ: N.Y. State Dept. of Social Welfare and Columbia Univ. Dept. of Social Science.

Erickson, Ethel. 1934. "The Employment of Women in Offices." *U.S. Women's Bureau Bull.* 120.

Esping-Andersen, Gosta, and Roger Friedland. 1982. "Class Coalitions and the Making of Western European Economies." In Maurice Zeitlin, ed., *Political Power and Social Theory.* Vol. 3. Greenwich, CT: JAI Press.

Estey, Marten. 1974. "The Retail Clerks." In Albert A. Blum et al., *White-Collar Workers.* New York: Random House.

Faunce, William A. 1970. "Automation and the Division of Labor." in Simon Marcson, ed., *Automation, Alienation, and Anomie.* New York: Harper.

Featherman, David L., and Robert M. Hauser. 1976. "Sexual Inequalities and Socioeconomic Achievement in the U.S., 1962–1973." *Am. Sociological Rev.* 41 (June): 262–483.

Fink, Gary M., ed. 1977. *Greenwood Encyclopedia of American Institutions: Labor Unions.* Greenwich, CT: Greenwood Press.

Firestone, Shulamith. 1970. *The Dialectic of Sex.* New York: Morrow.

Freidson, Eliot. 1973. "Professionalization and the Organization of Middle-class Labor in Post-industrial Society." In Paul Halmos, ed., *Professionalization and Social Change.* Sociological Monograph 20. Univ. of Keele. North Staffs., England.

Fuchs, Riet. 1971. "Different Meanings of Employment for Women." *Human Relations* 24 (December): 495–99.

Fuchs, Victor R. 1974. "Women's Earnings: Recent Trends and Long-run Prospects." *Monthly Labor Review* (May): 23–26.

Galbraith, John Kenneth. 1952. *American Capitalism.* Boston: Houghton Mifflin.

Gerth, Hans. 1940. "The Nazi Party: Its Leadership and Composition." *Am. J. Sociology* 45 (January 1940): 514–41.

Giddens, Anthony. 1973. *The Class Structure of the Advanced Societies.* London: Hutchinson Univ. Library.

Gifford, Courtney D., ed. 1982. *Directory of U.S. Labor Organizations, 1982–83.* Washington, DC: Bureau of National Affairs.

Ginger, Ray, ed. 1961. *American Social Thought.* New York: Hill and Wang.

Gioglio, Gerald R. 1975. " Stratification and Proletarianization in the Petit Bourgeoisie." Ms.

Glenn, Evelyn Nakano and Roslyn L. Feldberg. 1977. "Degraded and De-skilled: The Proletarianization of Clerical Work." *Social Problems* 25 (October): 52–64.

———. 1979. "Proletarianizing Clerical Work: Technology and organizational Control in the Office." In Andrew Zimbalist, ed., *Case Studies on the Labor Process.* New York: Monthly Review Press.

Goldthorpe. John H., et al. 1968. *The Affluent Worker: Political Attitudes and Behaviour.* Cambridge: Cambridge Univ. Press.

Gorelick, Sherry. 1982. "Class Relations and the Development of the Teaching Profession." In Dale L. Johnson, ed., *Class and Social development.* Beverley Hills, CA: Sage Publications.

Gouldner, Alvin W. 1979. *The Future of Intellectuals and the Rise of the New Class.* New York: Seabury Press.

Grandjean, Burke D., and Patricia A. Taylor. 1980. "Job Satisfaction among Female Clerical Workers." *Sociology of Work and Occupations* 7, no. 1 (February): 33–53.

Granovetter, Mark. 1984. "Small Is Bountiful: Labor Markets and Establishment Size." *Am. Sociol. Rev.* 49 (June): 323–34.

Gunderson, Morley. 1974. *Male-female Wage Differentials and the Impact of Equal Pay Legislation.* Working Paper 74–04, Faculty of Management Studies, Univ. of Toronto, Toronto, Canada.

Haavio-Mannila Elina. 1971. "Satisfaction with Family, Work, Leisure, and Life among Men and Women." *Human Relations* 24 (December): 585–601.

Haber, Barbara, and Alan Haber. 1969. "Getting By with a Little Help from our Friends." In Priscilla Long, ed., *The New Left.* Porter Sargent. (Orig. pub. 1966, 1967 by Students for a Democratic Society.)

Habermas, Jurgen. 1971. *Toward a Rational Society.* Boston: Beacon.

Hacker, Andrew. 1979. "Two 'New Classes' or None?" In B. Bruce-Briggs, *The New Class.* New Brunswick, NJ: Transaction Books.

Haller, Max, and Leopold Rosenmayr. 1971. "The Pluridimensionality of Work Commitment." *Human Relations* 24 (December): 501–18.

Halmos, Paul. 1966. *The Faith of the Counsellors.* New York: Schocken.

———. 1970. *The Personal Service Society.* New York: Schocken.

Hamilton, Richard F. 1967. *Affluence and the French Worker in the Fourth Republic.* Princeton, NJ: Princeton Univ. Press.

———. 1972. *Class and Politics in the United States.* New York: Wiley.

———. 1975. *Restraining Myths.* Beverly Hills, CA: Sage.

———. 1982. *Who Voted for Hitler?* Princeton, NJ: Princeton Univ. Press.

Harrington, Michael. 1972. *Socialism.* New York: Bantam.

Harris, Alice K., and Bertram Silverman. 1973. "Women in Advanced Capitalism." *Social Policy* 4 (July/August): 16–22.

Haug, Marie. 1973. "Deprofessionalization: An Alternate Hypothesis for the Future." In Paul Halmos, ed., *Professionalization and Social Change.* Sociological Monograph 20, Univ. of Keele, Nerth Staffs., England.

Hayghe, Howard. 1976. "Families and the Rise of Working Wives—An Overview." *Monthly Labor Review* (May): 12–19.

Hoch, Paul. 1972. *Rip Off the Big Game.* Garden City, NY: Doubleday.

Hoffer, Eric. 1951. *The True Believer.* New York: New American Library.

Howe, Louise K. 1977. *Pink Collar Workers.* New York: Putnam.

Hyman, Richard, and Robert Price, eds. *The New Working Class? White-Collar Workers and Their Organizations.* London: Macmillan Press.

Invernizzi, Emanuele. 1982. "Some Hypotheses on the Evolution of Office Work . . . in Italy." Paper presented at Annual Meeting of World Congress of Sociology, Mexico City.

Jaeggi, Urs, and Herbert Wiedemann. 1966. *Der Angestellte im automatisierten büro.* Stuttgart: Kohlhammer.

Jenkins, Clive, and Barrie Sherman. 1979. *White-collar Unionism: The Rebellious Salariat.* London: Routlege & Kegan Paul.

Johnson, Terence J. 1972. *Professions and Power.* London: Macmillan Press and the British Sociological Association.

Kadritzke, Ulf. 1975. *Angestellte—Die geduldigen arbeiter.* Frankfurt: Europäische Verlaganstalt.

Kassalow, Everett M. 1977. "White-collar Unions and the Work Humanization Movement." *Monthly Labor Review* (May).

Kistler, Alan. 1984. "Union Organizing: New Challenges and Prospects." *Annals AAPSS* 473 (May): 96–107.

Kocka, Jurgen. 1980. *White Collar Workers in America, 1890–1940.* Beverly Hills, CA: Sage.

Kraft, Philip. 1977. *Programmers and Managers.* New York: Springer-Verlag.

———. 1979. "The Industrialization of Computer Programming: From Programming to 'Software Production'" In Andrew Zimbalist, ed., *Case Studies on the Labor Process.* New York: Monthly Review Press.

——— and Steven Dubnoff. 1984. "The Division of Labor, Fragmentation, and Hierarchy in Computer Software Work." Paper presented at the Annual Meeting of the Eastern Sociological Society, Boston.

Lange, Hellmuth. 1972. *Wissenschaftliche intelligenz: Neue bourgeoisie oder neue arbeiterklasse?* Köln: Paul-Rugenstein Verlag.

Larson, Magali. 1975. *The Rise of Professionalism.* Berkeley, CA: Univ. of California Press.

Lasch, Christopher. 1977. "The Siege of the Family." *New York Review of Books* 24 November: 15–18.

Laslett, John H. M. 1979. "The American Tradition of Labor Theory and Its Relevance to the Contemporary Working Class." In Irving Louis Horowitz et. al., *The American Working Class.* New Brunswick, NJ: Transaction Books.

Lasswell, Harold D. et. al. 1952. *The Comparative Study of Elites.* Stanford, CA: Stanford Univ. Press.

Lederer, Emil. 1975. *Die privatangestellten in der modernen wirtschaftsentwicklung.* New York: Arno Press. (Orig. pub. Tübingen, 1912.)

Leggett, John C. 1968. *Class, Race, and Labor.* New York: Oxford Univ. Press.

Lens, Sidney. 1973. *The Labor Wars.* Garden City, NY: Doubleday.

Lerner, Daniel. 1951. *The Nazi Elite.* Stanford, CA: Stanford Univ. Press.

Lerner, Max, ed. 1948. *The Portable Veblen*. New York: Viking Press.

Leventman, Paula G. 1981. *Professionals Out of Work*. New York: Free Press.

Lipset, Seymour Martin. 1979. "The New Class and the Professoriate." In B. Bruce-Briggs, ed., *The New Class?* New Brunswick, NJ: Transaction Books.

———. 1981a. *Political Man*. Baltimore, MD: Johns Hopkins Univ. Press.

———. 1981b. "Whatever Happened to the Proletariat?" *Encounter* (June).

———, and Reinhard Bendix. 1959. *Social Mobility in Industrial Society*. Berkeley, CA: California Press.

Littek, Wolfgang, et al., eds. 1981. *Angestellte und reproduktionsrisiken*. Forschungsgruppe Industrieangestellte, Univ. of Bremen.

———. 1982. *Einführung in die arbetis- und industriesoziologie*. Frankfurt: Campus Verlag.

Lockwood, David. 1958. *The Blackcoated Worker*. London: Allen & Unwin.

Lorentz, Ellen. 1981. *"Rationalisierung und Feminisierung der Büroitarbeit." Diplom. thesis, J. W. Goethe-Universität, Frankfurt*.

Low-Beer, John R. 1978. *Protest and Participation: The New Working Class in Italy*. New York: Cambridge Univ. Press.

Maher, Amy G. 1932. "Bookkeepers, Stenographers, and Office Clerks in Ohio, 1914–1929." *U.S. Women's Bureau Bull* 95.

Mallet, Serge. 1963. *La nouvelle classe ouvrière*. Paris. (Also see Dick Howard and Dean Savage, eds. *Essays on the New Working Class*. Telos Press: 1975.)

Mandel, Ernest. 1968. "The Working Class under Neo-capitalism." *Guardian* (New York) 28 September.

———. 1969. "Where Is America Going?" *Leviathan* (September). (Also in *The Revolutionary Potential of the Working Class*. New York: Pathfinder, 1974; and *New Left Review* 54 [March/April 1959].)

Mann, Michael. 1973. *Consciousness and Action among the Western Working Class*. London: The Macmillan Press.

Mannheim, Karl. 1936. *Ideology and Utopia*. New York: Harcourt, Brace.

Marcuse, Herbert. 1964. *One-Dimensional Man*. Boston: Beacon.

———. 1969. "On Revolution." In Alexander Cockburn and Robin Blackburn, eds., *Student Power*. Harmondsworth: Penguin Books.

Martin, Shan. 1983. *Managing without Managers*. Beverly Hills, CA: Sage.

Mattila, J. Peter. 1974. *Labor Turnover and Sex Discrimination*. Working Paper 1974-01, Industrial Relations Center, Iowa State Univ.

Mercer, D. E., and D. T. Weir. 1983. "Instrumental Collectivism and Occupational Sectionalism." In Richard Hyman and Robert Price, eds., *The New Working Class?* London: Macmillan Press.

Michael, Donald N. 1962. "Cybernation: The Silent Conquest." In Morris Philipson, ed., *Automation*. New York: Random House.

Michels, Robert. 1949. *Political Parties*. New York: Free Press. (Orig. pub. 1911.)

Miller, Delbert C., and William H. Form. 1980. *Industrial Sociology.* New York: Harper. ·

Mills, C. Wright. 1951. *White Collar.* New York: Oxford Univ. Press.

———. 1958. *The Causes of World War III.* New York: Ballantine Books.

Mitchell, Juliet. 1971. *Woman's Estate.* New York: Random House.

Morse, Nancy. 1953. *Satisfactions in the White-Collar Job.* Ann Arbor: Univ. of Michigan.

National Commission on Working Women (NCWW). 1978. *Survey* (September).

Neuloh, Otto. 1966. *Die Weisse Automation.* Cologne: Grote.

Newman, Edward, and Jerry Turem. 1974. "The Crisis of Accountability." *Social Work* 19 (January): 5–16.

Nielsen, George Panter. 1982. *From Sky Girl to Flight Attendant.* Ithaca, NY: State School of Industrial and Labor Relations Press, Cornell University.

Noble, David. 1977. *America by Design.* New York: Knopf.

———. 1979. "Social Change in Machine Design." In Andrew Zimbalist, ed., *Case Studies on the Labor Process.* New York: Monthly Review Press.

O'Connor, James. 1973. *The Fiscal Crisis of the State.* New York: St. Martin's.

Ollman, Bertell. 1972. "Toward Class Consciousness Next Time: Marx and the Working Class." *Politics and Society* (Fall): 1–24.

Oppenheimer, Martin. 1979. "What Is the New Working Class?" In Irving Horowitz et al., eds., *The American Working Class: Prospects for the 1980s.* New Brunswick, NJ: Transaction Books.

——— and Jane C. Canning. 1979. "The National Security State." *Berkeley J. Sociology* 23: 3–33

Oppenheimer, Valerie Kincaide. 1968. "The Sex-Labeling of Jobs." *Industrial Relations* 7, no. 3 (May): 219–34.

Ortega y Gasset, José. 1932. *The Revolt of the Masses.* New York: Norton.

Orzack, Louis. 1974. "The Cross-National Analysis of Professionalization." Ms.

Papcke, Sven. 1979. *Der Revisionismusstreit und die politische Theorie der Reform.* Stuttgart: Kohlhammer.

———. 1982. "Kriegsdienst mit den Waffen des Geistes." *Vorgänge* 21, no. 2 (April).

Parkin, Frank. 1971. *Class Inequality and Political Order.* New York: Praeger.

Peak, Helen. 1946. "Observations on the Characteristics and Distribution of German Nazis." *Psych. Monographs* 59, no. 6: 1–44.

Perlman, Selig. 1922. *History of Trade Unionism in the U.S.* New York: Macmillan.

———. 1928. *A Theory of the Labor Movement.* New York: Macmillan.

——— and Philip Taft. 1935. *History of Labor in the United States, 1896–1932.* Vol. IV. New York: Macmillan.

Perucci, Robert, and Joel E. Gerstl. 1969. *Profession Without Community: Engineers in American Society.* New York: Random House.

Pidgeon, Mary E. 1930. "Women in the 5-and-10-cent Stores." *U.S. Women's Bureau Bull.* 76.

Podhoretz, Norman. 1979. "The Adversary Culture and the New Class." In B. Bruce-Briggs. ed., *The New Class?* New Brunswick, NJ: Transaction Books.

Poulantzas, Nicos. 1975. *Classes in Contemporary Capitalism.* London: New Left Books.

Praderie, Michel. 1968. *Ni Ouvriers, Ni Paysans: Les Tertiaires.* Paris: Seuil.

Pratt, Samuel A. 1948. "The Social Basis of Nazism and Communism in Urban Germany." M.A. thesis Michigan State College.

Presthus, Robert. 1964. *Men at the Top.* New York: Oxford Univ. Press.

Price, Robert. 1983. "White-Collar Unions: Growth, Character, and Attitudes in the 1970s." In Richard Hyman and Robert Price, eds., *The New Working Class?* London: Macmillan.

Przeworski, Adam. 1980. "Social Democracy as a Historical Phenomenon." *New Left Review* 122 (July–August): 27–58.

Rainwater, Lee, et al. 1959. *Working Class Wife.* Dobbs Ferry, NY: Oceana.

Reich, Charles. 1970. *The Greening of America.* New York: Random House.

Rosenblum, Gerald. 1973. *Immigrant Workers.* New York: Basic Books.

Roszak, Theodore. 1969. *The Making of a Counter Culture.* Garden City, NY: Doubleday.

———. 1973. *Where the Wasteland Ends.* Garden City, NY: Doubleday.

Safilios-Rothschild, Constantina. 1971. "Towards the Conceptualization and Measurement of Work Commitment." *Human Relations* 24 (December): 489–93.

Schevitz, Jeffrey. 1979. *The Weaponsmakers.* New York: Schenkman.

Schmoller, Gustav. 1897. *Was Verstehen Wir Unter dem Mittelstand?* Göttingen: Evang.-soz. Kongress.

Schumpeter, Joseph. 1953. "Das Soziale Antlitz des Deutschen Reiches." In *Aufsätze.* Tübningen. (Orig. pub. 1929.)

Seligman, Ben B. 1966. *Most Notorious Victory: Man in an Age of Automation.* New York: Macmillan.

———. 1970. "The Impact of Automation on White-Collar Workers." In Simon Marcson, ed., *Automation, Alienation, and Anomie.* New York: Harper.

Sennett, Richard and Jonathan Cobb. 1972. *The Hidden Injuries of Class.* New York: Random House.

Shalev, Michael, and Walter Korpi. 1980. "Working Class Mobilization and American Exceptionalism." *Economic and Industrial Democracy* 1, no. 1 (February): 31–61.

Shelp, Ronald K. 1981. *Beyond Industrialization.* New York: Praeger.

Simpson, Richard L., and Ida Harper Simpson. 1969. "Women and Bureaucracy in the Semi-Professions." In Amitai Etzioni, ed., *The Semi-Professions and Their Organization.* New York: Free Press.

Skinner, B. F. 1948. *Walden II.* New York: Macmillan.

Slater, Philip E. 1970. *The Pursuit of Loneliness.* Boston: Beacon.

Small, Albion W. 1913. *Between Eras: From Capitalism to Democracy.* New York: Inter-Collegiate Press.

Sobel, Richard. 1981. "White Collar Structure and Class: Educated Labor Re-evaluated." D.Ed. diss. Univ. of Massachusetts.

Social Research, Inc. 1973. *Working-Class Women in a Changing World: A Review of Research Findings.* Study no. 287/07.

Sommers, Dixie. 1974. "Occupational Rankings for Men and Women by Earnings." *Monthly Labor Review* (August): 34–51.

Sorensen, Jeff, and Jon Swan. 1981. "VDTs: The Overlooked Story Right in the Newsroom." *Columbia Journalism Review* (January–February).

Speier, Hans. 1934. "The Salaried Employee in Modern Society." *Social Research* (February): 111–33.

Stone, Katherine. 1975. "The Origins of Job Structures in the Steel Industry." In Richard E. Edwards et al., eds., *Labor Market Segmentation.* Boston: Heath.

Sullivan, Mary L. 1936. "Employment Conditions in Department Stores in 1932–1933." *U.S. Women's Bureau Bull.* 125.

Suter, Larry E., and Herman P. Miller. 1973. "Income Differences Between Men and Career Women." *Am. J. Sociology* 78 (January): 962–74.

U.S. Dept. of Commerce, Bureau of the Census. 1982. *Current Industrial Reports.*

———. Bureau of the Census. 1983. *Statistical Abstract of the United States, 1982–1983.*

———. International Trade Administration. 1982b. *Country Market Survey* January.

U.S. Dept. of Health, Education, and Welfare. 1973. *Work in America.* Report of a Special Task Force to the Secretary of HEW. Boston: MIT Press.

U.S. Dept. of Labor, 1979. *Directory of National Unions.*

———. Bureau of Labor Statistics. 1980. *Handbook of Labor Statistics.*

———. Bureau of Labor Statistics. 1980. *National Survey of Professional, Administrative, Technical, and Clerical Pay.* March.

———. 1982. *Labor Force Statistics Derived From Current Population Survey.* Vol. 1. September.

———. Manpower Administration. 1974. *Job Satisfaction: Is There a Trend?* Monograph No. 30.

———. Women's Bureau. 1970. *Automation and Women Workers.* February.

———. Women's Bureau. 1942. "Office Work in Houston, Los Angeles, Kansas City, Richmond, Philadelphia, in 1940." Bulletin 188.

———. 1975. *Handbook on Women Workers.* Bulletin 297.

Veblen, Thorstein. 1921. *The Engineers and the Price System.* New York: Huebsch.

Vogel, Ezra F. 1963. *Japan's New Middle Class: The Salary Man and His Family in a Tokyo Suburb*. Berkeley, CA: Univ. of California Press.

Vuskovic, Pedro. 1980. "Latin America and the Changing World Economy." *NACLA Report on the Americas* 14, no. 1 (January–February).

Wachtel, Howard M. 1975. "Class Consciousness and Stratification in the Labor Process." In Richard E. Edwards et al., eds., *Labor Market Segmentation*. Boston: Heath.

Waldman, Elizabeth, and Beverly J. McEaddy. 1974. "Where Women Work— An Analysis by Industry and Occupation." *Monthly Labor Review* (May).

Weber, Max. 1919. *Wirtschaft und Gesellschaft*. Tübingen: J. C. B. Mohr.

———. 1946. *From Max Weber*. New York: Oxford Univ. Press.

Wharton, Amy, and Val Burris. 1983. "Office Automation and Its Impact on Women Workers." *Humboldt J. Social Relations* 10, no. 2 (Spring/Summer): 112–26.

Willhelm, Sidney. 1980. "Can Marxism Explain America's Racism?" In Richard E. Edwards et al., eds., *Labor Market Segmentation*. Boston: Heath.

Wilson, Edmund. 1940. *To the Finland Station*. Garden City, NY: Doubleday.

Witt, Günter. 1975. *Leitende Angestellte und Einheitsgewerkschaft*. Frankfurt: Europäische Verlagsanstalt.

Wright, Erik Olin. 1978. *Class, Crisis, and the State*. London: New Left Books.

Yarrow, Michael. 1981. "How Good Strong Union Men Line It Out: Structure and Dynamics of Coal Miner Consciousness." Ph.D. diss. Rutgers Univ.

Index